They Were There

They Were There

Memories of the Great War 1914-1918 by
those who experienced it

Edited by

William Langford

Pen & Sword
MILITARY

First published in Great Britain in 2014 by
PEN & SWORD MILITARY
an imprint of
Pen & Sword Books Ltd,
47 Church Street, Barnsley,
South Yorkshire.
S70 2AS

Introduction © William Langford 2014

ISBN 9781783831050

The right of William Langford to be identified as Editor of this Work
has been asserted by him in accordance with the
Copyright, Designs and Patents Act 1988.

A CIP catalogue record for this book is available
from the British Library

Designed by Factionpress

Printed and bound by CPI Group (UK) Ltd, Croydon, CR0 4YY

Pen & Sword Books Ltd incorporates the imprints of
Pen & Sword Aviation, Pen & Sword Maritime,
Pen & Sword Military, Pen & Sword Select, Pen & Sword Military Classics,
Leo Cooper, Wharncliffe Local History

For a complete list of Pen & Sword titles please contact:
PEN & SWORD BOOKS LIMITED
47 Church Street, Barnsley, South Yorkshire, S70 2AS, England.
E-mail: enquiries@pen-and-sword.co.uk
Website: www.pen-and-sword.co.uk

Contents

Editor's Introduction　　6

One Man's Road to Adventure　　9

British Troops Arrive in Mons　　19

The First Shot Fired at Mons　　23

The First Hours at Mons　　25

He Rode With Fear　　31

Long Lines of Death　　43

Terror and Tribulation　　51

Saving Haig's Corps at Landrecies　　63

Affair of Mattresses in Landrecies　　65

Unseen Killers at Le Cateau　　67

Stragglers Lost For a Week　　71

Laughing Dawn of Despair　　75

Epic Story of St. Quentin　　83

The Rallying of Demoralized Men　　89

A Diary of the Great Retreat　　93

About to be Shot for a Spy　　101

Infantry Subaltern on the Retreat　　111

The Account of L Battery　　123

Wounded, Captured, then Rescued　　131

The Crossing of the River Marne　　143

Death in a Wood on the River Aisne　　153

German White Flag Treachery　　165

Doom Over Antwerp　　173

An Antwerp Adventure　　185

When They Lost Zonnebeke　　195

Cabaret of Death　　205

Stopping the Prussians　　215

They Saved the Day at Gheluvelt　　227

London Scottish Before Messines　　233

The Horror of Sanctuary Wood　　245

The Historic Christmas Truce of 1914　　251

German Bombardment of Hartlepool　　261

Editor's Introduction

IN SEPTEMBER 1938, tensions were increasing throughout Europe as the Führer of Germany strutted and loudly demanded self-determination for Sudeten Germans in Czechoslovakia. In a flurry of appeasement the British Prime Minister flew to Munich intent on placating the dictator. He returned on 30 September waving a piece of paper – an Anglo-German agreement, signed by 'Herr Hitler and myself' pledging that the two nations would never go to war against each other again.

This was the month when a new magazine was launched in Britain with the title *The Great War: I Was There*. It carried the sub-title *Undying Memories of 1914-1918*, and was published by The Amalgamated Press Ltd and edited by Sir John Hammerton.

In its editorial introductory letter it announced: 'The story of the Great War of 1914-18 has been told in many ways, but there has never before been collected in the scope of one work a narrative account of those years, every word of which has been written by an eye-witness of the actual events described.' The declared intent of the publisher was to make effective use of personal narratives of those who experienced the events of the 'war to end all wars'. Twenty years had elapsed since the Great War ended and in that period hundreds of books on the subject had been written by those who took part. It was from these published sources that extracts would be taken to bring to life the pages of the magazine *I Was There*. Each issue of the magazine would be on sale every Thursday for price of 9d (£2.10 present-day value). There would be fifty-one parts in the first series – taking its weekly publishing to 19 September 1939.

So it was, one year later to the month the final edition of *I Was There* was published and contained the announcement:

> 'In view of the outbreak of the European War subscribers to *I Was There* will not be surprised to learn that the publishers have decided not to proceed with the issue of a proposed New Series.'

With Hitler's invasion of Poland, Britain and France declared war on Germany on 3 September 1939. The Great War was about to be eclipsed by round two. The Second World War proved to be 'greater' in terms of loss of life, material destruction and suffering than the Great War of 1914-1918. The First World War brought massive changes to the extent that the world of mankind would never be the same again, as empires disappeared and social norms altered forever; and the Second conflict completed those changes and ended with an even greater threat to security of mankind with a nuclear age and 'mutually assured destruction' – or MAD.

What lessons are really learned from history? And when learned, are applied by the decision makers in government to present-day affairs so as to bring about true peace? The League of Nations, set up after the First World War, had failed to prevent the dictator Mussolini from offensive actions in Libya, Ethiopia and Albania and finally collapsed with the outbreak of global conflict once more. It seems that mankind does not have the inherent ability to direct his own steps by means of self government.

Yet the stories of those who took part in the first world conflict of the twentieth century have a message for later generations – that there is nothing glorious in armed conflict; the stories these witnesses tell are of fear, great suffering and the onset of a callousing with regards to the plight of his fellow man, who by politics and birth, must be viewed as 'enemy'.

Those who had made a career of the army had been brought up on a diet of glory, on stories of daring-do as the heroes of the British Empire sorted out the cruel and blood-thirsty pagan natives in far away places such as Africa, India and the Far East.

Around the turn of the twentieth century there had been uneasy indications that all was not well with British imperialism; during the fighting with the Dutch settlers in South Africa. The Boer farmers, with their Mauser rifles and hit-and-run commando tactics, had, on numerous occasions, bested the British Army and dealt it a bloody nose. However, the British Regular soldier and the Territorial warrior (part-time soldiers or 'Saturday Night Soldiers') would find out about the hardships and privations on a far greater scale in the conflict breaking out in Europe in 1914.

In John Lucy's eye-witness account of the fighting in Sanctuary Wood, November 1914, he describes how a sergeant fell near him when a piece of shrapnel entered the back of his head: 'He lay unconscious all the day nodding his holed head as if suffering only from some slight irritation, and did not become still until evening.' One young soldier wanted to put him out of his misery by shooting him. An older and more experienced man pointed out that the sergeant was already as good as dead and was not suffering. In the same account a German attempting to surrender is shot out of hand in reprisal for the death of another British sergeant who had been shot whilst attempting to rescue a wounded German. Yes, there are also tales of bravery and selfless acts which took place among that murderous activity, yet the callousness comes through.

As the next four years dragged on disillusion would set in among those who were wielding the weapons. The potential for this can be discerned in these accounts at the beginning of the Great War: near rebellion of elements of the demoralized British Expeditionary Force occured following the fighting at Mons. Furious soldiers could only look on helplessly as their headquarters staff crowded the last trains out of St Quentin leaving them, thoroughly exhausted by the retreat, to resist the enemy hordes bearing down on the British rearguards. Two British colonels took steps to surrender their commands to the Germans. There is the account of a British major, Tom Bridges, who rallied the surrendered men just before the enemy arrived to take them into captivity. How he twarted the surrender of two battalions and led them off to join the general withdrawal is remarkable. Tom Bridges achieved the amazing transformation with stirring words – along with a tin drum and a toy whistle.

There followed the Battle of the Marne, which the French called a miracle when the invaders were stopped before Paris and the Allied counter-attack drove the Germans back to the River Aisne. The two sides carried out a series of outflanking movements, wheeling their tired formations in cross-country sweeps, which is refered to in history as the Race to the Sea. The First Battle of Ypres took place when the Germans were halted in the north. With the Channel coast blocked and denied to the Germans the belligerents dug in, and glared at each other across a strip of ground which would become known as 'No Man's Land' and which ran for 300 miles.

This rework – *They Were There* – has allowed their stories of 1914 to be aired once more in personal accounts – from Mons to the Christmas Truce and the German naval bombardment of East Coast of England.

We hope you agree, these stories are well worth ressurecting and presenting to readers of the twenty-first century. In this, another age, judgements will be made afresh and opinions formed, and some may even wonder how the strange belligerent behaviour arose in the first place. Present-day readers may be led to consider the dividing influences existing among humankind: nationalism, patriotism, religion, which still fuels prejudice down to this hour, and which a further world peace-keeping organization the United Nations seems unable to control. Some might conclude that a benevolent world dictatorship is the only, as yet untried, answer.

In the editing of these stories originally typed-up seventy to a hundred years ago it has meant making some minor alterations. For example some abreviations familiar back then require spelling out today. Reference to certain people, events and their usage would be unfamiliar: Blondin was, in the nineteenth century, a well known French tightrope walker, but is not part of present-day awareness (and could now be confused with a female popstar). Usage of military terms has settled down and is here standardized. Some words have faded into the background such as 'hence' and 'whence'; 'intercourse' nowadays conveys something different to 'conversation' and so on. Where confusion is unlikely the words and sentences have been left as originally written, as it helps the flavour of what is being reported.

So – *I Was There* has become *They Were There* and it is hoped that what these men had to say over a generation ago is informative and interesting to readers today.

9-23 August 1914

ONE MAN'S ROAD TO ADVENTURE

Captain Arnold Gyde

As a member of the original British Expeditionary Force in 1914, Arnold Gyde was serving as a second lieutenant commanding No. 7 Platoon, B Company, 2nd Battalion, South Staffordshire Regiment, at the Battle of Mons.

After about two days' stay, the battalion moved away from the rest camp and, setting out before dawn, marched back through those fatal streets of the port of Le Havre, at this time deserted in the moonlight, to a sort of shed, called by the French authorities a troop station. Here as usual the train was waiting and the men had to be entrained. The carriages could not be called luxurious, to be frank, they were cattle trucks. But it takes more than that to damp the spirits of 'Thomas Atkins'. Cries imitating the lowing of cattle and the bleating of sheep broke out from the trucks. Officers were, of course, in carriages.

The train moved out of the depot and wended its way in the most casual

British troops about to be transported to the Belgian border in cattle trucks. The sign indicates 32 to 40 men or 8 horses. The chalked 'strike' message is with reference to the workers' intentions to fight rather than them taking industrial action.

British officers of the 11th Hussars at a railway stop on the way to the British Expeditionary Force concentration area at Rouen, 18 August 1914.

manner alongside the streets of Havre. This so amused Tommy that he roared with laughter. The people who rushed to give the train a send-off, with many cries of '*Vive les Anglais*,' and '*A bas les Boches*,' were greeted with more bleatings and brayings.

The journey through France was quite uneventful. Sleeping or reading the whole day through, this subaltern only remembered Rouen, passed at about midday and Amiens late in the evening. The train had paused at numerous villages on its way, and in every case there had been violent demonstrations of enthusiasm. In one case a young lady of prepossessing appearance had thrust her face through the window of our carriage and talked very excitedly and quite incomprehensibly, until one of the fellows in the carriage grasped the situation, leant forward and planted a kiss. The damsel withdrew blushing.

At Amiens various rumours were afloat. Somebody had heard the colonel say the magic word 'Liège'. Images of battles to be fought that very night thrilled some of them not a litle. Dawn found the Battalion hungry, shivering and miserable, paraded by the side of the track, at a little wayside station raled Wassigné. The engine shunted away, leaving the Battalion with an overpowering feeling of desolation. A staff officer, rubbing sleep from his eyes, emerged from a little *estaminet* and gave the colonel the necessary orders. During the march that ensued the Battalion passed through villages where the other battalions in the Brigade were billeted. At length a village called Iron was reached and various billets were allotted to each Company. The subaltern's Company settled down in a huge watermill; its officers being quartered in the miller's private house. A wash, a shave and a meal worked wonders. And so the journey was finished and the Battalion found itself at last in the theatre of operations.

The battalions which composed the first Expeditionary Force had been spread in small groups over the whole length and breadth of Britain. They had been mobilized, embarked, piloted across the Channel in the face of an undefeated enemy fleet, rested, and carried by train to their various areas of concentration to take their place by the side of their French Allies. All this was accomplished without a major hitch, and with a speed that was astonishing.

Peace reigned for the next five days and they were to prove to be the last taste of careless times that many of those poor fellows were to have. A route march generally occupied the mornings, and a musketry parade the evenings. Meanwhile, the men were rapidly accustoming themselves to the new conditions. The officers occupied themselves with polishing up their French, and getting a hold upon the reservists who had joined the Battalion on mobilization.

The French did everything in their power to make the Battalion feel at home. Cider was given to the men by the bucket-full. The officers were treated like the best friends of the families with whom they were billeted. The fatted calf was not spared and this in a land where there were not too many fatted calves to be found.

The Company struck a particularly soft spot. The miller was serving in the colours and he had left behind him his wife, his mother and two children. Nothing they could do for the five officers of the Company was too much trouble. Madame Mère gave up her bedroom to the major and his second-in-command, while madame herself slew the fattest of her chickens and rabbits for the meals of her hungry officers.

Conversations that were attempted by the British officers must have been amusing, for their French was halting and ungrammatical. Of all the companies' messes, this one took the most serious view of the future, and earned the nickname 'Les Misérables'. The senior subaltern said that calm preceded a storm. The papers they managed to get hold of, such as the *Le Petit Parisien* and other such-like, talked vaguely about a successful offensive on the extreme right. Mulhouse, it was said, had been taken. But of the rest, of Belgium, there was silence. Such ideas as the subaltern himself had on the strategical situation were but crude. The line of battle, he fancied, would stretch north and south, from Mulhouse to Liège. If it were true that Liège had fallen, he thought the left would rest sucessfully on Namur. The British Army, he imagined, was acting as general reserve, behind the French line, and could not be employed until the time had arrived to hurl the last reserve into the *melée*, at the most critical point. And all the while, never a sound of firing, never a sight of the red and blue of the French uniforms. The war might have been two hundred miles away.

Meanwhile Tommy on his marches was discovering things. Wonder of wonders, this curious people called baccy 'tabac'. 'And if yer wants a bit of bread yer asks for *pain*, strewth!' Tommy loved to hear the French gabble to him in their excited way; he never thought that, reciprocally, his talk was just as funny. But, on the whole, he admired sunny France, with its squares of golden corn and vegetables; and when he passed a painted Crucifix, with its cluster of flowering graves, he would say: 'Golly, Bill, ain't it pretty? We oughter 'ave them at 'ome, yor know.' And of course he kept on saying what he was going to do with 'Kayser Bill' if he got his hands on him.

One night the men of the Company gave a little concert outside the mill. The flower-scented twilight was fragrantly beautiful and the mill stream gurgled a lullaby accompaniment as it swept past the trailing grass. Nor was there any lack of talent: one reservist, a miner since he had left the army, roared out several songs concerning the feminine element at the seaside, or voicing an inquiry as to a gentleman's companion on the previous night. Then, with an entire lack of appropriateness, another got up and recited 'The Wreck of the *Titanic*' in a most touching and dramatic manner. Followed by a song with a much-appreciated chorus:

> Though your heart may ache awhile,
> Never mind!
> Though your face may lose its smile,
> Never mind!
> For there's sunshine after rain,
> And then gladness follows pain,
> You'll be happy once again,
> Never mind!

The ditty deals with broken vows, faithless hearts and blighted lives; just the sort of song that Tommy loves to warble after a good meal in the evening. It conjured to the subaltern's eyes the picture of the dainty little star who had sung it on the boards of the Coliseum. And to conclude, there was heard madame's voice, French, and sonorously metallic, coming from the dining-room, striking up the *Marseillaise*. Tommy did not know a word of it, but he yelled 'Marchon!' (a very good translation of *Marchons*) and sang 'lar-lar' to the rest of the tune.

Thus passed peacefully enough those five days calm before the storm. The Battalion had arrived at Iron on a Sunday morning. It had rested there, while the remainder of the British Army was being concentrated, until Friday morning. On Thursday night the Battalion Orders made it clear that a start was to be made. Parade was to be earlier than usual and nothing was to be left behind. Everyone was very sorry to be leaving their French

**Flowers and fruit were showered on the British
Tommies as they moved towards the front.**

The last tented camp before these men of the BEF began their march to Mons.

friends and there were great doings that night. Champagne was produced, and a horrible sort of liquor called 'alcohol' was introduced into the coffee. Such was the generosity of the miller's people that it was only with the greatest difficulty the captain induced madame to accept any payment for her kindness.

MARCHING TOWARDS MONS

So in the chill of that Friday morning the Battalion marched away, not without much hand-shakings and blessings from the simple villagers. The subaltern often wonders what became of mesdames, and that excitable son Raoul, and charming Thérese, whom the subalterns had all insisted on kissing before they left.

The Battalion joined its Brigade, and the Brigade its Division and, before the sun was very high in the sky, thousands were swinging along the *route nationale*, due northwards. The day was very hot and the Battalion was hurried, with as few halts as possible, towards Landrecies. As, however, this march was easily surpassed in 'frightfulness' by many others, it will be enough to say that Landrecies was reached in the afternoon.

Having seen his men as comfortable as possible in the schools where they were billeted for the night, the subaltern threw off his equipment, and having bought as much chocolate as he and a friend could lay their hands on, retired to his room and lay down.

At about seven o'clock in the evening the three subalterns made their way to the largest hotel in the town, where they found the rest of the Officers' Mess already assembled at dinner. He often remembered this meal afterwards, for it was the last that he would be properly served for some time. In the middle of it the colonel was summoned away by an urgent message. Before they dispersed to their billets the unwelcome news was received that Battalion parade was to be at three o'clock next morning.

'This,' said he, 'is the real beginning of the Show. Henceforth, horribleness.'

A hunk of bread eaten during the first stage of the march was all the breakfast he could find. Maroilles, a suburb of Landrecies, was passed, and an hour later a big railway junction. The march seemed to be directed on Maubeuge, but a digression was made to the north-west, and finally a halt was called at a tiny village called Hargnies. The subaltern's men were billeted in a large barn opening on to an orchard.

After a scrap meal he [the subaltern] pulled out some maps to study the country which lay before them, and what should meet his eye but the field of Waterloo, with all its familiar names: Charleroi, Ligny, Quatre Bras, Genappe, the names which he had studied a year ago at Sandhurst. Surely these names of the victory of ninety-nine years ago were a good omen.

A horrible rumour went about that another move was to be made at five o'clock the same evening, but this hour was subsequently altered to two o'clock the next morning. That night a five-franc postal order was given to every man as part of his pay.

Even in the height of summer there is always a feeling of ghostliness about nocturnal parades. The darkness was intense. As might be expected, the men had not by any means recovered from the heat and exertion of the previous day and were not in the best of tempers. The subaltern himself was so tired that he had to lie down on the cold ground at each hourly halt of ten minutes. With his cap for a pillow, he slept soundly for at least eight of those minutes. Then whistles were sounded and the men would rise wearily and shuffle back into their equipment with the single effort that is the hallmark of a well-trained soldier. The captain, passing along the Company, called their attention to the village they were passing. It was Malplaquet. The grey light of dawn revealed large open fields. 'I expect this is where they fought it out,' said the captain.

Keeping a close eye upon the map, he could tell almost to a hundred yards where the boundary of Belgium crossed the road. A few miles further

Men of the 2nd Battalion, Seaforth Highlanders crossing a canal in Belgium on their way to Mons.

on, a halt for breakfast was ordered, as it was about 8 am. The colonel called for company commanders and while they were away Sir John French, followed by Sir Archibald Murray and a few members of the General Staff, passed by in motors.

Among the hundred and one images the subaltern will always carry in his mind of the opening stages of the campaign, this one stands out most vividly. The sun was shining, but it was still cool. On the right of the road was a thick forest of young firs; on the left, a row of essentially suburban villas were being built, curiously out of place in that agricultural district. The men were sitting on the banks of the road or clustered round the cookers, drawing their breakfast rations of bread and cold bacon. Then the major came back; there was an expression on his face that showed he was well aware of the dramatic part he was about to play. Imagine him standing by the wayside, surrounded by his officers, two sergeant-majors, and some half-dozen senior sergeants, all with pencils ready poised to write his orders in their Field Service note-books. There was a pause of several seconds. The major seemed to be at a loss quite how to begin:

'There's a lot that I need not mention, but this is what concerns this Company,' he said jerkily 'When we reach' (here he mentioned a name which the subaltern has long since forgotten), 'we have to deploy to the left, and search the village of Harmignies to drive the enemy from it, and take up a position...'

It was a blow. Officers were frowning over their note books as if afraid they had not heard correctly. The enemy here, in the western corner of Belgium? The major's orders petered out. They saluted and returned to their platoons, feeling puzzled and a little shaken.

The subaltern had come to this campaign with such fresh hopes of victory. This was not to have been a repetition of the Franco-Prussian War of 1870. Surely France would not have gone to war unless she had been strong and ready. Inspired with the spirit of the First Republic, the French armies, they had convinced themselves, would surge forward in a wave of victory and beat successfully against the crumbling sands of the Kaiser's military monarchy. It should have been an early victory, drenching Germany with the blood of her sons and adding a lustre to the Sun of Peace that should never be dimmed by the black clouds of militarism. So then, all this was not to be.

He had yet to learn that Liège had fallen, let alone Brussels, the Belgian capital, and here were the Germans right round the Allied flank. It was astounding, irritating. In a vague way he felt deceived and staggered. It was a disillusionment. If the Germans were across the River Sambre, the French could scarcely launch their victorious attack on the Rhine.

The excitement dispelled his fatigue but, the men were openly incredulous: 'The ruddy 'Oolans 'ere all ready? They're only telling us that, to make us march.'

The first fight; how would it turn out? How would the men shape-up? Could the ammunition supply be depended upon? But, above all, what would he be like ? Would he feel afraid? If so, would he be able to hide it? Would his men follow him well? Perhaps he might be wounded (parts of him shrank from the thought), or killed. No, somehow he felt it was impossible that he would be killed. These and a thousand more such questions flashed through his brain as the march continued northwards.

The hourly halts were decreased from ten to about three minutes. The excitement of the future disolved the accumulating fatigue of the three days. The very weight of his sword and haversack was forgotten.

It was Sunday morning. The bells of the village churches were ringing and the women and children, decked in their Sunday best, were going calmly to church, just as if the greatest battle that, up to then, history had ever seen was not about to be fought around their very homesteads.

A waterworks was passed, and at last the cross roads were reached. There was a wait while the battalion in front of them deployed. Officers were loading their revolvers. They threw aside a hastily improvised barricade of ploughshares and hurried on to the place which was to be their especial care in the impending battle, known, rather inadequately, as Mons.

German cavalry advancing through Belgium in August 1914. These troops were the spearpoint of the massed army of infantry and artillery.

21 August, 1914

BRITISH TROOPS ARRIVE IN MONS

Georges Licope

As a fourteen-year-old boy, Georges Licope, witnessed the arrival of the advance guard of the British Expeditionary Force in his home town. The patrol of Lancers was given an enthusiastic welcome by the Belgian inhabitants of the suburbs of Mons. He also witnessed the Canadians re-entering Mons as the war ended on 11 November 1918.

It was Friday, 21 August, a glorious summer's day, blazing with sunshine, as if Nature was intent on revealing all her splendour. The civilized world, in a torment of anxiety, turned its gaze towards that ancient land of Belgium, where, once more the destiny of Europe was to be decided. Already the eastern half of the country was under the heel of the enemy and King Albert's little army, after having waged a lone struggle for eighteen long days against an enemy a hundredfold stronger in numbers and material, was withdrawing slowly upon the fort of Antwerp.

At Mons, capital of the province of Hainaut, close by the ancient battlefield of Malplaquet, where the Duke of Marlborough won fame two centuries before, the war had not yet made itself felt, and the inhabitants awaited anxiously to know their fate.

From early morning, alarming news had spread from mouth to mouth: Brussels had been occupied the previous evening and German Uhlans had been sighted at Manage, some sixteen miles north-east of Mons.

The *Garde Civique* had been on a war footing since the beginning of August and was holding the bridges and crossroads on all the highways leading into the town. This force, corresponding in some degree to the French *Garde Nationale*, or the English Yeomanry, was composed of men who had not served in the army. Armed with Comblain single-shot rifles, firing a leaden bullet, this corps could not be utilized in war time, except for service in the rear, because of its obsolete equipment. The *Garde Civique*, only active in peace time in the towns, assembed every Sunday on the parade ground or at the rifle range. These displays were either a time of relaxation or an imposition, according to whether the citizens who took part in them were martially or peacefully inclined. Their manoeuvres invariably ended at the cafe, where a few pints of good Belgian beer put everybody into high spirits.

On that particular morning, however, a company of the *Garde Civique* from La Louvière had come to reinforce their comrades at Mons and promptly took up position at 'La Bascule', an important strategic point at which the roads from Mons to Binche and Charleroi, and to Givry and Beaumont, crossed about a mile and a half south-east of the town on the northern slopes of Paniael Hill. Sentries had been stationed all along the roads and were conscientiously scanning the horizon, whilst their comrades made themselves comfortable and slaked their thirst at the Belle Vue café.

Suddenly I noticed about six or seven hundred yards away a cloud of dust approaching swiftly along the Beaumont road from the south-east. Indisputably, it was caused by galloping cavalry. A few seconds later I could clearly make out lances and khaki silhouettes wearing flat service caps, and galloping at full tilt. The sentry close by me missed no detail of this. I watched as he hid behind a big elm tree, loaded his single-shot rifle, and waited.

Who could these strange horsemen be, armed with lances and coming from the direction of the Ardennes – who else but German Uhlans? They certainly were not Belgian Lancers, and I for one was not aware that the French army included any mounted regiments armed with lancers.

The sentry methodically took aim with his rifle. In another few seconds a shot would have rung out.

Suddenly the horses stopped dead, the leaders drawing up on their haunches but the rider did not dismount. Seeing the sentry, the riders waved their caps, shouting 'English! English!' The sentry, somewhat reassured, beckoned them and aroused the company.

There followed a fine commotion; the *Gardes Civiques* were instantly on their feet. While senior officers who knew English were trying to talk with the members of the patrol, others gave orders: 'Company fall-in in two ranks! Slope arms! Present arms!'

In a few minutes all the nearby inhabitants were joining the *Gardes Civiques* in welcoming our Allies and offering them cigarettes, eggs, chocolate and beer.

Never shall I forget that moment when we first knew for certain that the British Army was drawing near and was going to fight the invader for our soil.

My two eyes were hopelessly incapable of taking in fully the martial glamour and magnificent equipment of our Allies. The highly polished leather rifle holsters; the ropes and pickets for tethering the horses and, above all, the bags of feed to care for their mounts. All were objects of comment and high praise by the admiring crowd.

The horsemen, still in the saddle, seemed in a tremendous hurry. Having asked the way to Obourg, they rode off again, amid excited cries of '*Vivent les Anglais!*' and '*Vive L'Angleterre!*' The mounted troopers raised their hands to acknowledge our spontaneous welcome and

Obsolete Belgian Comblain rifles armed the *Garde Civique*.

Caught on camera, the moment the British Lancers rode into Mons.

shouting 'Hurrah!' in a salute to Belgium, they trotted off. As a precaution, an officer of the *Garde Civique* escorted them on his bicycle to Obourg. This was as much to grant safe passage against any trigger-happy members of the *Garde Civique*, as to show them the way. I cannot recall whether these horsemen belonged to the 9th Lancers (2 Brigade) or to the 5th Lancers (3 Brigade).

Over the years I have dwelt upon that event which I witnessed because it gave us all inestimable encouragement at the very moment when we needed it most. Two days after that event I witnessed the gallantry of the Brtish infantry (8 Brigade, General B.J.C.D. Doran), which then consisted of 4th Middlesex, 2nd Royal Irish Regiment, 1st Gordon Highlanders, and 2nd Royal Scots. For a whole day on 23 August they resisted, almost alone, the brunt of the attack by the German IX Corps in the Mons Salient and on the heights of Panisel and Bois-la-Haut. I pay equal tribute to the King's 15th Hussars, who fought in the same part of the line in the capacity of divisional cavalry, and to the 6th, 23rd and 49th Batteries of 40 Brigade of the Royal Field Artillery. The civilians of the district where they fought for the first time in the Great War have never forgotten, nor will they ever forget, the sacrifices they made.

22 August, 1914

THE FIRST SHOT FIRED AT MONS

Sergeant E. Thomas, MM

It seemed rather odd that it was twenty-four years after the event that I was finally asked to tell about how I fired the first shot for the British Army in the Great War. Of course, when I did that I had not the slightest idea I was doing anything of the kind. However, it was officially proved to the satisfaction of those in a position to judge these things that I did have the distinction of firing the first of untold billions of shots that were discharged in the succeeding four years of terror and distress throughout the battlefields of the world.

The strange thing about the episode was, as far as I can remember and it seems as clear to me as if it took place last week, that I had not the slightest feeling of being in battle, not the remotest idea that I was taking a very active part as far as rifle fire was

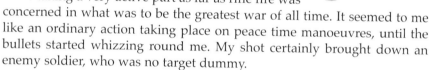

concerned in what was to be the greatest war of all time. It seemed to me like an ordinary action taking place on peace time manoeuvres, until the bullets started whizzing round me. My shot certainly brought down an enemy soldier, who was no target dummy.

My regiment, 4th Irish Dragoon Guards, had left Tidworth for Southampton, embarking at noon on 15 August, 1914, on HMT *Winnfrian* and disembarked at Boulogne the following day. After a few days camp we entrained and Haupont was reached by the 19th. We pushed forward, with no sign of the enemy. C Squadron, to which I belonged, was then detached from the regiment and sent forward on reconnaissance. The squadron moved forward to St. Denis, where we stayed the night, sending out patrols.

I need not say anything more of the cavalry advance to Mons, as that had nothing to do with the critical moment I am going to descrbe, but it so happened that on the morning of 22 August, 1914, when the countryside was flooded with the loveliest sunshine, its level rays making the haystacks in the spreading fields alongside the Mons-Charleroi road stand out boldly with their long black shadows to the west, that I, being a member of C Squadron, was waiting on the south-east of the road near to and almost within the shadow of the Chateau de Ghislain, under cover, when one of our scouts reported 'enemy coming down main road'.

Major Bridges, DSO, who went on to become Lieutenant General Sir Thomas Bridges, gave the order:

'4th Troop, dismount and prepare to give covering fire,' he called. '1st, Troop, draw sabres and prepare to charge.'

I can recall no tremendous sense of the moment – of men about to engage in battle; or thrill of anticipation of an encounter at that moment in time. Or, indeed, anything that seemed more exciting than some peace-time exercise back in England.

Then I saw them, a troop of Uhlan coming down the road towards us at a leisurely pace. The officer in front was smoking a cigar. Anxiously we watched their every movement. Then suddenly they halted, as if they sensed something was amiss. They had seen us. They turned quickly about. Captain Hornby called out for permission to charge after them with the sabre troop. Permission was granted and down the road they galloped. My troop was ordered to follow on in support, and we galloped on through the little village of Casteau. Then it was we could see the 1st Troop using their swords and scattering the Uhlans left and right. We caught them up and Captain Hornby gave the order, '4th Troop, dismounted action'.

We found cover for our horses by the side of the chateau wall. Bullets were flying past us and all round us, and I was first into action. I could see a German cavalry officer some four hundred yards away astride his mount in full view of me, gesticulating to the left and to the right as he directed his dismounted men and issued orders for them to engage us.

Immediately I saw him I took aim, squeezed the trigger and almost instantly it seemed, he fell to the ground, wounded or killed. As far as I am aware it was never ascertained which.

That was the first shot that was fired by a rifle in the British Army in the Great War and I cannot repeat too often that, at the time, it seemed to me more like rifle practice on the plains of Salisbury. However, within a second or two, it all changed. From every direction, or so it seemed, the air above us was thick with rifle and machine-gun bullets. There was the whistling noise of them and the little flurries of hay which errupted like smoke as bullets tore through the stacks all around us. The straw offered meagre cover to the troops. At once all this was something very different from our days of peace-time soldiering.

Still, it was really astonishing how few were injured in this first affair of the cavalry. None of our men was hit by the enemy fire, which just shows you what a lot of bullets it takes to drop a man. That now historic moment over, and the job that we had been appointed to do discharged, our C Squadron patrol under Captain Hornby safely wthdrew to our position at the little village of Casteau, off the main road of Soignies. With us were five German prisoners captured in the first sabre charge of the war.

23 August, 1914

THE FIRST HOURS AT MONS

Major A. Corbett Smith

Major Corbett Smith was an officer in the Royal Field Artillery during the Battle of Mons. His impressions of that memorable day in the little town, from its first beginning to its melancholy close, form the subject of this chapter. Corbett Smith was Mentioned in Dispatches for his valuable services during the fighting.

The dawn of Sunday the 23rd broke dim and misty, giving promise of heat. From the late afternoon of the previous day, squadrons and reconnaissance patrols from Chetwode's Cavalry Brigade had been pushing well forward on the flanks and front of the British line. It was pretty, though delicate, work, this feeling forward to get into touch with enemy outposts and patrols. Nor was there a troop which did not have some story to tell that evening of a tussle with enemy cavalry.

But as our cavalry pushed farther and farther northwards they found themselves confronting ever-increasing numbers and retirement became necessary. Thus were the first shots fired.

The morning wore on. The countryside was not unlike one of our own mining districts, the little villages and low-roofed houses giving that curious smoky, grimy effect of mean suburbs of a large industrial town. Here and there great heaps of slag or disused pits and quarries; gaunt iron girders carrying great wheels and heavy machinery.

The soldiers were billeted all through the houses or in odd barns and yards. Looking over the garden gate of one little house I saw the company cooks of one regiment getting the Sunday dinner ready, peeling the potatoes, swinging the pots on to the camp fires.

From a barn close by came the sound of singing. A padre had looked in as the rollicking chorus of 'Who's your lady friend?' rang out into the roadway, and with gentle interruption he improvised a short service, suggesting 'Rock of Ages' as a substitute for the music-hall ditty.

Down the road a couple of sergeants of the West Ridings leant idly over a gate, smoking and watching the folk going off to Mass. Into this peaceful scene a motorbike dispatch rider hurled himself, causing astonishment to a group of West Kents. 'Where's the officer? Get moving, you're wanted up

The village main street of Frameries, 24 August. Brigadier-General F. C. Shaw, commanding 9 Infantry Brigade, is seated with his staff. Down the street a barricade can be seen. Already, occasional shots are coming down the road from the far side of the barrier.

there!' and he jerked his thumb over his shoulder. The men rushed for their kit and rifles. Away to the west there was the crack of an 18-pounder. Down the street the cyclist panted. A subaltern burst in on the Sunday dinner of the Bedfords.

'Fall in outside at once!'

All down the line there errupted the crack of rifles. Beyond the canal, outposts of the Lincolns, Royal Scots and others were coming in at the double. A curtain of shell fire was lowered behind them as the British batteries came into action. A curtain fire rolled down before them as the German guns took the range. It was now close upon one o'clock, and enemy shells had begun to creep nearer and nearer, in from the suburbs and upon Mons itself. North of the town where our lines bulged out, making a salient, the fighting became desperate. Here three regiments, especially the Middlesex, Royal Irish and Royal Fusiliers, lost very heavily as they sturdily contested every yard of ground. This point had, from the first, been recognized as the weakest in our lines.

Barely an hour since the first shots were fired and now, by one o'clock, practically every gun and every rifle of the British Force was blazing away as though the powers of hell were let loose.

As yet it would seem that the ammunition was being merely wasted for the sake of making a noise. There was no enemy in sight save in the air the circling aeroplanes, and away on the flanks dimly seen clouds of horsemen. A modern battlefield, with its curious emptiness, has so often been described that here one need only record the fact in passing. There was nothing to be seen. The men were firing, in the first flush of excitement, at corners of possible concealment, the line of a hedge, the edge of a wood, the very occasional flash of a field-gun.

On the left, in the Second Corps sector, the British fire slackened somewhat as the men pulled themslves together. No one had the foggiest notion of what was really happening. It was the officers' business of the moment to steady the ranks and keep them under cover.

But away on the right, out towards Binche, where the Guards were, the storm had burst forth in fullest fury. No slackening there. The German gun fire was incessant and amazingly accurate. The effect of shells from their heavier guns, later so familiar, was at that time overwhelming.

Still, the British guns out towards Binche went gallantly pounding on, hopelessly outmatched though they were.

The fighting on the right, where General Lomax had the 1st Division, did not slacken for a moment, but steadily became more intense. Now, for the first time, the enemy was really seen. And, as his infantry began an

German infantry marching to their attack position

advance, the German shell-fire redoubled in intensity. Every house where British soldiers could be concealed, every possible observation post, every foot of trench, every hill-crest and 400 yards behind it, was swept and devastated by the fiery tornado.

What communication between units was possible in such a storm? Now battalions and batteries found themselves cut off from their neighbours, each fighting and carrying on alone.

Chetwode's Cavalry Brigade was caught in the thick of it. The Guards held on almost by their teeth.

The cavalry had to withraw and the Munsters and Black Watch lost horribly as they covered the retirement. No finer fighting regiments in the world than these on the right, but nothing human could stay there and live. The little town of Binche was abandoned – the first enemy success.

It must have been about 2.30 in the afternoon that this happened. But it was before the fall of Binche that the German infantry attacks began all along the line.

One end of the 1st Battalion, King's Own Yorkshire Light Infantry's trench ended in a little stone-walled pigsty. At least it was a pigsty about church time that morning, but a German gunner thought it would look better without any roof or walls. There was still a fragment three feet high on the weather side and the KOYLI commanding officer found it to be a convenient shelter.

For some minutes he had been watching intently through his glasses

German infantry receiving orders just prior to a mass attack on the British positions.

and observing the corner of a wood about 500 yards in front. He handed the binoculars to a sergeant

'What do you make of it? That corner over the little shed.'

The sergeant had a look and returning the glasses slowly nodded.

'It might be an entire brigade, sir, from the number of them.'

'Yes,' said the CO, 'I thought it was about time they turned up. Get word along that there is to be no firing until the order is given.'

'Very good sir!' The sergeant scrambled to his feet, saluted, ducked hastily as a shell whistled past alarmingly close, and promptly took a dive into the enlarged rabbit burrow in which his men were squatting.

The officer commanding a British battery, in position some distance to the rear, had evidently spotted that particular target, for puffs of bursting shrapnel had begun to appear over the wood and round its edges. Then there was a distinct movement of troops coming from behind the wood. It was a movement which could barely be discerned, for the packed ranks merged in against the grey-green countryside.

Suddenly, at about the same time the advancing troops became evident, it seemed as if all the guns in the world had been turned on to those few miles of British front line and on to the artillery batteries situated behind.

The KOYLI commanding officer held his fire until the last moment. When he did give the order for rapid fire (fifteen aimed shots a minute per man) it was impossible to miss. You cannot help hitting the side of a house, and that was what the massive grey-green target looked like. It was just slaughter. The oncoming ranks simply melted away.

The massed attack still came on. Though hundreds, thousands of the grey coats were mown down, just as many more crowded forward to refill the ranks.

Nearer still, and with a hoarse yell, the Yorkshires, Dorsets, Cornwalls and others were out of the trenches, officers ahead of them, with bayonets fixed and heading straight at the enemy. A murderous machine-gun fire met them, but it did not stop them, and within minutes they were thrusting and bashing with rifles, fists and stones, in amongst the enemy ranks.

Again the German gunners dropped their range and poured shells indiscriminately into friend and foe alike. It was all too much for the attacking regiments and they broke up, turned and began to struggle back. It was impossible to attempt any recall of our men. They pursued until they were overwhelmed by sheer numbers and were killed or captured. Some did struggle back to our lines as best they could in knots of twos and threes, or wandered aimlessly on to the flanks and got lost.

Such was one single attack. But no sooner was it broken than fresh regiments would march out to begin it all over again. Here was no Pass of Thermopylae where a handful of men could withstand for indefinite time an army. What could the British Army hope to do against such overwhelming numbers?

The cavalry, the only reserves available, were working hard, surely, as no cavalry has ever worked before. Squadrons were everywhere at once. Wherever a gap was threatened they were there in support. And wherever they went there also went the Horse Gunners, working hand in glove with them. Charge and counter-charge upon the flanks of the attacking infantry, dismounting to cover with their fire a British infantry rally; fierce hand-to-hand encounters with enemy squadrons. Wherever they were wanted, each man and horse was doing the work of ten.

But this could not last for long. Now it was becoming only too evident that far from there being a reasonable superiority against us, the British were everywhere along the line hopelessly outnumbered in every arm.

At 6.00 pm the enemy had concentrated their fire upon the town of Mons and it became untenable.

Only six hours – six short hours since the Belgian townsfolk had come peacefully home from Mass to their Sunday *déjeuner*, proud and hopeful in the presence of their British allies. Now their houses, their town, was a heap of smoking ruins.

In those short hours how many women had seen their children crushed by falling walls or blown to atoms by bursting shells? How many children were left helpless and alone in the world, with no mother or father to take them by the hand and guide them from the hell of destruction?

About 2 am, 24 August, orders to begin retiring were issued from General Headquarters (GHQ). Some four hours before a few of the units – those north of the canal – had begun to fall back and so the beginning of the move was made. As the last of these crossed the bridges the detonator fuses were fired and the bridges blown up.

For the rest, the men crouched ever in their places. Bayonets fixed, rifles always ready, waiting, waiting.

23 August, 1914

HE RODE WITH FEAR

Lieutenant Colonel Arthur Osburn

Arthur Osburn was at Mons as a medical officer with the 4th Dragoon Guards, the first British regiment to fire a shot in the war. After serving in the ranks in the Yeomanry during the Boer War, he went on to qualify as a doctor in 1902. He was commissioned in the Royal Army Medical Corps in 1903. He was promoted major in 1915 and awarded the Distinguished Service Order in 1916.

Sunday, 23 August and we had arrived at Thulin on the bank of the canal that stretches from Mons to Condé. We had had no sleep worth talking about for some days and we had been the first unit in the British Army in contact with the enemy. On the Saturday, Captain Hornby, with a half squadron had got as far as Soignies, where from the church tower the battlefield of Waterloo was just visible. They had pursued and charged some German cavalry: Bavarian ploughboys kitted out in German uniforms, that was all they really were. These youngsters carried long metal lances, like lengths of gas-piping, they could hardly manage. Some of the lads had been killed and three or four wounded and captured. Fair, resolute, genial and a keen soldier, Captain Hornby with his troop, magnificently mounted – as indeed we all were – all yelling at full charge, their long, straight swords a glittering row of steely points, would have struck terror into far more hardened soldiers.

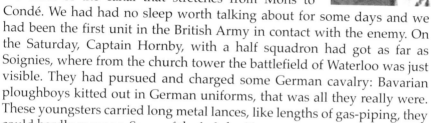

   After forty-eight hours of almost continuous movement we had finished up with a long night ride through the wretched slums of Frameries, Wasmes, and Paturages. That ride had been a nightmare; a thin drizzle had turned the coal dust that lay everywhere into a greasy slime. Our horses, half-asleep like ourselves, had staggered on, stumbling over the uneven cobbles and cinder heaps, slipping and falling on the endless network of tram and trolley lines. So on that Sunday we were all drowsy and slack, yet the tension in the air was unmistakable.

Early in the afternoon there had fallen an ominous silence. Everyone and everything, even the great line of elm trees opposite our billet, seemed to be attentive, as if waiting for something to happen.

A sense of impending disaster pervaded the silent village. We knew that the Germans were not far way. Twenty minutes later we were engaged in the battle of Mons; five hours later we had begun the Long Retreat.

I shall not easily forget the overture of that extraordinary battle. At 3.30 pm on that sultry Sunday afternoon there rose, apparently about 800 yards in front of us, a crackling sound, exactly like the noise of an October bonfire into which a cartload of dry holly boughs has been suddenly thrown: a fierce, steady crackle that grew ominously louder and angrier and nearer, nearer moment by moment. I had heard nothing like that in the Boer War!

My heart sank. There surged over me the first and worst moments of dismay – of fear – in the war. Afterwards I was often partly indifferent to danger from sheer exhaustion, nerve strain and fatigue, yet not seldom – like, I think, most others – I walked and rode with Fear, or at least, apprehension. Fear, like a tall, grey figure stalking by my side or never very far away. The deep thunder of our own or enemy artillery fire could be stimulating, but the angry crackle of massed rifles I shall always loathe.

FIRST HOT ENGAGEMENT

The regiment mounted, and we moved off a few hundred yards to the left and dismounted again. A German and an English plane, firing viciously at one another, circled overhead.

The infantry in the line ahead of us were evidently in for a hot time. We, as cavalry, were merely standing-to for eventualities. Presently wounded from the infantry regiments just in front of us began to limp and stagger down the road on our right. I left the regiment and walked over to some cart sheds just across this road, which I had already marked down as my prospective 'dressing station'. My groom and servant and my corporal led our horses over, and I knelt down in the shed to dress the first of the British troops who had been wounded. As I did so the first bursts of German shrapnel were coming over with a venomous buzz, like swarms of angry hornets. Soon I was up to my eyes in work, the knees of my riding-breeches soaked with the blood that was running all over the place from those who were badly wounded.

More and more, in twos and threes, sixes and sevens, then in streams, the wounded poured in, some walking, some carried pickaback or in hand-seats, and a few on stretchers. Men of the Manchester Regiment and Duke of Cornwall's Light Infantry (DCLI), King's Own Scottish Borderers (K.O.S.B.) and several other regiments. But where were their doctors? There seemed to be not a sign of one. At that point I did not realize the almost hopeless task that the infantry doctors were engaged in. My orderly and myself made desperate attempts to cope with the streams of wounded

Men of the British Cavalry Division, commanded by Major General E.H. Allenby in the opening weeks of the war.

men. The whole of the cart shed was now full of wounded that lay or sat about in the mud and sodden straw. Every post was being clung to by those able to stand; some slipped down and fainted. There were now streams of men, presumably wounded, passing right and left across the fields, going I know not where.

It never occured to me that anyone was retreating. More shrapnel was coming over and our own Royal Horse Artillery was replying.

We must have been there for hours, but it seemed only a few minutes before we were lighting candles and lanterns to see what we were doing. So numerous now were the wounded that I could only find time to look at the worst, and then do little more than tighten an amateur tourniquet or plug a gaping wound in the chest wall with gauze, and give morphine in heroic doses to those who appeared to be in the most pain.

I got up and went out. A blaze of burning hayricks and a night glow from a hundred thousand rifles in rapid fire lit up the darkening northern sky just beyond some trees. Down the centre of the road on the other side of which I had left my regiment were coming streams of wounded, hopping, crawling, walking or being carried, but the dry ditches on either side of the road just outside my dressing-station were full of whispering shadows.

'What's the matter with you all there?' I demanded.

There was no reply from the huddled forms in the darknessof the ditch. I was really too weary to be indignant, but I pretended to be.

'It you do not immediately rejoin your regiment in the firing line, I'll take every man's name and regiment and send him to his adjutant. You know what that means – court martial for desertion in the face of the enemy!'

There was a silence and then a few, only a few, of the huddled forms sullenly emerged with their rifles and walked with slow, depressed step; back towards that pink glow and that 'holly-bush' crackling beyond the trees.

Getting suddenly alarmed at all the possibilities, I collected my gear, with some haste and we mounted, leaving, alas, many wounded, some partly with wounds dressed and others unattended. I left them in charge of a senior non-commissioned officer who was only slightly wounded. I reminded him of the most simple forms of tourniquets, and giving him an armful of dressings, advised him when the carts came back to take all the rest of the wounded were to be taken to Thulin, the village about half a mile back on the road behind us. This I think he did, for carts with wounded began arriving while I was attending to those already in the town hall there. This was not the only time in which it was quite impossible to fulfil my duty to my unit and to the wounded of other units. We entered the little town of Thulin in darkness and silence; indeed, I was rather surpised how silent everything had suddenly become. There was but one building that had any light in it. As we passed it I was besieged by a party of Belgian priests and nuns.

'M'sieur is a doctor? Please come in at once – in here! There are many English wounded. There are no doctors and we do not know what to do.'

I dismounted and entered what was evidently the *Mairie,* or town hall.

The steps were thronged with a jostling crowd of wounded. Many excited Belgian peasants and Sisters of Mercy were carrying in mattresses, straw, jugs of water and old sheets for bandages.

The scene inside was one with which I was soon to become only too familiar. It was packed with wounded, lying down, crouching or standing; the stairs were blocked with sitting cases, the passages with loaded stretchers. There were several whose hastily applied tourniquets had evidently slipped, lying in a dead faint from loss of blood.

Everywhere lights and confusion and a babel of tongues – Cockney, French, Flemish, and broken English. I spoke but little French, and getting hold of the most responsible priests and the older Catholic sisters, I urged them to keep the badly wounded cases on the ground floor and all the slightly wounded cases up to the rooms on the upper floors of the building. They had started doing the very reverse.

'But why, m'sieur?'

'Because in case of fire you will never get the stretcher cases down again in time, if you carry them up those narrow stairs.'

'Fire! But why should there be a fire? The bad cases will be much more comfortable upstairs. Besides there are far too many slight cases to put up in the small rooms above. And some of the upper rooms are locked, half full of the town's records.'

'Never mind,' I said. 'Break the doors open. Let all the wounded who can walk go up and leave the stairs and passages free. They can sit down on the floor in the upstairs rooms.'

We began gradually to get the place in some sort of order. The palliasses and mattresses which were being brought in we arranged in rows. Straw had been put down where there were no mattresses, much too much straw, for the harvest time was just beginning.

Thulin Town Hall *(Marie)* where Captain (later Lieutenant Colonel) Osburn set up a temporary dressing station. It was from here that he made his escape when the Germans arrived unexpectedly.

The sisters were giving the men cigarettes. I tried to dissuade them. 'Don't encourage them to smoke here, or you will soon have all this straw alight.'

'Soldiers! Poor English soldiers! Not smoke! After such a brave battle!' They gazed at me, astonished. I might as well have ordered them to stop the men breathing. Soon I was terribly busy with the worst cases. Only two can I remember in all that confusion. One badly wounded in the head, yet conscious enough to point to the man lying next to him.

'Sir, that man alongside blew off his own right hand recharging a fuse to blow up a bridge across that canal which the Germans had just captured.

He went back alone of his own accord to do it himself. The first charge wouldn't go off. If he hadn't stopped the Germans they would have enfiladed our entire line.

The two men were, I feel sure, both Royal Engineers. I dressed the stump of the hero of the bridge and hastily scribbled his name and number in my notebook.

'You won't, be forgotten,' I said. You deserve a VC. I'll see that the General hears about it.'

I was in the midst of giving instructions as to each wounded man not injured in the stomach having at least a litre of milk a day, when an excited sister seized me by the arm.

M'sieur! Go at once! The Germans are here.'

'Here?'

'Yes, m'sieur. In the street outside. No! Not that way! By the side door to the right. Quick! Quick!'

I dashed to the side door and there found my groom and orderly looking pale and excited. They, too, had just seen the Germans; indeed had actually rubbed shoulders with them in the darkness outside. We all three flung ourselves on our horses and dashed away from the *Mairie*, not knowing in the least which direction to take.

A light rain had begun to fall and the cobble stones were greasy. Shots behind added wings to our speed. Galloping madly in the darkness, slithering and skidding through those silent streets, we were nearly down half a dozen times.

Where was everybody? What had become of the British Army? Why had nobody told me? Where were we galloping to?

I called out, 'Ou sont les Chasseurs anglais?' to no one in particular. 'Ou sont les Dragons de la Garde?' I shouted through the echoing streets – the excitement playing havoc with my scanty French. There was no answer to my ill-judged question as to where the English cavalry in general was, and where were the Dragoon Guards in particular. Only shots and the echoes of our clattering hoofs could be heard.

Suddenly we were fired at point-blank from in front; the flash showed a group of dismounted cavalry on the left of the road. Someone challenged us with an unmistakable English accent: 'Qui va la?'

'Who's that? We're 4th Dragoon Guards.'

'Ninth Lancers,' answered the voice. 'Where the hell have you come from?'

We had bumped into the rear troop of the rearguard of 2 Cavalry Brigade, which was under the command of Brigadier General de Lisle. Geoffrey à Court, I think it was, in charge of the rearguard, he and his men were guarding the

Brigadier General
Beauvoir De Lisle.

railway crossing. There was a hurried explanation, and the sliding metal gates rolled back for us to cross the lines. I found our regiment half a mile back, in a soaking cornfield, whose every sheaf drenched us as we touched it. No lights were to be shown and it was almost out of the question to lie down, for the ground was sodden. We had had only a very few light casualties in the regiment; Pat Fitzgerald, our machine gun officer, had his cheek slit open with a bullet. I sewed up the wound, which was several inches long, by the screened light of a candle as he and I crouched behind a sheaf.

The road past the field was crowded with Belgian peasants and their children hurrying away in the dark. For a moment or two I watched the refugees, trying to think what on earth could be happening. It was unbelievable that any part of the British Army should have begun to retire in the first few hours of 'Armageddon' [Biblical war to end conflict for ever]. Would not some of us be court martialled? The Army and Navy had for years been looking forward in confidence to a sharp decisive scrap with Germany. In the naval ward-rooms I had visited and the military messes I had lived in, conversation constantly returned to the subject. We had all been cheerfully assured of victory; prepared as we were to the last range-finder, and ready to the last gaiter button – and now this.

UP IN FLAMES

Presently a bright light flared up behind us; some of the refugees turned, their white faces lit by the glare.

'What's that?' I asked.

'It must be the town hall, m'sieur. It is the only building of that size in Thulin.'

So the expected had happened. I have always had a horror of fire, especially in hospitals; I thought of that crowded building, with so many nearly helpless men and confused and frightened priests and sisters; of the suffocating blaze and smoke from damp straw, khaki clothing and matresses. With all those men smoking it needed no prophet to see what was almost a certainty. And my VC hero, too weak from loss of blood from that jagged stump to walk. Poor devil! He had looked as white as a sheet; was he at that moment being burnt alive?

I fumbled for my notebook. At least this gallant soldier should have a posthumous honour for his mother and his relations. Then there was his corps and his country, they should know of his self sacrfice.

My notebook was gone.

I had had it in my hand when the sister warned me. That panic-stricken dash from the town hall, the mad ride over those greasy cobble-stones, accounted all too easily for the loss. I learnt afterwards that the Germans, all things considered, devoted great care and skill and were very kind to our wounded.

Direction of German advance

Mons, looking along the length of the Mons-Condé Canal from the church tower. This is looking westward towards St Ghislain and the Mariette Bridge. The slag heap in the centre is at Jemappes.

CONFUSED FIGHTING

Gradually our men were being pressed back to the outskirts of Élouges [24 August]. It is hard to describe clearly what happened, or just when and where the trouble began; but as concerns one of the most famous incidents of the retreat from Mons, it may be worthwhile to make some attempt, though I was but a puzzled spectator, not a participant. The difficulty in giving a clear account was increased by the confusing nature of the country. Within a radius of about three thousand yards of Élouges and of one another lay at least six little villages: Angre, Angreau, Audregnies. Montignies, Onnezies and Wihéries, similar in size, each situated in a little valley, their names having to English ears a similar sound. Outside each village, and as alike as two peas, were one or more little cemeteries surrounded with brick walls. In or near this area, strange to us on that eventful morning, dotted as it was with conical slag-heaps about sixty feet high, and intersected with many sunken roads, railways and trolley lines, no fewer than three brigades or twenty-seven squadrons of our cavalry were active between 8 am and noon, in addition to several battalions of infantry and many artillery units. If my account of what I saw appears muddled, confusing, it is my only excuse. It must have been about 11 am when the brigade turned about at the shrine and rode back through the two villages towards the small cemetery at Wihéries.

The brigade halted twice. Artillery fire had begun on our right; this I supposed to be our guns on the hillside to the south and east of us. Then heavy firing began from the German positions both to the north and east and also on our left. Some shrapnel was coming over. I had the impression that an important move was about to take place, and as my position in an action should be alongside my own colonel, who was on ahead, I decided to overtake him. I saw him and a few of his staff turn up to the right and then halt. The remainder of the regiment, all three squadrons, as I thought, turned to the left, toward the Germans.

I missed my groom and stopped for a moment to look for him; then a squadron of the 9th who had got just in front of me turned about, and I had perforce – because of the narrowness of the lane – to turn about with them. They turned down to their right between two walls and there they halted, facing the Germans. I turned about again, intending to rejoin the

German battery of 77 mm field guns laying down supporting fire for attacking infantry.

headquarters of my own regiment. Instead of overtaking them, I found myself with some of the 18th Hussars riding up a slope above some railway lines to where our field and horse batteries were halted. The firing had become much heavier. Some of the cavalry were riding towards the railway lines between us and the Germans, making, apparently, for the tall brick buildings of a sugar factory. A perfect hurricane of shelling began. Then the whole scene was blotted out in smoke and dust. Like most of the others, I had heard no orders and did not know a charge was taking place. I don't think anyone except those taking part in it did, and many of them told me afterwards that they thought it was only a reconnaissance.

The noise was now terrific. Shells were bursting higher up the hill; some seemed to be skimming just overhead. With two mounted signallers and a man of the 18th Hussars, I rode in between two walls, close to the cemetery, where we sheltered. The broad slope of the hill above and behind, to the south of us, was now one white cloud of bursting shells. Then some of the 9th and 11th came galloping past us excitedly. Everybody seemed to be shouting, though the din was so deafening we could not hear what they said; but with the signallers I followed some of them, only to find myself again in one of the villages we had passed through nearly an hour before.

BRITISH CAVALRY CHARGE

It must then have been about 11.30 am. The Hussar – an officer's servant – had followed after us. He and I rode up to the hilltop crowned by the little shrine at the fork roads. The artillery fire all round was very heavy.

I could see infantry moving down below me across our front, but whether English or German I could not be certain (probably the Cheshires, or part of our 19 Brigade). Unaware that my regiment – and indeed the whole brigade – were dispersed and disorganized, temporarily non-existent, I started off again to find them.

Only by piecing together the conflicting accounts and experiences of survivors did I manage during the next week to get a hazy idea of the day's events. At 10 am the 2nd Cavalry Brigade, sixteen or seventeen hundred officers and men, Dragoons, Lancers and Hussars, had been virtually intact; yet before noon the brigade was so broken and scattered as to be for the time being non-existent. By 7 o'clock that evening about two hundred men and a few officers had arrived in Wargnies-le-Petit, believing themselves to be the only survivors. Whole batteries of horse and field artillery had apparently been exterminated.

One account was that General de Lisle, hearing that the 5th Infantry Division on our right was in difficulties and trying to extricate itself from the German attack, had placed his brigade at the disposal of the GOC. To delay the advance of the Germans on our retreating infantry and prevent the capture of our field batteries, our brigade was to make some sort of demonstration in force. This was to be preceded by a reconnaissance of the ground by two troops of the 18th Hussars or the 9th Lancers.

Either the orders were confused or confusing – or the general's commands were given direct to the troops and squadrons concerned, (always a fatal mistake, instead of being passed as they should have been through the regimental commanders).

At all events the two troops sent out to reconnoitre had been followed, by practically the entire brigade. The Germans, seeing a comparatively large mass of cavalry suddenly let loose and galloping towards them, got a bad attack of nerves – why, it is hard to understand, for the network of hedges, wire fences, allotments, trolley lines and other obstructions made it unlikely that our cavalry would ever reach their infantry or guns. But nearly every German gun within range had at once been put on to the small area on which our cavalry were moving.

Presumably to counter this, our field and horse artillery had also been compelled to open fire, thus disclosing prematurely and fatally their own position. They in turn had been hopelessly hammered by the German massed artillery. A first-class battle had in fact developed with the rapidity of a whirlwind from this muddled order. For the German infantry, imagining themselves to be seriously threatened by this charge of British cavalry, had taken it seriously and halted their advance.

German infantry resting during their advance.

Every rifle and machine gun on their side was now blazing away at our desperate and rather objectless cavalrymen.

What our men did exactly when they emerged from the cover of those walls into a perfect hail of shell and machine-gun fire, and the clouds of dust and ashes disturbed from the slag heaps, no one seems to know. Some eventually got over to a sugar factory, from which they were driven out again by a concentration of machine-gun fire. Horses tripped over signal wires, railway lines, plunged into ballast pits alongside the railway lines, killing and injuring their riders. Men and horses managed to reach a hedge and wooden fence surrounding some allotments on the far side of the railway, terrifying the Germans in that sector. That reckless and meaningless onrush unnerved them, as a German told me after the war.

Incredibly, some men actually galloped under this terrific fire through a half-circle of two miles and survived.

The Vicomte de Vauvineur, our principal French liaison officer, was blown to pieces, with many of the 4th Dragoon Guards around him. Most of the other French officers attached to us were either killed or wounded. Major Tom Bridges had his horse shot from under him and in the resulting fall the bones of his face were badly damaged as he crashed onto the railway lines. Climbing into the sugar factory, at which half a dozen German machine guns were firing, he got out of a window and, dropping onto the back of a riderless horse, somehow got away. Although the casualties eventually turned out to be less heavy than at first supposed, about three hundred of our magnificent horses – many of them had come from Rothschild's stables – had been killed.

The London papers, hard up for any cheering news, transmuted this unfortunate affair into 'a magnificient charge of the 9th Lancers – German gunners sabred!'

Colonel David Campbell, commanding the 9th Lancers, was, as we were told, offered a VC on the strength of it all, an honour he was said to have indignantly refused. 'I want my squadrons back again, not VCs or any other medals.

23 August, 1914

LONG LINES of DEATH

Corporal John F Lucy

The author of this description of his experiences at Mons, was a corporal in 1914. He and his brother had run away from home and enlisted in the Royal Irish Rifles in 1912. He rose through the ranks and was commissioned a second lieutenant in 1917, retiring as a captain. He was invalided home with multiple wounds during the Second Battle of Ypres in 1915. He wrote a famous war memoir, There's a Devil in the Drum.

In 1915 John Lucy was promoted sergeant. He is seen here with his sergeant stripes.

A staff officer came perspiring from behind, and overtook us. He trotted past in a hurry, asking for the commanding officer. A hundred voices answered him: 'At the head of the column, sir,' and eight hundred pairs of eyes viewed him with that feeling of amusement peculiar to a mass of men finding entertainment in the efforts of an isolated individual.

The soldiers criticised his accent, his face, his seat, and his mount in turn, and then they cursed him because of the result of his coming. This was the order to turn about, and go back the road they had come, to the trenches abandoned that very morning.

So about we went, and passing back to the rear of the line of trenches, took to open country in artillery formation, and thus extended went forward to occupy the earthworks.

The old Army was familiar with the siting and digging of trenches, although it was trained for open warfare. The type of trench here was called a kneeling trench, as it was roughly only three feet deep, this being considered good

British soldiers manning shallow trenches near Mons, August 1914.

enough for temporary occupation by infantry not expected to remain in it for the entire course of a battle. Our motto was 'Attack, or counter-attack', and we had very little time for entrenchments, which, though they might be useful during a short period of temporary defence, were generally despised. With many jokes the men settled into their defences and cheerfully waited for the enemy, presenting in his direction a line of first-class riflemen, each trained to fire fifteen well-applied shots a minute. Our two machine-guns poked their squat muzzles in support from their emplacements.

A battery of field-guns wheeled away from the main road, and drew up on the back slope of our position about three hundred yards to the rear. The menacing mouths of the eighteen-pounders slewed round in our direction and remained, while the horses were led rapidly away under cover. The activities of the smart-looking gunners slowed down, and the teams

British 18-pounder gun crew at Mons.

German artillerymen hauling a 120 mm heavy Krupp Howitzer into place.

became still behind their gun shields. A young subaltern came forward to our height as observation officer.

All then was ready, as far as we were concerned, for the battle of Mons.

FOUND BY THE ENEMY

At half-past three in the afternoon, as nearly as I remember, the Germans discovered us before we saw them, and three or four dull thuds to our distant front followed by a whirring noise rapidly approaching us marked the discharge of enemy guns, and our first moment under shell-fire.

The salvo of shells passed over our heads, and burst about eighty yards in our rear with a terrific clattering crash. We were fascinated. More shells came and still more, all going over. The heads of our curious men appeared above the trenches looking back to see the bursts.

'Look', they shouted, 'a black one!' or 'one only!' or 'four more whites'. Some laughingly imagined themselves on butt duty on the rifle ranges at home, and shouted advice to the German gunners: 'washout!' 'another miss,' and 'lower your sights.' One wag, simulating great terror, cried: 'Send for the police; there's going to be a row on here,' and another, in mock despair: 'Oh, mother, why did I desert you?' Then the enemy gunners shortened, and the shells exploded above our trenches; and the men, already told off for exposing themselves, crouched low.

I had been standing about by my ammunition carts on the open road immediately behind and parallel to our trenches, and not far from the commanding officer, who was, with his adjutant, fully exposed on a little rise nearer to the entrenched companies, when fragments of a bursting shell ripped and slashed all round us. Someone shouted 'Take cover," and my men and I, leaving the carts to the drivers, took shelter as best we could in the roadside ditch, amateurishly choosing that side of the road farthest from the enemy.

The Germans now ranged well, and their shell-fire seemed to concentrate heavily on the trenches. The acrid smoke of the explosions

German infantry awaiting orders to advance.

blew about us, and screaming pieces of metal and shrapnel balls flew in all directions. One shrapnel bullet hit my pack and – instinctively – I moved a little farther along the ditch to a burly sergeant, who laughed at me when I handed him the still hot ball for his inspection. I was too young to discern nervousness in the laugh. A dispatch-rider coming towards us on the road from the west fell off his motor-cycle when a shell burst over him. His antics distracted and amused us. The shell-fire became hotter and hotter, and we crouched farther down in our ditch. The commanding officer still remained exposed to all the fire, and his adjutant kept taking messages to

A British machine gun team operating a British Maxim in the summer of 1914.

the entrenched companies. Finally the shelling ceased, and we put up our heads to breathe more freely. Then we heard conch-like sounds – strange, bugle calls. The German infantry, which had approached during the shelling, was in sight and about to attack us.

DREADFUL RAIN OF SHELLS

Not a shot had been fired from our trenches up to now, and the only opposition to the Germans had been made by our field-gun battery, which was heavily engaged behind us, and making almost as much clamour as the enemy shelling. To my mind it seemed that the whole battalion must have been wiped out by that dreadful rain of shells, but apparently not.

In answer to the German bugles or trumpets the cheerful sound of our officers' whistles and the riflemen, casting aside the amazement at their strange trial, sprang to action and a great roar of musketry rent the air, varying slightly in intensity from minute to minute as whole companies ceased fire and opened-up again. The satisfactory sharp blasts of the directing whistles showed that our machinery of defence was working like the drill book, and that the recent shelling had caused no disorganisation. The clatter of our machine guns added to the din.

For us the battle took the form of well-ordered, rapid rifle-fire at close range, as the field-grey human targets appeared, and were struck down.

A field of German dead after a mass attack in the late summer of 1914.

The enemy infantry advanced, according to one of our men, in 'columns of masses', which withered away under the galling fire of the well-trained and coolly led Irishmen. The leading Germans fired standing, from the hip, as they came on, but their scattered fire was ineffective and ignored. They crumpled up – mown down as quickly as I tell it, their reinforcing waves and sections coming on bravely and steadily to fall over as they reached the front line of the slain and wounded. Behind the death line thicker converging columns were being blown about by our field-guns.

Our rapid fire was appalling even to us, and the worst marksman could not miss, as he only had to fire into the massed ranks of the unfortunate enemy, who on the fronts of two of our companies were continually and uselessly reinforced at the short range of three hundred yards. Such tactics amazed us, and after the first shock of seeing men slowly and helplessly falling down as they were hit, gave us a great sense of power and pleasure. It was all so easy

The German survivors began to go back here and there from the line. The attack had been an utter failure. Soon all that remained was the long line of the dead heaped before us, motionless except for the limb movements of some of the wounded. Every battle seems endless to those taking part in it. All sense of time is lost, and the minutes appear to be hours. The sequence of events is lost, and the most unlikely tales are told by survivors. I am hazy as to what happened after the first attack. I believe the Germans tried to come on again, but I am not sure. At any rate they did not succeed.

We were not without casualties, but for such a terrific lot of shooting they were very few indeed, and were actually the least we had in any battle in the war. Only three or four men were killed and the same number wounded.

Most of the German shrapnel shells had burst too high, and their rifle-fire was hopeless.

A German shell burst on one of our machine gunners, killing him instantly. His place was immediately taken at the gun by a lance-corporal who was shot almost at once through the arm. He, though wounded, continued to fire the machine gun, but he rather puzzled those near him by weeping at intervals, either with pain or fright. He would not, however, leave his gun until his arm stiffened. One seldom hears a soldier crying, or raising his voice in any way, for that matter, when wounded. A shot through joints like the knee, or through the stomach, often makes a man shout out in great pain, but most wounds are merely numbing for the time. Most of the pain comes afterwards when the wounds are being dressed in hospital.

Our commanding officer still stood on the high ground overlooking the scene of action. He now had fears for our ammunition supply. I had doled out a large number of boxes, and an officer presently came along and

The summer of 1914: a line of concealed British infantry firing on the massed ranks of German attackers.

ordered all my carts away to be refilled. The sounds of battle had died down, and all was quiet except for some intermittent shelling from the Germans. I was to take my carts off to a refilling point controlled by the artillery a mile or so away to the south-east. It was getting dark and the lights of enemy camp fires could be seen in the distance.

Nearer, their red-cross lanterns appeared here and there on our front, showing that they were attending to their wounded.

A mounted bombardier came to guide my carts, and off we went, passing along a road that appeared to me times to traverse No Man's Land for we passed British infantry facing north, on our right hand. They greeted us and joked at us from their trenches.

We had had orders to hurry, and in the rush of our departure no check was made of the total amount of ammunition still in hand. In order to travel lightly we had also been told to leave our packs behind us in our ditch. Having gone some distance in the darkness, I noticed that three of our four carts gave forth the heavy rumble of well-weighted vehicles, and I called a halt to examine them. I found the three almost full, and completing them from the fourth I took matters into my own hands and brought them back at once to the battalion, terrified lest it should be without a reserve of ammunition in case of another enemy attack. The fourth cart I ordered on to the refilling point, with two of my men and the bombardier.

It was after midnight when I rejoined the battalion, and reported my action. The officer who had sent me merely said 'Good, now go and rejoin the machine gun section.' I found the section fallen in on the road behind the trenches, and saw that our companies were also evacuating their positions.

All was very still and peaceful. Quiet words of command were passed along: 'Number'; Form fours'; 'Right'; 'Keep silence'; 'Quick march.' And off we went stealthily, in columns and in ranks of four from the battlefield of Mons.

In the morning the entire British Army was marching south in retreat.

23-25 August, 1914

TERROR and TRIBULATION

Captain Arnold Gyde

The writer of this chapter is pictured here as a subaltern shortly before the war. He served at Mons in the 2nd Battalion, South Staffordshire Regiment, which formed part of 6 Infantry Brigade; his Platoon was No. 7, B Company.

In war it is well known that he who sees most is likely to take least away. It was not the soldier's duty to gaze about him to see what was happening. He must enlarge his bit of trench, and be ready to meet the enemy when he himself is attacked. Therefore, if you asked a veteran of Mons about the battle, all he would be able to tell you – as likely as not – would be, 'marching and digging, and then marching mostly'.

The company on the left was astride a railway embankment in front of a large mine. B Company was directly in front of the village itself [Harmignies]; another company to the right, and the fourth in local reserve. The work of entrenchment began immediately. There was not time

British positions at Mons, August 1914.

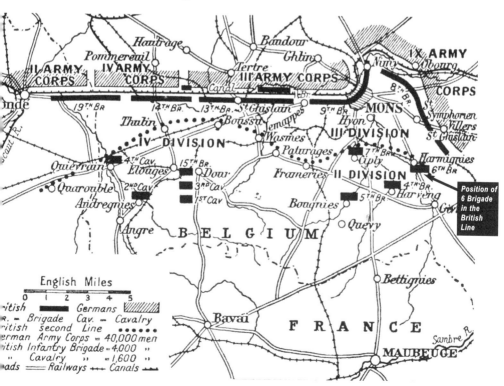

to construct a trench as laid down in the *Manual of Field Engineering*. Each man had to scrape with his entrenching tool as big a hole as he could before the enemy came upon him.

A subaltern had many things to arrange: the 'field of fire' had to be cleared and any refuge behind which the enemy might lurk within two hundred yards of the trenches had to be, if possible, cut down. Sheaves of corn standing upright presented the first problem for the defence. Should he burn as many of them as he could, or overturn them, or beat them down? No, he decided, sheaves were not bullet-proof, a man could be shot behind them easily.

He told off a small party to improve what natural obstacles – in this case wire fences – lay in front. He next went to arrange for the methods of effecting a retirement, if it should be necessary, breaking through one or two fences so that this could be effected in perfect order. As some of the houses were still occupied, he went to the owners, and not knowing the French for pick and shovel, said: 'Monsieur, voulez-vous me preter des choses pour faire des troux dans la terre?' [would you lend me things to dig the earth?].

'Ah, oui, Monsieur, des pioches!' [pick] As many of these as possible were sent forward to the men, together with many pounds of biscuits which he bought from a shop, and buckets of water for the wounded.

So busy had he been that he had almost been unable to concern himself in the battle which was already beginning to develop on the left. While he was in the village a stretcher was carried through. The body on it was covered with a mackintosh sheet, but the man's face was visible and if he had not been so occupied, the ashen face might have upset him a little. The face was absolutely calm, and its expression was contorted neither by pain nor hate nor fear – the face of one who appeared indifferent, and very, very weak.

With that he returned to the trenches.

'Ere yer are, sir, I've started this 'un for yer,' one man shouted. He threw off his equipment and began to dig as he had never dug before. Each spadeful was safety for another inch of his body. It was fighting against time for protection of life and limb. The work was engrossing, exhilarating. Some of the men were too tired, too apathetic, too lazy to dig trenches as deep as they might have done. They had to be urged, cajoled, enticed, ordered.

The day was beautiful, hotter a great deal than those the men were accustomed to. The senior subaltern had been occupying a small hut as an advanced post. The enemy came within his range in some force, but having the presence of mind to restrain himself from firing, he managed to withdraw without loss. All the while the British cavalry were being rapidly driven in.

This was about three o'clock, and the sound of a terrific bombardment

British soldiers preparing a street barricade and defending trench at Mons.

could be heard from some miles to the left. This puzzled them, as it was naturally expected that the battle would develop from the north-east. The regiment on the right had been occupying a small copse this was set alight to the rear of them, and they were forced to draw back through it, which must have been a terrible operation.

Fresh meat, in the form of a stew, was brought out to the trenches at about three o'clock. The bombardment on the left, like a terrific thunderstorm, rolled on till dusk. A few aeroplanes flew overhead, looking like huge birds in the blue sky. As yet the troops found it very hard to distinguish the Germans from the English, although several pamphlets had been issued on the subject of aircraft identification.

As evening drew on, the trenches began to assume a more workmanlike aspect, although when one got down deeper than three feet the ground was

A section of infantry preparing a line of withdrawal across the Condé-Nimy canal at Mons.

German Uhlans in a charge.

like chalk and very difficult to cut. Thus ended that memorable Sunday, when the English line, the last hope of the French, was pierced at Mons, when the appearance of a huge force, above all strong in cavalry, appeared on the left of the English line, and rendered the whole strategic position of the Allies so dangerous that there was nothing for it but to fall back in order to avert a terrible catastrophe.

Intermittently throughout the whole night firing continued. A searchlight had been played continually on the lines and, if anything, the artillery duel began before it was light. This was his first opportunity to watch shell fire. The shells sailed overhead so slowly that we half expected to see them in their flight. The noise they made was very difficult to describe. They hurtled, they whizzed, they shrieked, they sang. He could imagine the thing spinning in its flight, creating a noise something like steam escaping jerkily from an engine.

An English battery was firing from somewhere unseen on the right, to meet an attack apparently launched on the left. Furious messages were passed up the line that the artillery were firing on their own men and, whether this was true or not, soon afterwards the attack ceased. At about seven o'clock the major gave orders to withdraw his platoon when the company on his right should retire. This surprised him; for, knowing nothing of the general situation, he had felt that they would hang on and fight the battle out then and there, to the last gasp. He gave orders to his section commanders, and then lay down to await the development of events.

At about nine o'clock a general retirement seemed to be taking place on the right. It is a very difficult thing to pick upon exactly the right moment to retire. If you retire too early, you allow the enemy to advance without having inflicted sufficient loss, that is, you allow him to succeed too cheaply, to say nothing of rendering the position of units on your flanks precarious. On the other hand, if you hang on to your position too long, you become committed to a close fight from which it is almost impossible to withdraw without the most serious losses.

There are no hedges in Belgium; the ground was perfectly open, and west of the line showed signs of envelopment. Eventually, however, the retirement to the village was effected quietly and without loss. He led his platoon to a second defensive position about a mile behind the village, but already shells were beginning to drop around and even beyond it.

THE BRITISH RETREAT

It was from this point that the great 'Retreat from Mons' really began. The road in front of the battalion was hit by one or two shells. Apparently it was being 'searched', and so the battalion was hastily moved into the open fields, assuming what is known as 'artillery formation', i.e. small collections of troops, moving on the same objective, with 'irregular distances and depths'. By this means many lives must have been saved. After about a mile of very hurried marching through turnip fields and stubble, the road was again reached, and the battalion was apparently out of the range of the German guns. The heat was beginning to be intense.

The men had marched for the last three days almost incessantly and without sufficient sleep. Sunday night in the firing line had been full of excitement of battle, and all Monday morning had been spent at digging trenches. Imagine the state of the men: dirty from digging, with a four days' growth of beard, bathed in sweat, eyes half closed with want of sleep, 'packs' missing; lurching with the drunken torpor of fatigue, their own mothers would not have known them. There was no time to rest and sleep, when rest and sleep were the most desirable things on earth. Those men assuredly knew all the agonies of a temptation to sell for a few moments' sleep their liberty and lives. During a halt the subaltern threw himself so heavily in a cabbage patch that his revolver became unhitched from his belt, and when the halt was over he lurched to his feet and went on, without noticing its loss. Careless? Perhaps, but one of his men lost his rifle and never noticed it, because he was carrying a spade. There was, however, one consolation: the Germans had, for the time, been shaken off: although the noise of battle could still be heard uncomfortably near on the left. But if a man waits long enough, the hottest sun must go to rest, and drag its horrible day with it.

About six o'clock that evening the battalion at last came up with its 'cookers' and transport. Glory of glories, rest had at last been achieved. Never had bacon been so welcome, never tea so desirable, so stimulating, so wonderful. The quartermaster-sergeant had some terrifying tales for the company about disasters on the less fortunate of the line; but there was no time to go into the matter, for the battalion was ordered to parade immediately. This was the last straw. The men had been looking forward to, and longing for, a good sleep that night. Every aching limb of their bodies cried out for rest, and here they were going to be put on outpost duty for yet another night. Imagine their state off mind. Is there a word to cope with the situation? Assuredly not, though great efforts were made. Darkness fell so swiftly that the officers had scarcely time to site the position of their trenches. Then the weary business of entrenching began again. Have you ever heard the tinkering, tapping, thudding sounds made by entrenching implements or spades? None of the men who heard it that night will ever forget it. It will give them a memory of energy, promoted by the desire for safety, clogged by heat and fatigue.

At about eleven or twelve that night a fair cover had been made, and the long-sought for rest became possible at last – not, however, the sleep that the subaltern had been longing for all day, not complete oblivion to body and mind, for the fear of surprise was upon him even in his sleep, and he knew that if his precautions should prove insufficient, he would have to answer for sixty good lives. In addition, there was the cold of the cloudless night, and the clinging wetness of the dew. These things would not have allowed him to sleep, even if he could.

A fresh day began very similar to the last. There were no signs of the enemy to the immediate front, so the work of entrenching continued. A fatigue party went to draw rations, which were distributed at about seven o'clock. This was their first introduction to bully beef and hard biscuits.

Also, wonder of wonders, mail was distributed. He was lying in the corn just beginning to eat a biscuit and read a letter when the voice of a senior subaltern called him from somewhere up the line. Thinking he had got another letter, or something of that sort, he did not wait to put letters and rations in his haversack but reported to his senior officer.

'A party of Uhlans, about a 100 strong have broken through the line further up. We have to prevent them from taking us by surprise on this flank. So you had better take a couple of sections to keep them off.'

Commands on the battlefield must never be didactic and narrow. Tell a man what to do, give him his mission – and how he will carry it out, the methods he will employ are for himself to determine. He hurriedly collected his men and took up a position astride a road that ran behind and was parallel to the lines. In peacetime manoeuvres one had generally been told the direction from which to expect the enemy hours before he actually came; now, when the great game was being played in real earnest, he found he had to guess the direction of the threat. The Uhlans might have come unsuspecting along the road, in which case the game would be his or they might come blundering along from somewhere in the rear and enfilade him, in which case the game would most assuredly be theirs. Fortunately the Uhlans did not come at all.

Meanwhile, a rare and fortunate circumstance was beginning to be

British cavary during the retreat from Mons.

apparent. The enemy were actually attacking from the direction they were expected. The senior subaltern was left to hold out in a small cottage in the firing line until the rest had got away. With characteristic forethought and presence of mind he not only got his men away without loss, but seized all luxuries in the place.

As on the day before, in getting clear away from the enemy the company had to pass a large stretch of ground which was being literally peppered with shrapnel. The noise was louder than it had seemed on the previous day. Thunder seemed muffled beside it. Moreover, thunder rolled – seemed to spread itself into space – but not so with bursting shells. The clap of sound caused by one is more confined, more localized, more intense. The earth seems to quiver under it. It suggests splitting, a terrible splitting. Only the nerves of the young and healthy can stand it. It would not be so bad if one could see the thing whistling through the air, or even when it bursts; but one cannot. After the explosion a man may scream or moan, totter and fall, but for all one can see he might have been struck down by the wrath of God.

The road safely reached, the retreat was continued, but under very trying circumstances for the company. The brigadier in charge of the rearguard action, not having sufficient cavalry at his disposal, ordered the company to take up the role of flank-guard to the retreating column. The company, extended over a long front, had to move across rough country, intersected with all sorts of obstacles, at the same rate as the infantry on the road, which, as the wise Greek Euclid says, 'is impossible'. In war, however, the logically 'impossible' is not impossible really, only very fatiguing.

Things grew from bad to worse. The men could no longer keep their places in the ranks. If one had seen them and not known the spirit of the British Army, one would have thought that they were a dispirited, defeated rabble. Yet, in their own minds, the officers and men had no doubts about what was going to happen: they were going to fight even though they might not sleep, and their determination was shaken not one whit. There was a very welcome halt for an hour in the town for the men to fill their water-bottles and rest.

The men's feet were beginning to suffer terribly, for the road along which they were marching had been cobbled – cobbles, not as we know them in England, but rounded on the surface; cobbles that turned one's ankles; cobbles that the nails of one's boots slipped on, that were metallic, that gave not the fraction of a millimetre. Hobnails in the subaltern's boots began to press through the soles. To put his feet to the ground was an agony, and they swelled with the pain and heat. The bones of them ached with bearing his weight. They longed for air, to be dangling in some cool, babbling stream.

The mental strain of the morning's action was as nothing compared to the physical pain of the afternoon. The colonel, seeing his plight, offered to lend him his horse, but he thanked him and declined, as there is a sort of grim pride in sticking it. The men, too, took an unreasonable objection to seeing their officers avail themselves of these lifts. Then the heavens were kind and it rained; they turned faces to the clouds and let the drops fall on their features, unshaven, glazed with the sun, and clammy with sweat.

They took off their hats and extended the palms of their hands. It was refreshing, invigorating, a tonic. Somebody had heard Brigadier General Davis say that they should have a rest, a real rest, that night. High hopes filled weary hearts. It was rumoured that they were to be billeted in that suburb of Landrecies through which they had just passed, Maroilles.

At about five o'clock on that aching day Maroilles was reached. All through the streets there were halts and delays, intolerable to those in whom the want of rest had become a positive passion. At last the members of the billeting party were sighted – here at last was rest and sleep.

The general, followed by the brigade-major and an orderly, came trotting down the road. A few hasty commands were thrown at the adjutant, accompanied by gesticulations towards the road leading out of the town. Assuredly some fresh devilment was rife, and for the moment, anyway, an attack on the town was expected by a large detachment of cavalry. The wretched men had to be hurried out to line a row of hedges to the west of the town. They waited about half an hour, but saw not a sign of the famous square-crested Uhlan helmet. It appeared that the enemy had been content with destroying the canal bridge, which formed the communication between Maroilles and Landrecies and had then withdrawn. There was a whole brigade in Maroilles, which was therefore cut off from the rest of the division and from its natural line of retreat. That, however, did not greatly upset the rank and file, and billets were at last achieved.

The subaltern found that he was billeted in the same house as the

During the retreat British transport pass a memorial (which stands today) to the Battle of Malplaquet, which was fought 11 September 1709. The memorial practically marks the Franco–Belgian border.

Taking a much needed and well-deserved rest during the Retreat.

headquarters of the battalion – colonel, his second in command, adjutant, etc. The subaltern's servant brought him his valise from the regimental transport and he began to change the offending boots for a fresh pair, without nails. Someone procured a footbath and ablutions began.

The medical officer came in to say that the colonel seemed to be very ill. The subaltern was glad he had declined the offer of his horse. He then began to shave and wash. Just as he was in the middle of this, with his boots and puttees off, his captain came in to say that his platoon was being sent off as infantry escort to a battery of artillery.

By the time he had re-dressed himself, the battery and his platoon had both gone. The streets were filled by French peasants, as usual excited and garrulous, and by men settling down to their billets. The subaltern failed absolutely to discover what route his platoon had taken, but pursuing the road along which they had come, he soon left the town.

It was raining and blowing most fiercely; the darkness was intense, otherwise absolute silence reigned. Suddenly, excitedly, a voice, saturated with fear, cried out from the darkness, 'Who goes there?' A face, with a bayonet in front of it, loomed up from the side of the road. 'Friend' – this tersely. 'Sentry, have you seen a battery of artillery and a platoon of South Staffordshires pass here? 'No, sir; you're nearly in the outpost line. There's only Royal Berkshires in front, sir.' So they had evidently not come this way. Where next? They must be found. He felt that to lose his men would be a sort of dishonour. Even while he was thinking a shout was wafted on the wind out of the darkness and chasing it, overtaking it almost, a rifle shot. It was as if a match had been applied to the whole line. With, the rapidity of wind the crackling spread to either side.

Soon the whole line in front was blazing away into the darkness. Should the subaltern stop and try to lend assistance where he was, or hurry back to his own unit? Before long a couple of men rushed along the road crying out for stretcher bearers, and he learnt from one of them that in the darkness and confusion of the retreat, British had been fighting with British. The pitch darkness shrouded every action with a ghastly uncertainty.

Then news came through that another bridge had been captured by the Germans. A fresh company arrived in reinforcement. There was nothing for it but to effect a retreat before the morning light could betray their weakness to the Germans. Apparently, however, the capture of the bridge had only been a precautionary measure, for the enemy did not press his attack home. The subaltern saw that the best thing he could do would be to return to the remainder of his battalion at Maroilles. If he were to grope about the countryside in the dark, looking for that battery, he would most likely be shot down for a spy; moreover, in a little over two hours the morning would dawn. So he trudged back to Maroilles.

He felt that he ought to have been on the verge of exhaustion from lack of food and from fatigue, and he vaguely wondered why he was not. The truth was that the excitement of the attack, coupled with the chill of the night, had restored him in mind and body, although he had marched over twenty miles on the previous day, had had no sleep that night and no meal since the evening of the Battle of Mons.

The battalion was taking its rest as well as it could on the pavement of the street, so as to be ready to move at a minute's notice. The subaltern found his major and reported that he had failed to find his platoon. The major was too sleepy to be annoyed. 'I expect they'll turn up,' he said. We got some food in that house there; I should go and see if there is any left if I were you.'

There followed a couple of hours or so of interrupted sleep, disturbed by the cold. Then came dawn, and with it the shells whizzing and bursting over the town. The retreat of the brigade had been cut off by the breaking of the canal bridge the previous evening, so the battalion had to retire to the east, and not to the west. As the subaltern marched along he reflected with grim amusement on the ease with which the most confirmed Sybarite [seeker of pleasure and luxury] can get accustomed to hardships. At home, if he did anything early on an empty stomach, he very soon felt faint and tired. Now, this was taken as a matter of course, one was only too glad to restore the circulation to the limbs, cramped with the cold and damp of dawn.

An hour or so later they ran into a French battalion, apparently preparing to occupy an outpost position along the bank of the road. This was a cheering sight. Tommy, who had expected to fight mixed up in some weird way with 'le petit Piou-Piou', had not yet seen a Frenchman in

A French unit withdrawing before the invading German army, though one man finds time to light his pipe.

action. In a vague way he fancied that 'the Frenchies' had let him down'. He knew nothing of the battles of Charleroi and Namur, nor of the defence of Verdun, and the French were getting dreadfully un-popular with him. Things were thrown at anyone who ventured to sing the Marseillaise.

'Oh, 'ere they are; so they 'ave come. Well, that's somethink.'

The Marseillaise broke out once again.

'Look 'ere, Bill, there's too much of this ruddy Marslasie abaht this show.'

'Ow d'you mean, Sam?'

'Why, it's all march on, march on and I'm sick of it – and I'm bloody-well sick of the singing that goes with it!'

25 August, 1914

SAVING HAIG'S CORPS at LANDRECIES

Captain R. Wolrige Gordon, MC

Captain Wolrige Gordon was with the 2nd Battalion Grenadier Guards from 12 August to 16 September 1914. He was present at the fighting at Landrecies on 25 August, which, but for the quick action he describes, might have resulted in a serious blow to I Corps under Sir Douglas Haig

On 25 August we marched on past Maroilles to Landrecies. Here we were told we were quite safe and could get a good rest. We were billeted in a school, the officers all provided with nice clean beds, but no sooner were we comfortable than the alert was sounded. And so we had to stand to arms.

I remember seeing the man who brought the message riding through the streets. A French gendarme, he galloped on shouting 'Les Allemands! Les Allemands!' and never stopped even to answer questions. We again turned-in, but we were cautioned to be ready to fall in at a moment's notice. By this time it was almost dark and we proceeded to get on with our dinner, when suddenly heavy machine-gun fire broke out from the north-west side of the town. The alarm – the only time I ever heard the bugle during the entire war – was sounded and we had to fall in – alas, without our dinner.

The 3rd Battalion Coldstream Guards went forward at once and were forced to occupy the outposts in the town where the shots appeared to be coming from. Their Nos. 2 and 3 Companies went across the canal and railway bridges to support, if required, and formed two sides of a square. No. 1 Company occupied the canal bridge and banks, while 4 Company went to guard the roads to the east – the one by which we had come in and the one leading south to Etreux and Guise.

The story of Landrecies is roughly this:

When the Coldstream arrived at the outskirts of the town, one of their companies under Captain Monk went forward with their machine gun to establish out-posts. They heard in the distance men coming along singing 'La Marseillaise'. Monk and his sergeant-major and runner went forward to meet them. They appeared to be French. Directly they saw Monk they advanced, and two or three of them gathered around shouting 'Vivent les

Anglais!' Something or other warned the sergeant-major, who went back in front to the company. The supposed Frenchmen followed. Directly they reached the machine-gun they knocked Bingham, the officer in charge, into the ditch and seized the machine gun. The company bayoneted them.

They turned out to be Germans dressed up as Frenchmen who intended to creep unawares into the town. It was just getting dark, and all the Coldstream could do was to put a bell on a rope 150 feet distant across the road. It was not long before the Germans attacked in force, coming down the road in fours.

The Coldstream waited until the bell tinkled and then all fired five rounds rapid fire. The German losses must have been colossal. The Germans did this three times. Then they brought up two field guns and started shelling right down the road. These shells were taking some Coldstreamers' heads off and bursting in the town 2,000 yards away. The situation was most serious. The Coldstream were in three ranks, lying, kneeling and standing in this road, and were having heavy casualties. I can see General Fielding to this day with his sword drawn, drawing a line on the ground, calling, 'Remember, not one man of the Coldstream goes back over this line.' Luckily, two of our guns happened to get direct hits on the guns of the Germans, and the Germans fell back.

Meanwhile, everything was confusion behind us. Houses had all been put into a state of defence and barricades were across the streets, most of the officers' kits forming a considerable part of some of the barricades. We were considering what was to be done when the Germans suddenly cleared off. About 3 am the Irish Guards came up to make a counter attack at dawn, but the artillery supporting the enemy having retired, we started evacuating the town. First the 3rd Coldstream went, then the Irish Guards, and finally the Grenadiers, The 2nd Coldstream was sent on some time before to take up a position to cover the retirement of the rest of the brigade.

No. 12 Platoon was the last to go. Such was our night's rest. The 3rd Battalion Coldstream Guards lost two officers killed and three officers wounded. Also ninety men killed and wounded. We lost Second Lieutenant Vereker and ten men wounded. The German casualties were about 800 killed, almost entirely from rifle and machine-gun fire.

The brigade retired down the Guise road and we discovered that we had lost our food cart. The march was very slow, as the men were dead tired. Why the Germans let us get away so easily is difficult to understand; they did not shell Landrecies heavily until long after we had left the place. They missed the opportunity to annihilate the brigade as it withdrew.

25 August, 1914

AFFAIR OF MATTRESSES IN LANDRECIES

Brigadier General Charteris, CMG, DSO

General Charters, in August 1914 was Military Secretary to Sir Douglas Haig, had a most anxious part to play in the attack on Landrecies, but he revives here some humorous aspects of those critical hours.

Just about 4 pm we reached Landrecies, where we were to stop for the evening and until 2 am, when we were to march again. Though I had been riding almost all day, I was pretty tired, for I had been up most of the previous night. As soon as I had got my billet I lay down to sleep. I had just dozed off when a great disturbance in the street awakened me. Refugees were streaming in, shouting that the Uhlans were hard at their heels and some of them flourished Uhlan lances and accoutrements to prove their statements. DH [Sir Douglas Haig] told me to get on my horse and, with one orderly, ride back and investigate. Just north of Landrecies, where the refugees reported the Germans to be, there was a thick wood [the Forêt de Mormal]. There the two main roads converged on to a bridge over a river.

Mounting my horse, *Dukani*, and along with an orderly, I rode over a mile up one road, and then back to the bridge and up the other road. There was absolutely nothing to be seen or heard and I returned to Landrecies and reported to DH that it seemed to be a false alarm, or, in any case, an exaggerated report. There could be no large body of troops within some miles of us. It must have been about 6 am and I lay down again to rest.

I think I was asleep, though it cannot have been more than ten minutes later, when I was aroused by sharp rifle-fire and some shelling. Almost immediately after, reports came in that Landrecies was surrounded. There was a good deal of confusion and some amusing incidents. DH ordered the whole town to be organized for defence, barricades to meet across the roads with furniture and anything else handy, all secret papers, etc., to be destroyed.

DH sent me off to prepare a big school building for defence, giving me a couple of companies of Guards as a working party. For once he was quite jolted out of his usual placidity. He said, 'If we are to be caught, by God, we'll sell our lives dearly.'

It was a weird scene in the village street; soldiers were throwing mattresses and chairs out of the windows for the barricades, which others were making as best they could. The few inhabitants left were protesting feebly. The Guards had arrested and tied up a French officer who had lost his head, and was making an ass of himself. It was then I saw one rather pompous and unpopular Staff officer walking towards me and one of the men at an upper window taking deliberate aim with one of those great soft French mattresses. It was a direct hit and to the immense glee of the men down went the pompous one totally smothered in the feather mattress. He was, of course, none the worse for it, but very, very angry.

Suddenly, there was a great rattle of revolver shots quite close and I saw an officer, obviously very excited, discharging his revolver down a street. I asked a military policeman who was near by what was in the street. 'Nothing, sir,' he said with a smile, 'but some officers' horses.' So I asked him, 'Why the... don't you stop him?' 'Well, you see, sir,' he said, 'he is a full Colonel, and his own horse is there with the others, and besides he's very excited and it may ease him up.' So I asked the 'full Colonel' if he would care to come and help me with my job instead of shooting at horses, and he quite amicably agreed. So off we went together.

The next day, Wednesday, was the first full day of the retreat, and it was a very anxious time for the Staff and terrible for the troops. We started at 5 am and marched steadily until 4 pm (it seemed much longer than that), steadily plodding along a dusty road in a glaring, blazing sun. We only halted a few minutes in each hour's march. Always there was the sound of the guns – now distant, now seeming much closer. The battalion commanders knew what we were in for, and made the men lie down at every halt. At first the men resented this, but as the hours slowly passed they dropped as if hit immediately a halt was ordered and were asleep almost before their bodies touched the ground.

25 August, 1914

UNSEEN KILLERS AT LE CATEAU

Private. R. G. Hill

Private Hill went to France on 22 August, 1914, with the 1st Battalion Royal Warwickshire Regiment. Except for a few days in hospital in 1915, he served in this battalion until April 1917, when he was wounded and then discharged medically unfit in March 1918. His story of the wild fighting at Le Cateau and of the nightmare of marching in retreat graphically describes the epic of the British infantrymen of 1914.

We detrained just outside Le Cateau railway station. The town was in confusion, as the Battle of Mons had just been fought; refugees, troops, and ammunition columns created a dust that choked us. Civilians offered us jugs of weak beer, but discipline was so strong that to accept it would have meant a court martial.

We marched out of the town along a typical French road. Just when we were about all in, a halt was called for dinner, which we never had as an outburst of artillery fire was heard. It must'have been miles away, but we were given orders to open out to artillery formation and proceed once more. We saw no enemy that day, and at night bivouacked in a cornfield, where we enjoyed a long-delayed dinner. We marched off in column of fours [four men wide] next morning at dawn in a new direction. At noon we halted, piled arms, and rations were issued – the last for many days. Men were told off to dig trenches on rising ground to our left.

Whilst so engaged an aeroplane hovered over us. It had no distinguishing mark, and we assumed it was French, but were soon disillusioned, as it scattered coloured lights over us [flares for artillery]. Too late, we opened fire on it. Soon large black shells were bursting in the beet field just in front of our improvised position. Rain then started and the shelling ceased.

A regiment of our cavalry came galloping up and jumped over us in our hastily constructed trenches. We stayed there till nightfall, incidentally wiping out a small Uhlan patrol that blundered upon us. When we withdrew we could hear the jingle of accoutrements of many men approaching. That night we seemed to march round and round a burning farmhouse.

Day broke and we were still dragging our weary limbs along in what seemed to us to be an everlasting circle. At last the word came to halt and fall out for a couple of hours' rest. We had been marching along a road with a high ridge on the right and cornfields on the left. High up the ridges ran a road parallel to ours, on which one of our regiments had been keeping pace with us. We had no sooner sunk down in the cornfield on our left than shrapnel began to burst over us. Our officers were fine leaders. 'Man the ditch on the road,' came the order. In the meantime the battalion on the ridge had been caught napping by a squadron of Uhlans, who charged

British troops resting in a Belgian village during the retreat. Note the uneven, cobbled street.

Fighting a rear guard action during the retreat. The ubiquitous sunken roads provided a parapet, but left the backs of the men unprotected.

them while they were falling out for a rest. Our eager young officers went frantic with excitement. On their own initiative they led us up the hill to the rescue of our comrades. With wild shouts we dashed up. At first the ground was broken and afforded cover for our short sharp dashes. We then came to a hedge with a gap about four yards wide. A dozen youngsters made for the gap, unheeding the advice of older soldiers to break through the hedge. Soon that gap was a heap of dead and dying as a machine-gun was trained on it.

We reached an open field, where we were met with a hail of shrapnel. Officers were being picked off by snipers. A subaltern rallied us and gave the order to fix bayonets when a piece of shrapnel carried half his jaw away. Upwards we went, but not a sign of a German. They had hidden themselves and waited for our mad rush. Officers and sergeants being wiped out, and, not knowing where the enemy really were, our attack fizzled out. A staff officer came galloping amongst us mounted on a big black charger. He bore a charmed life. He shouted something unintelligible, which someone said was the order to retire.

The survivors walked slowly down, puzzled and baffled. They had attained nothing, and had not even seen the men they set out to help. We lost half the battalion in that wild attack. Then came our turn to do something better. The survivors, under the direction of a capable major, dug in and waited to get their own back. A battery of eighteen-pounders started to shell the ridge. Suddenly shells started falling round the guns. One direct hit, and a gunner's leg fell amongst us. The battery was wiped out. Tired and worn out, we waited. Towards afternoon shrapnel played on us, fortunately without serious result. Then it was our turn to laugh. German infantry were advancing in close formation. They broke at our first volley. Something seemed to sting my leg. I found a shrapnel bullet had ploughed a shallow groove down the fleshy part of my thigh.

The enemy advanced. Another volley and they broke again.

My leg began to pain me, so I hobbled along the road to a house which was being used as a dressing station. A long queue of wounded men were waiting to be dressed, while a crowd of thirst-maddened un-wounded were crowding round a well in the garden. Despairing of medical aid I begged a field dressing, and, catching sight of a sunken road, there dressed my wound.

In this sunken road I found battalion headquarters. At dusk they retired, I with them. I learnt afterwards that all our wounded were captured that night, and small bodies of our troops, trying to retire in the darkness, had fired-on each other. This was our part in the Battle of Le Cateau.

Then began the retreat. I must have fainted, for I remember hobbling along with some chums and next I found myself tied to the seat of an ammunition limber. We came to a village jammed with retiring troops, where an artillery officer bundled me off. Fortunately some of my own regiment passed, and, seeing me lying in the road, helped me along. My leg seemed easier and I was able to proceed at the pace my footsore companions were going. It was nightmare marching. Our party was now about 150 strong. Sleep was out of the question and food was begged from villagers.

Reaching St. Quentin, we had great hopes of rest, but were told that we were surrounded. We lay down to die through sheer weariness, but a staff officer rounded us up, and got us out just as the enemy entered. Tramp, tramp, again. Engineers told us to hurry over the bridge at Ham, as they were just about to blow it up. A little scrap a bit farther on, then Noyon, where we snatched a night's sleep.

26-27 August, 1914

STRAGGLERS LOST for a WEEK

Private Frank Richards, DC, MM

Author of the memoir, Old Soldiers Never Die, *he went to France with the 2nd Battalion Royal Welch Fusiliers in 1914. He saw continuous active service until 1918. Here he describes with characteristic understatement the exploits of an 'Old Contemptible' in the historic retreat from Le Cateau.*

At dawn we marched out of Le Cateau with fixed bayonets. My mate Duffy said, 'We'll have a bang at the bastards today'. And we all hoped the same. We were all fed up with the marching and would have welcomed a scrap to relieve the monotony. But we were more fed up before the day was over. The Second Argyll's, who went to the assistance of the East Yorks, lost half of their battalion during the day, but we simply marched and counter-marched during the whole time that this was going on.

We kept on meeting people who had left their homes and were making their way south with the few belongings they could carry. One little lad, about twelve years of age, was wheeling his old grandmother in a wheelbarrow. They all seemed to be terror-stricken. In every village we marched through the church had been converted into a field-hospital and was generally full of our wounded. At about twilight we lined up in a sunken road. I was the extreme left-hand man of the battalion, Billy and Stevens being on my right.

Our colonel was speaking to our company commander just behind us when up the road came a man wheeling a pram with a baby in it and two women walking alongside. They stopped close by me, and the man, speaking in English, told me that the two women were his wife and mother-in-law, and that his only child was in the pram. He was an Englishman, the manager of some works in a small town, but his wife was French. They had been travelling all day. If they had delayed another hour they would have been in the enemy's hands.

Just at this moment a staff-officer came along and informed our colonel that all our cavalry patrols were in, and that any cavalry or troops who now appeared on our front would be the enemy. He had hardly finished speaking when over a ridge in front of us appeared a body of horsemen galloping towards us. We immediately got out of the sunken road, and standing opened up with rapid fire at six hundred yards. I had only fired two rounds when a bugle blew the cease-fire. This, I may say, was the only time during the whole of the war, with the exception of the German bugle at Bois Grenier, that I heard a bugle in action. The light was very bad, and the majority of the bullets had been falling short because we couldn't clearly see the sights of our rifles, but several horses fell. The horsemen stopped and waved their arms. We had been firing on our own cavalry who, I was told later, belonged to the 19th Hussars. I never heard whether any of them had been killed.

MARCH, MARCH – HOUR BY HOUR

When we got back down in the sunken road the women were crying and the child was bawling, but the man seemed to have vanished. Stevens said 'Where has he got to?' I asked the women, but couldn't get a word out of them, only crying, when out from under the cover of the pram crawled the man. He commenced to storm and rave and wanted to know what we meant by all that firing which had terrified his wife and child. (He didn't say a word about his mother-in-law.) He said that he would report us. Billy got hold of him and said: 'Call yourself an Englishman! What the hell do you reckon you were going to do under that pram? For two pins I'd bayonet you, you bloody swine!'

'Fall in!' came the order, and we were on the march again. It was now dusk and I expect that family fell into the hands of the enemy during the night.

We retired all night with fixed bayonets, many sleeping as they were marching along. March, march, for hour after hour, with no halt: we were now breaking into the fifth day of continuous marching with practically no sleep in between. We were carrying our rifles any old way and it was only by luck that many a man didn't receive a severe bayonet wound during the night. Stevens called out 'There's a fine castle there, see?' pointing to one side of the road. But there was nothing there. Very nearly everyone was seeing things, we were all so dead-beat.

At last we were halted and told that we would rest for a couple of hours. Outposts and sentries were posted, and we sank down just off the road and were soon fast asleep. Fifteen minutes later we were woken up, and on the march again. We had great difficulty in waking some of the men. About ten yards from the side of the road was a straw rick, and about half a dozen men had got down the other side of it. I slipped over and woke them up. One man we had a job with, but we got him going at last. By this time the company had moved off, so we were stragglers. We came to some cross-roads and didn't know which way to go. Somehow we decided to take the road to the right.

Dawn was now breaking. Along the road we took were broken-down

British cavalry on the road from Mons.

motor lorries, motor cycles, dead horses and broken wagons. In a field were dumped a lot of rations. We had a feed, crammed some biscuits into our haversacks and moved along again. After a few minutes, by picking up more stragglers, we were twenty strong, men of several different battalions. I enquired if anyone had seen the 2nd Battalion Royal Welch Fusiliers, but nobody had. By the time that it was full daylight there were thirty-five of us marching along, including two sergeants. We got into a small village – I had long since lost interest in the names of the places we came to – where we met a staff-officer, who took charge of us. He marched us out and up a hill and told us to extend ourselves in skirmishing order at two paces interval and lie down, and be prepared to stop an attack at any moment. About five hundred yards in front of us was a woodland; the attack would come from that direction.

The enemy commenced shelling our position, but the shells were falling about fifteen yards short. The man on my left was fast asleep; he was so dead-beat that the shelling did not even rouse him and the majority of us were not much better. We lay there for about half an-hour, but saw no signs of the enemy. The staff-officer then lined us up and told us to attach ourselves to the first battalion we came across. I had to shake and thump the man on my left before I could wake him up. We marched off again and came across lots of people who had left their homes. Four ladies in an open carriage insisted on getting out to let some of our crippled and dead-beat men have a ride. We packed as many as we could into the carriage and moved along, the ladies marching with us. Late in the afternoon we took leave of the ladies. The men who had been riding had a good day's rest and sleep. If the ladies had all our wishes they would be riding in a Rolls-Royce for the rest of their lives.

During the evening when passing through a village, I got news that the battalion had passed through it an hour before. I and a man named Rhodes decided to leave the band and try to catch them. During the next few days we attached ourselves to three different battalions, but immediately left them when we got news of our own. We wandered on for days living on anything we could scrounge. It seemed to us that trying to find the battalion was like trying to chase a will-o-the-wisp. But we were going the right way – all roads seemed to lead to Paris.

One day when we were on our own and not attached to any unit, Rhodes and I came across a band of gypsies in a wood and made them understand that we were very hungry. They invited us to the meal they were about to have. I think we surprised them by our eating abilities. We thanked them heartily and, with bellies like poisoned pups, staggered off once more. It was the first square meal we had enjoyed since leaving Amiens. The next day we came to a railhead. A train was in and an officer asked if we had lost our unit; upon hearing that we were indeed stragglers he ordered us onto the train which was full of troops in the same fix as ourselves.

27 August, 1914

LAUGHING DAWN of DESPAIR

Frederic Coleman

A pioneer motorist and one of the early members of the Royal Automobile Club (RAC) Frederick Coleman volunteered his services and his car at the outbreak of war. Constantly on the move in the battle area, American national Coleman had a close-up view of much of the fighting. His observations of the retreat through St. Quentin on the morning of 27 August differs from the unhappy picture drawn by some eye-witnesses who were there.

The morning of Thursday 27 August found us in the direct path of what, in the early hours of the day, we believed to be the remnant of the shattered Left flank of the British Army. Like the dawn of the day before, the morning broke clear and warm, promising a hot summer day. The perfect mornings on the retreat were some compensation for our short hours of rest.

St. Quentin that Thursday saw rare scenes and strange sights. An orderly, well-disciplined army had been through a great fight. Its infantry, unbeaten by the infantry that opposed it, and yet it had been ordered to retire. 'Gawd knows why,' hundreds of Tommies were saying. The vastness of the scale of operations, the uncertainty of the General Staff itself as to just what was happening in some quarters of the field, and the universal ignorance of the rank and file as to what had happened elsewhere than in their own immediate vicinity, all tended to bring on discouragement.

After inflicting such terrible losses as the German foot soldiers suffered at Cambrai-Le Cateau, the British Army had taken a hammering which seemed to many of them to be totally unnecessary. To fight stubbornly and victoriously against an advancing enemy, hurling back his masses as fast as they are poured forward, had been soul-inspiring. To leave such occupation for a scamper over a shell-swept field, comrades falling to right and left as they run, was not. Units that had just proven to themselves their seeming invincibility were smashed and disintegrated in the very obeying of an unwelcome order to retire.

Jumbled together, inextricably mixed, every group convinced that their little remnant contained the only survivors of their individual command, confusion worse confounded was only to be expected. The work of sorting out the men from the steady flowing stream of humanity as it moved

British troops on the march in Belgium before the Big Retreat.

southward, of re-forming an army that had lost most semblance of form, was the task set before the British officers in St. Quentin that morning at sun-up. It did not take them long to set about it. Stationed here and there along the main route through the town, each officer of staff became an usher, urbanely advising each little knot of stragglers where to proceed to find the nucleus of their particular unit, and obtain food, drink and news of their comrades.

The wounded were in considerable numbers. Ambulances drew up at the railway station and unloaded. A couple of sweet little old French ladies bustled about on one side of the station square, giving out tea as fast as they could make it.

TASKED WITH CHEERING THEM UP

Moving about St. Quentin in a motorcar that morning was slow work, as the roads were full to overflowing. Not far from the *Mairie* a wounded officer, his vitality all but spent, was placed in my car. I took him as quickly as possible to the station. Badly wounded in the chest, he said with a pale smile, 'I've been about a hundred miles, it seems, since I was hit, and in pretty well every sort of conveyance except a motor-car. Two miles on a limber nearly finished me.'

He looked, poor chap, as though he had reached care and attention none too soon.

For a time I was to act as usher at a point a bit north of St. Quentin. Placed on the road by a staff officer, and told where the men of the various units were to be directed, I chose to stand by a French lady, who, with her daughters, was supplying coffee, steaming hot, to the passing Tommies. Never shall I forget that staff officer's parting instructions.

Cheer them up as you keep them on the move. They are very downhearted. Tell them anything, but cheer them up. They've got their tails down a bit, but they are really all right. No wonder they are tired worn out to begin with, then fighting all day, only to fall back all night, no rest, no food, no sleep poor devils. Yes, they are very downhearted. Tell 'em where to go, and cheer 'em up – cheer 'em up.

Of all the jobs that have ever fallen to my lot, I thought, this promises to be one of the most hopeless. Cheer them up, indeed. A fine atmosphere this, for good cheer. Ragged and muddy and foot-sore they looked, straggling along for all the world like a beaten army.

The first individual who caught my attention particularly was a tall captain, an old acquaintance. He showed me his service cap, through the crown of which two neat bullet-holes had been drilled. Both of the vicious little pellets had missed their intended mark, though one had ploughed a slight furrow along his scalp, leaving an angry red welt. No one had examined his head to find what damage had been caused, and he asked me to investigate. He bent over, and I poked my finger here and there, asking where it hurt and how much – in short, doing the best I could to accommodate his thirst for information. As I was intent on my amateur probing, a voice from behind commented,

'A close shave the little divil made that toime, shure.'

Turning at the soft brogue, I was surprised to see a Jock, in a kilt that looked as if its wearer had been rolled in the mud. Capless, his shock of red hair stood on end, and a pair of blue Irish eyes twinkled merrily. I was genuinely surprised. It was before I learned that an Irish man in a Scotish regiment was no rarity – nor a Cockney in a battalion dubbed 'Irish' on the rolls, for that matter.

As if entering himself in a competition of close shaves, the Irishman held his right ear between thumb and linger.

'And what do ye think o' that?' he queried.

Right through the lobe of his ear, close to his cheek, a Mauser bullet had drilled a clean hole.

'Close that, I'm thinking,' said the proud owner of the damaged member, 'And I niver knew how close me ear was to me head till that thing come along.

A burst of laughter from the group that had gathered was infectious.

The men went off together chatting over other stories of close shaves, leaving me thankful the Irish lad had come by, cheered that lot up, and so saved me the task.

The next group to reach me contained a sergeant and a dozen or so Tommies, of most disreputable appearance.

'To what lot do you belong, sergeant?' I called.

'We're *Riles*, sir,' said the sergeant.

'You're what?'

'*Riles*' with decided emphasis.

Suddenly it clicked, Riles = Royals. I remembered that the Royal Fusiliers were in 9 Brigade of the 3rd Division and directed the group accordingly.

'You oughter know who we are, said the sergeant, somewhat haughtily. 'We're the lot what was first in Mons and last out we are.'

'That's right,' piped up a squeaky voice that came from a diminutive member of the squad; 'Buck up, you beggar, buck up. Tell him the full tale.'

A grin on half a dozen faces indicated that the small one might be expected to produce some comment when occasion permitted. The sergeant turned:

'What's ailin' you, Shorty? the sergeant demanded.

'Tell 'im the tale,' croaked the little man. 'Fust in Mons we were and last out. In at three miles an hour and out at eighteen? That's us, you bet your life,' and he snorted as the squad roared in appreciative mirth.

So they drifted on, anything but downhearted, if one could judge from the running fire of banter between Shorty and his sergeant, which kept their comrades in continual chuckles as they toiled along. Truly I thanked Shorty for his assistance in the 'cheer 'em up' department.

Groups of weary men went past, at times keeping in step, whistling or singing. Some were obviously too footsore to walk normally, but they heroically tried to keep pace with the rest, and made a brave show of it.

One big, lantern-jawed chap, as he caught sight of me, insisted on his score of companions forming single file. They brought rifles to shoulder-arms and stepped out in fine style with an indescribable swagger. The Sphinx would have broken into a smile at the sight of them. As the leader, much begrimed, came up I explained that hot coffee was to be had from jugs held by three little pig-tailed French schoolgirls under a tree close by.

PROPER REARGUARDS

As the boys drank, the leading spirit chatted away. I gathered from casual remarks, if they were to be believed, that talking was a habit with him. In fact, remarks were proffered, *sotto voce*, that he had not ceased talking, except to sleep, since leaving England. The comments of his soiled band seemed meat and drink to his soul. He fairly revelled in them.

'Pals we are, all right,' he said with a grin, 'though no one would think it to hear 'em, would they? Know how to fight they do, but can't talk – that's their big drawback. Don't know no words you see.'

A hot strong draught of good black French coffee caused him to pause, but a moment later he was at it again. I told him where to go. As he tramped off he said, 'Come on, you buggers! Don't block the road. You ain't no bloomin' army now, you're just a forlorn 'ope, that's what you are. Nice-lookin' lot o' beggars. 'Op to it!' And they hopped to it, to the music of his cheery abuse. God bless him!

Not long after a very woebegone procession hove into sight. There were few in that squad and they seemed especially worn and tired. Red-eyed from flack of sleep, barren of equipment, many a cap missing and not a pair of sound feet in the lot. Every man had his rifle, but they were all about done in. Here are the pessimists at last, I thought. It will take something to cheer this bunch up.'

I discovered their regiment and informed them of the whereabouts of their follows. 'Yes,' said I, 'three streets on after you get to the fountain, then to the right, and there you'll see a big building on the left – that's where you need to be.'

'We've been *rearguarding*' said a cadaverous corporal who acted as

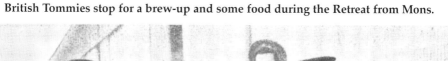

British Tommies stop for a brew-up and some food during the Retreat from Mons.

spokesman. 'We're proper *rearguards*, we are. Been doin' nothin' else but bloody *rearguardin*.'

'Right,' said I, 'now don't forget, third turning after the fountain. There's plenty of food there.'

'*Rearguards*, we are,' insisted the lugubrious corporal. 'Proper *rearguards*. Ain't done nothing else for three days.'

'Quite, quite and... cheerio!' I insisted, 'three streets on after the fountain and then...'

'Proper *rearguards*...' he started again.

'But,' I interrupted in turn. 'I am telling you where there is food, my boy.'

'And I am telling you sir, if you don't not mind,' he continued gravely, 'that we're proper *rearguards*, we are. And we 'ave learned one thing about proper *rearguards* in this 'ere war right off, and that is us *rearguards* ain't expected to eat. So we 'ave given it up, we 'ave. It's a bad habit, anyhow. Ain't that so, boys?'

A famous Scots battalion withdrawing in good order. Note the cyclist has cut his trousers to make cycling shorts for easier pedaling.

Tired but cheery British soldiers withdrawing through a Belgian village.

Off they trudged all grinning at me as they passed. Then the funereal visage of the spokesman turned and indulged in a sombre wink, whereas they laughed to a man – and I with them.

'Proper rearguards don't eat.' He had had his joke, and played it out to his heart's content. Ah, well, it was an experience.

I had not been long on that roadside when I realized that many of us had been labouring under a great delusion. It was not that someone was needed to cheer up the dispirited Tommy; it was that most of us needed the Tommy to cheer us up.

The indomitable pluck of the soldier in the ranks and his effervescent cheeriness was to save that retreating army of Smith-Dorrien's as no staff work could have saved it had the Tommy not possessed those characteristics to such remarkable degree. Many an officer whose hair had grown grey in the Service said that day that Tommy was of finer metal than he had ever dreamed it possible of any soldier. The very air was full of unostentatious heroism.

One grizzled brigadier, seated on his horse, watched that straggling army pass, tears dropping now and then unheeded on his tunic, his lips pressed hard. One of his staff heard the old warrior mutter, as one unit passed, soiled, but with bold eye and shoulders well back:

'Ah they may be able to kill such men, but they will never be able to beat them.'

I began to look at the men with new eyes as the morning passed. If the thousands struggling by but continued to come, I thought, many more must have been saved than any of us had imagined. Beneath the grime and dirt and weariness I saw clear eyes and firm jaws, even when men were almost too worn out to walk further. Those who appeared to be positively unable to go on were stopped at St. Quentin station, to be sent south by rail.

1 realized that in front of me was passing a pageant such as men had rarely seen in the ages. It was a pageant of the indomitable will and un-conquerable power of the Anglo-Saxon.

Early in the day I was relieved and sent back to the station. Horse wagons full of wounded jostled the ambulances in the station yard. Even the motor transport lorries, as they rolled past, paused to drop off their quota of maimed and bandaged men in khaki.

One young subaltern passed, sound asleep in his saddle and unmindful of all about him, his horse following the human current. At times a pitiable group of refugees went by, though for the most part, the refugees had been crowded off the main roads by the retreating army, or diverted to other routes.

SMITH-DORRIEN'S WINNING SMILE

A sergeant of the East Surrey Regiment, of Fergusson's division, came up. His face was haggard. He reported that two hundred and fifty men, with five officers, were all that was left of that battalion.

Standing near the bridge, close by the station, I saw General Smith-Dorrien a few feet distant. He turned, and I caught his eye. He was speaking to a passing officer. I hardly remember his words. Something about plenty more of the same command being down the road a bit, I think. It was good to see Smith-Dorrien's face and hear his voice. I had heard much of him during those days, and never was he spoken of save in terms of affection. As he looked my way he smiled, with the sort of smile that everyone within range takes to himself as his own property. It was of inestimable value that morning in St. Quentin – Smith-Dorrien's smile. It must have put heart into many a man.

General Sir Horace Lockwood Smith-Dorrien GCB, GCMG, DSO, ADC (26 May 1858 – 12 August 1930). He commanded II Corps during Mons and the Retreat.

27 August, 1914

EPIC STORY of St. QUENTIN
The Saving of Two Regiments

Lieutenant Colonel Arthur Osburn, DSO

The then Major Arthur Osburn was at Mons and the Retreat,
and was the medical officer with the 4th Dragoon Guards. This
narrative shows how the surrender of two British battalions at
St.Quentin was averted by firm action on the part of a gallant
cavalry officer.

As we turned into the Grand Place at St. Quentin on that late August afternoon not a single German was to be seen. The whole square was thronged with British infantrymen standing in groups or wandering about in an aimless fashion, most of them without either packs or rifles. Scores had gone to sleep sitting on the pavement, their backs against the fronts of the shops. Many, exhausted, lay at full length on the pavement. Some few, obviously intoxicated, wandered about firing in the air at real or imaginary German aeroplanes. The great majority were not only without their arms but had apparently either lost or thrown away their belts, water bottles and other equipment.

There must have been several hundred men in the Square, and more in the side streets; yet apparently they were without officers – anyway, no officers were to be seen. On the road down to the station we found Major Tom Bridges with part of his squadron and a few Lancers, horse-gunners and other stragglers who had attached themselves to his command. We followed him down to the station.

Apparently some hours before our arrival the last train that was to leave St. Quentin – Paris-wards – for several years, had steamed out, carrying with it most of the British General Staff. A mob of disorganized soldiery had collected at the station, and I was told some had booed and cheered ironically these senior Staff officers as the Staff train steamed out.

Certainly many of these infantrymen were in a truculent mood. Bridges, who had sized up the situation, harangued this disorganized mob that only a few short hours before had represented two famous regiments of the BEF 4th Division.

Dismounted and standing far back in the crowd I could not hear what he said, but his words of encouragement and exhortation were received with sullen disapproval and murmurs by the bulk of those around him. One man pointed his rifle at Bridges and shouted out:

'Our old man [his colonel] has surrendered to the Germans, and we'll stick to him. We don't want any bloody cavalry interfering!'

I failed at first to understand how all these English soldiers could have surrendered to the Germans whom we had left several miles outside the city. But I was tired and hungry and I did not much care what happened. Losing interest in what was taking place at the station I rode back up to the Grand Place, hoping I should find some food and a sofa on which I could lie down. As I rode up from the station many of the men in the street stared at me disdainfully, their arms folded; scarcely one saluted – I was for them only 'one of the bloody interfering cavalry officers'. The events of the last three or four days had evidently diminished the prestige of the officer caste. I began to wonder whether Bridges would be really shot if he continued his harangue at the railway station.

In the Grand Place I seemed to be the only officer.

MISTAKEN HOSPITALITY

I tied my horse to a lamp post, intending to find a shop where I could buy some food and get permission to lie down. But nearly every shop was closed or else the door was blocked by an indignant proprietor and his wife who insisted, as I was an officer, that I should go in at once and clear out the English soldiery who had entered and were lying asleep in the bedrooms and had helped themselves to food.

'Your men are all drunk, will you order them out of the house? I have young daughters in my house – the men have entered my kitchen – it is disgraceful! Why is there no order? Why are there no officers? Your troops have been here for hours and up to no good: please order them to go away!'

'It is all your fault,' I said angrily, 'I have seen your people giving our tired men white wine to drink; and you know they can have had nothing to eat for twenty-four hours. Why on earth do you not give them all some bread and butter and make them some coffee?'

They looked at me in amazement. French peasants will often give wine away – but who ever heard of a French shopkeeper giving away butter.

The townsfolk were exaggerating – only a few of the men were drunk. Certainly in nearly every house and shop I entered there were a few English soldiers. In a chemist's shop where I tried unsuccessfully to buy some soap (the proprietor was very rude), two British soldiers were lying fast asleep, not on, but underneath the couch in the chemist's back parlour.

But I saw few actually drunk. Eventually I got some bread and a bottle of white wine, and to avoid the recriminations of the shop people I decided I would sleep out in the Grand Place as so many men were doing. The pavement looked hard and the cobble-stones in the square too uneven. Eventually, for the first time in my life – may it be the last – I decided to sleep in the paved gutter which looked dry and cleaner than the road.

Rolling up my Burberry for a pillow, I lay down in the gutter close to my horse. When I awoke it was dusk and two or three officers of the 4th Dragoon Guards were in the square with Bridges. Apparently, Bridges was having a discussion with some official – I believe the mayor of St. Quentin – urging him to provide horses and carts to take those of our men who were too sore-footed to be able to march out of the town. I walked over to listen. As far as I could understand, the official – mayor or whoever – was very indignant; he kept on saying :

'You understand, m'sieur *le Majeur,* it is now too late. These men have surrendered to the Germans.'

'How? The Germans are not here.'

'Their colonel and officers have signed a paper giving me the numbers of the men of each regiment and the names of the officers who are prepared to surrender and I have sent a copy of this out under a white flag to the commander of the approaching German army.'

'But you have no business, m'sieur, as a loyal Frenchman, to assist allied troops to surrender.'

'What else? Consider, *m'sieur le Majeur,* the alternatives. The German army is at Gricourt? Very well: I, representing the inhabitants of St. Quentin, who do not want our beautiful town unnecessarily destroyed by shell-fire because it happens to be full of English troops, have said to your colonels and your men: "Will you please go and fight the German army outside St. Quentin?" But your men, they say, "No; we cannot fight! We have lost nearly all our officers, our Staff have gone away by train, we do not know where to fight. Also, we have no artillery, most of us have neither rifles nor ammunition, and we are all so very tired." Then, m'sieur le Majeur, I say to them, "Then, please, if you will not fight, will you please go right away, and presently the Germans will enter St. Quentin peacefully; so the inhabitants will be glad to be tranquil and not killed, and all our good shops not burnt." But they reply to me, "No, we cannot go away. We are terribly, terribly tired. We have had no proper food or rest for many days, and yesterday we fought a great battle. We have not got any maps, and we do not even know where to go to. So we will stay in St. Quentin and have a little rest." Then I say to them, "Since you will neither fight nor go away, then please you must surrender." So I send out a list of those who surrender to the German commander and now all is properly arranged.'

All arranged! Yet the logic of the argument was irresistible but for one point, which Bridges had quickly seized upon. The men could be got away if every horse and cart in St. Quentin was collected for those men too tired to march; his cavalrymen would escort them out of the town. So the shops and streets would be cleared of tired and drunken men, and then there would be no more firing off of rifles. But there was to be no more of this wine, only tea or coffee and bread.

So eventually it was arranged. Bridges had saved the situation which, though bad, was understandable. Disorganized stragglers had arrived by the hundred, many out of sheer fatigue, having thrown away their packs and rifles. They had tramped beneath the blazing August sun with empty stomachs, dispirited and utterly weary; many had received quantities of wine from friendly French peasants to revive them in those dusty lanes. Literally, in many cases their bellies were full of wine and their boots were half-full of blood; that I saw myself.

The English soldier's feet, like his head but unlike his heart, are not his strong point.

To me it seems there was every excuse for the two colonels and the one or two pale, exhausted-looking, subalterns whom I had noticed mingling with the crowd down at the station. Without Staff, without maps or orders, without food, without ammunition, what could the remnants of broken infantry do before the advance of a victorious army whose cavalry could have mopped them up in an hour? Probably looking back on it now, the two colonels did almost the only thing feasible and the brave thing. Middle-aged men, both of them looked utterly exhausted. From their appearance they were suffering severely from the sun; that alone might account for their not having thought of using the mayor as a collector of country carts.

So Bridges sent the remnant of his squadron round St. Quentin to encourage and collect in the square as many as possible of the infantrymen who were willing to join us in making our escape. The shots in different parts of the town still continued. Perhaps a few drunken soldiers were still having an imaginary wrestle with the 'Angels of Mons', or something more repulsive. White wine can raise many images. Or did some of Bridges' squadron shoot a few who too truculently scorned their suggestion that there was still time to run and fight another day?

Bridges asked me to count the men who were collecting in the square and get them into fours. I counted one hundred and ten fours; that is to say, four hundred and forty men. Then he asked me to do something else – I forget what it was. A few men had whistles and Jews' harps – perhaps they had them in their haversacks, as soldiers often do – and they formed a sort of band. We persuaded one of the colonels to march in front of his men. My recollection is that he looked very pale, entirely dazed, had no Sam Browne belt and leant heavily on his stick, apparently so exhausted with fatigue and the heat that he could scarcely have known what he was doing. Some of his men called to him encouraging words, affectionate and familiar, but not meant insolently, such as: 'Buck up, sir!' 'Cheer up, daddy! Now we shan't be long ! We are all going back to Hang-le-Tear.' [England].

Actually I saw him saluting one of his own corporals, who did not even look surprised. What with fatigue, heat, drink and the demoralization of defeat, many hardly knew what they were doing. I was so tired myself that I went to sleep on my horse almost immediately after I remounted and nearly fell off, much to the amusement of some of the infantry, who supposed I was as drunk with white wine as some of their comrades.

By this time it was quite dark. It seemed to have taken hours to collect the men, yet we did not move off. I began to feel quite sick with impatience. Over-tired or sheer funk? What on earth were the German cavalry doing? At about five that afternoon they had been at Gricourt. We had held on there, keeping them back until about six o'clock, and it was now nearly eleven o'clock, and Gricourt was but a few miles outside the town. Why had they not entered the town and mopped up this disorganized mob? Had they been informed by their aeroplanes circling over the town of the situation, already?

It was nearly half-past twelve before we left St. Quentin. The sultry August day had passed, to leave a thick summer mist. Our small army was at last collected. Every kind of vehicle had been filled with men with blistered feet. In front of them, on foot, were several hundred infantry, mostly of two regiments, but containing representatives of nearly every unit in the 4th Division, and behind, to form the rearguard to this

The Grand Place of St. Quentin. The cobbled stones were the scene of moving events in August 1914. Upon them 4th Division men in retreat from Le Cateau flung themselves down in a sleep of utter exhaustion, and were only roused by the heroic energy of Major Tom Bridges, who got them away in the nick of time.

extraordinary cavalcade, Tom Bridges' mounted column – the gallant little band of 4th Dragoon Guards, with driblets of Lancers, Hussars, Irish Horse, Signallers and the rest of the stragglers. In front of all rode a liaison officer and a guide sent by the mayor and, I think, Tom Bridges. By his side, walking, armed with a walking-stick, was one of the two colonels, a thick-set man, who had surrendered (the other had disappeared). And immediately behind them the miscellaneous 'band' made up of Jews' harps and penny whistles.

So through the darkness and the thick, shrouding fog of that summer night we marched out, literally feeling our way through the countryside, so thick was the mist. At about two in the morning we had reached the villages of Savy and Roupy. Just as we started to leave St. Quentin I woke up to the fact that my precious map case was missing and I had to return to look for it in the now deserted Grand Place.

As for a moment I sat on my horse alone there, taking a last look round, I heard an ominous sound – the metallic rattle on the cobbles of cavalry entering the town through one of the darkened side streets that led into the Grand Place.

The Germans must have entered St. Quentin but a few minutes after the tail of our queer little column disappeared westward through the fog towards Savy.

The two commanding officers who surrendered, Lieutenant Colonels John Elkington and Arthur Mainwaring, were subsequently court-martialed. They were cleared of cowardice but cashiered from the service. Elkington went on to join the French Foreign Legion and gave valuable and courageous service, was restored to the British Army and awarded the DSO. Mainwaring disappeared from public view.

27 August, 1914

THE RALLYING of DEMORALIZED MEN

Major Tom Bridges

Major Tom Bridges was the officer who rallied the deadbeat British soldiers at St. Quentin to the strains of 'The British Grenadiers' played on a toy drum. This is that officer's personal account of the dramatic incident when the British soldiers had surrendered to the Germans and yet were encouraged to continue with their withdrawal.

Approaching St. Quentin the situation of the infantry became precarious. Marched literally off their feet, they straggled into the town in a demoralized condition. In the early afternoon our Brigadier had called the officers together and said we were in a very tight corner, but must fight it out and die like gentlemen. He appointed me rearguard commander with two squadrons and two companies of French Territorial infantry in support. My orders were to hold the Germans off and retire through St. Quentin at 6 pm. (I was not actually clear of it until six hours later.) I made my dispositions and pushed out patrols to keep touch with the enemy. One of these, a corporal and three men, got cut off and joined a French cavalry regiment, but eventually found their way back to us a fortnight later.

The Germans were slow in coming on. During the afternoon a car loaded with ladies drove up on to a hill close by and had a good look round. The car was so like a Staff Benz that we thought the sex of the ladies doubtful. We sent a patrol to investigate but it quickly turned and drove off

The Frenchmen were dug in north of the town, a nice position with a clear line of fire. I arranged with the commandant that he should stay there till 4 pm, but after visiting the outposts and returning about 2 pm, there was not a pair of red trousers in sight anywhere. This was my first experience of Allied co-operation. The French, in spite of their gallantry and inherent military qualities, were often unreliable and unpunctual. It may be that their methods were different from ours. They came and went like autumn leaves. Where we would hold a position they would abandon it and retake it with a brilliant counter-attack. One had to remember that *Marianne* [a national emblem of France and an allegory of Liberty and Reason] was a woman and would keep you guessing. Heroic in danger, she would run from a mouse. She would rise to the heights and descend to the depths. Like the Hebrew prophet Habakkuk [Bible] she was *capable de tout* [capable of anything; unpredictable]. Our interpreter officer, Harrison (4th Hussars), went into St. Quentin to find out if the infantry were clear as, barring an occasional lame duck, they had ceased coming down the road from Le Cateau.

On his return he reported the place swarming with stragglers. He could find no officers, and the men were going into the houses and lying down to sleep. I then dispatched Sewell with some hefty henchmen, farriers and the like, to clear out the houses and get everyone into the market place. He was also to find the Maire and commandeer bread and cheese and beer for our men, who were now on short rations and to have it put down ready by portions on the pavement outside the Mairie, so that if we were pressed, as seemed quite possible, we should not have to waste time issuing rations.

We gradually fell back into the town, leaving two troops and machine guns to hold the bridge over the river. There were two or three hundred men lying about in the Place and the few officers, try as they would, could not get a kick out of them. Worse, Harrison now reported that the remains of two battalions had piled arms in the railway station, and that their commanding officer had given a written assurance to the *Maire* that they would surrender and fight no more, in order to save the town from bombardment. I had to relieve the *Maire* of this document at once, and sent Harrison back to tell the two commanding officers that there was a cavalry rearguard still behind them, and they must hurry up and get out. Apparently a meeting was then held and the men refused to march on the grounds that they had already surrendered and would only come away if a train was sent to take them. I therefore sent an ultimatum giving them half an hour's grace, during which time some carts would be provided for those who really could not walk, but letting them know that I would leave no British soldier alive in St. Quentin.

Upon this they left the station and gave no more trouble. I quote this unpleasant incident to show to what extremes good troops will be driven by fatigue. I conducted these negotiations through an intermediary, as I knew one of the colonels well and had met the other, and they were, of course, both senior to me. The men in the square were a different problem, and so jaded it was pathetic to see them. If one only had a band I thought. Why not? There was a toy-shop handy which provided my trumpeter and myself with a tin whistle and a drum, and we marched round and round the fountain where the men were lying like the dead, playing, 'The British Grenadiers' and 'Tipperary' and beating the drum like mad. They began to sit up and started to laugh and even cheer. I stopped playing and made them a short exhortation and told them I was going to take them back to their regiments.

They began to stand up and fall in, and eventually we slowly moved off into the night to the music of our improvised band, now reinforced with a couple of mouth-organs. When well clear of the town I tried to delegate my

A photograph taken a decade after the event when Major Tom Bridges had taken a toy drum from this shop in St Quentin and, along with his battalion trumpeter playing a tin whistle, rallied dispirited British troops and marched them towards Paris and out of the clutch of the Germans.

functions to someone else, but the infantry would not let me go. 'Don't leave us, major,' they cried, 'or by God we'll not get anywhere.' So on we went, and it was early morning before I got back to my squadron. Our rearguard was unmolested by the Germans and it looked as if 'more haste, less speed' might well have been the description of this part of the retreat.

Both the colonels above mentioned were afterwards court-martialled and cashiered. One of them, Elkington, joined the French Foreign Legion and worked his way to a commission. He was badly wounded and received the Legion of Honour. For his gallantry in the field King George V reinstated him in the British Army and awarded him the DSO.

SWORDS IN THE MOONLIGHT

The night of the anniversary of Sedan found us riding through the Forest of Compiègne in the white moonlight with drawn swords, ready to fall upon our enemy, whom we were informed (quite inaccurately) had now surrounded us. There is no doubt, however, that the Germans were making strenuous efforts to round up the British. Hate was the motif of the hour. The word 'contemptible' tickled the queer sense of humour of the British soldier, and was a valuable slogan for the first seven divisions, and no doubt gave impetus to recruiting, but this translation of the word is hardly a fair one. 'Insignificant' would probably meet the case.

Although we found a fleet of supply wagons in the wood with engines still running, and other queer things, including German soldiers in grey-green cut in half at the waist – I never knew how (was it an illusion caused by the ground mist or did I dream it, for I rode in a trance?) We emerged into the open without further contact. It was a relief to halt at last within the defences of Paris, for even the most unimaginative were by that time wondering when and where the chase would end. On the doctor's advice I got leave and borrowed a car to go into Paris and saw a specialist about my face. Paris was a dead city, the shutters were up, the streets entrenched, and the Government gone to Bordeaux.

The specialist had a German name; he rubbed his hands and beamed at me, 'Your army has had a bad time, yes? The Germans are supermen – Paris will now surrender to them?' Time, he said, would heal my cheekbone.

The Battle of the Marne, already in preparation by the British and French, must have come as a shock to him when it stopped the Germans and pushed them back the way they had come.

23 August – 5 September, 1914

A DIARY of the GREAT RETREAT

by Corporal Bernard John Denore

This diary of Corporal Denore, 1st Battalion Royal Berkshire Regiment, 2nd Division, I Corps, covers the Battle of Mons and the subsequent retreat. Four weeks later Corporal Denore was severely wounded at Zonnebeke during the First Battle of Ypres and was invalided home.

The diary begins with the entry made when the battalion arrived at Mons:

August 23

We had been marching since 2.30 am and at about 11.15 am an order was passed down for A Company (my company) to deploy to the right and dig in on the south bank of a railway cutting. We deployed and started digging in, but as the soil was mostly chalk, we were only able to make shallow holes. While we were digging the German artillery opened fire. The range was perfect, about six shells at a time bursting in line directly over our heads. All of us except the company commander fell flat on our faces, frightened and surprised; but after a while we got up and looked over the rough parapet we had thrown up and could not see much. One or two men had been wounded and one was killed.

There was a town about one mile away on our left front, and a lot of movement was going on round about it. There was a small village called Binche on our right, where there was a lot of heavy firing going on – rifle and artillery.

We saw the Germans attack on our left in great masses, but they were beaten back by the Coldstream Guards. A squadron of German cavalry crossed our front about 800 yards distant and we opened fire on them. We hit a few and the fact that we were doing something definite improved our morale immensely, and took away a lot of our nervousness.

The artillery fire from the Germans was very heavy, but was dropping behind us on a British battery. The company officer, who had stayed in the open all the time, had taken a couple of men to help get the wounded away from the battery behind us. He returned about 6.30 pm, when the firing had died down a bit and informed us that the battery had been blown to bits.

I was then sent with four men on outpost to a signal box at a level crossing, and found it was being used as a clearing station for wounded. After dark more wounded were brought in from the 9th Battery RFA (the battery that was cut up). One man was in a very bad way, and kept shrieking out for somebody to bring a razor and cut his throat and two others died almost immediately.

I was going to move a bundle of hay when someone called out, 'Lookout, chum. There's a bloke in there'. I saw a leg completely severed from its body, and suddenly felt very sick and tired. The German rifle-fire started again and an artilleryman to whom I was talking was shot dead. I

The first contacts between the opposing armies in the World War were made by the cavalry of the Allies and the Central Powers. Above is the point of a German Dragoon regiment in pursuit of the withdrawing British.

was sick then. Nothing much happened during the night except that one man spent all his time kissing his rosary beads, and another swore practically the whole night.

August 24

Just about dawn a party of Germans came near and we opened fire on them and hit quite a number. We thought of following them up, but a corporal brought an order to retire. We joined the company again behind the trenches, and learnt that the town we could see was Mons.

After a while we joined up with the rest of the battalion on the road and went back the same route that we covered coming up. All the time there was plenty of firing going on by Givry [Quévy], and about midday we deployed and opened fire on a regiment of German cavalry. Whereupon they dismounted and returned our fire, which was all 'rapid' and was telling on them. Then suddenly they mounted and disappeared out of range. We continued marching back for about four hours. Then again we deployed and opened fire on more German cavalry, but this time they kept out of range and eventually moved off altogether. My platoon was sent forward to a small village, where we stayed all night, firing occasionally at what we hoped were German cavalry.

August 25

We started off about 5 am, still retiring, and so far we had had no food since Sunday the 23rd. All day long we marched, and although a lot of firing was going on we did none of it. About 6.30 pm we got to a place called Maroilles and my platoon spent the night guarding a bridge over a stream. The Germans attacked about 9 pm and kept it up all night, but didn't get into Maroilles. About forty-five of the company were killed or wounded, including the company officer. A voice had called out in English, 'Has anybody got a map?' and when our OC stood up with his map, a German walked up and shot him with a revolver. The German was killed by a bayonet thrust from a one of the men.

August 16

The Germans withdrew at dawn, and soon after we continued retiring, and had not been on the march very long before we saw a French regiment, which showed that not all of them had deserted us. We marched all day long, miles and miles it seemed, probably owing to the fact that we had had no sleep at all since Saturday the 22nd, and had had very little food to eat, and the marching discipline was not good. I myself frequently felt very sick.

We had a bit of a fight at night, and what made matters worse was that it happened at Vénérolles, the village we were billeted in before we went up to Mons. Anyway, the Germans retired from the fight.

August 27

At dawn we started on the march again. I noticed that the *curé* and one old fellow stayed in Vénérolles, but all the other inhabitants went the previous night. A lot of our men threw away their overcoats while we were on the road today, but I kept mine.

The marching was getting quite disorderly; numbers of men from other regiments were mixed up with us. We reached St. Quentin, a nice town, just before dark, but marched straight through and dug ourselves in on some high ground, with a battery of artillery in line with us. Although we saw plenty of movement in the town, the Germans didn't attack us, neither did we fire on them. During the night, a man near me quite suddenly started squealing like a pig, and then jumped out of the trench, ran straight down the hill towards the town, and shot himself through the foot. He was brought in by some artillerymen.

August 28

Again at dawn we started on the march, and during the first halt another

German dragoons crossing a shallow river. Their shining helmets covered with cloth, but they still carry lances, as did all the German Dragoons in the early days of the war. It was such a squadron as this that the 1st Berkshire Battalion encountered.

fellow shot himself through the foot.

The roads were in a terrible state, the heat was terrific, there seemed to be very little order about anything, and mixed up with us and wandering about all over the roads were refugees with all sorts of conveyances: prams, trucks, wheelbarrows, and tiny little carts drawn by dogs. They were piled up with what looked like beds and bedding, and all of them asked us for food, which we could not give them, as we had none ourselves.

The men were discarding their equipment in a wholesale fashion in spite of orders to the contrary; also many of them fell out, and rejoined again towards dusk. They had been riding on limbers and wagons and officers' chargers, and generally looked worse than those of us who kept going all day. That night I went on outpost, but I did not know where exactly, as things were getting hazy in my mind. I tried to keep up with my diary, although it was against orders. Anyway, I could not realize all that was happening, and only knew that I was always tired, hungry, un-shaven and dirty. My feet were sore, water was scarce, in fact, it was issued in half-pints, as we were not allowed to touch the native water. The regulations were kept in force in that respect – so much so that two men were put under arrest and sentenced to field punishment for stealing bread from an empty house. Then, again, it wasn't straight marching. For every few hours we had to deploy and beat off an attack, and every time somebody I knew was killed or wounded. And after we had beaten off the attacking force, on we went again – retiring.

August 29

A despatch was read to us, from General French, [sic – he was a Field Marshal], explaining that the BEF was on the west of a sort of horseshoe, and that the retirement was to draw the Germans right into it, when they would be nipped off. That afternoon we went to a place called Chauny to guard the river while some REs blew up the bridges. It was a change from the everlasting marching, and we managed to get some vegetables out of the gardens and cook them. A few Uhlans appeared, but got away again in spite of our fire. So far as I could tell there wasn't a single civilian in the town, and all the houses were barricaded; while outside of them were buckets of wine – pink, blue, red, whitish, and other colours. We were not allowed to drink any.

August 30

Just as we were leaving Chauny, about 4 am, two girls were found and were taken along with us.

Although all the bridges were blown up, the Germans were after us almost immediately. God only knew how they got over so soon. Their fire was heavy but high; the few we saw were firing from their hips as they advanced. We fired for about half an hour. Then the artillery came into action, and we retired about two or three miles under cover of their fire. Then we waited till the Germans came up, and we began all over again, and then again, and then again, all day long. It was terribly tiring, heart-

German infantry pressing hard on the British rearguard units.

breaking work, as we seemed to have the measure of the Germans, and yet we retired. During the evening the Guards Brigade took over the rearguard work while our Brigade went on to Castle Isoy [sic] and bivouacked and slept for about six hours.

August 31

Again we were rearguard, but did little fighting. We marched instead, staggering about the road like a crowd of gipsies. Some of the fellows had puttees wrapped round their feet instead of boots; others had soft shoes they had picked up somewhere; others walked in their socks, with their feet all bleeding. My own boots would have disgraced a tramp, but I was too frightened to take them off and look at my feet. Yet they marched until they dropped, and then somehow got up and marched again.

One man (Ginger Gilmore) found a mouth-organ, and, despite the fact that his feet wore bound in blood-soaked rags, he staggered along at the head of the company playing tunes all day. Mostly he played 'The Irish Emigrant', which is a good marching tune. He reminded me of Captain Oates [Antarctic Explorer]. An officer asked me if I wanted a turn on his horse, but I looked at the fellow on it and said, 'No thanks'.

The marching; was getting on everyone's nerves, but as I went I kept saying to myself, 'If you can, force your heart and nerve and sinew'. Just that, over and over again. That night we spent the time looking for a Uhlan regiment, but didn't get in touch with them, and every time we stopped we fell asleep; in fact we slept while we were marching, and consequently kept falling over.

September 1

We continued at the same game from dawn till dark, and dark till dawn – marching and fighting and marching. Every roll call there were fewer to answer – some were killed some wounded, and some who had fallen out were missing. During this afternoon we fought for about three hours – near Villers-Cotterêts, I think it was, but I was getting very mixed about things, even mixed about the days of the week. Fifteen men in my company were killed, one in a rather peculiar fashion. He was bending down, handing me a piece of sausage, when a bullet ricochetted off a man's boot and went straight into his mouth and out of the top of his head. We got on to the road about 200 yards in front of a German brigade, and then ran like hell for about a mile, until we passed through the South Staffs Regiment, who were entrenched each side of the road. I believe about six of the battalion were captured. Still we marched on until dusk, then on out-post again, and during the night the South Staffs passed through us.

September 2

At 2 am we moved off and marched all day long. It was hot and dusty and the roads were rotten, but as we got mixed up with hundreds of refugees we were obliged to keep better marching order. About 6 pm to 8 pm we reached Meaux. I believe we did about twenty-five miles that day, but no fighting. We bivouacked outside Meaux, but I went into the cathedral when we halted near it, and thought it was very beautiful. Also, I saw some of the largest tomatoes I have ever seen in my life growing in a garden. I was rounding up stragglers most of the night until 1 am and at 3 am we moved off again.

September 3

The first four or five hours we did without a single halt or rest, as we had to cross a bridge over the Aisne before the REs blew it up. It was the most terrible march I have ever done. Men were falling down like nine-pins. They would fall flat on their faces on the road, while the rest of us staggered round them, as we couldn't lift our feet high enough to step over them; and as for picking them up, that was impossible, as to bend meant to fall. What happened to them God only knows. An aeroplane was following us most of the time, dropping iron darts. We fired at it a couple of times, but soon lost the strength required for that. About 9 am we halted by a river, and immediately two fellows threw themselves into it. Nobody, from sheer fatigue, was able to save them, although one sergeant made an attempt and was nearly drowned himself. I, like a fool, took my boots off, and found my feet were covered with blood. I could find no sores or cuts, so I thought I must have sweated blood. As I couldn't get my boots on again I cut the sides away and when we started marching again my feet hurt like hell. We marched till about 3 pm – nothing else, just march, march, march. I kept repeating my line 'If you can, force, etc.' Why, I didn't know. A sergeant irritated everyone who could hear him by continually shouting out: 'Stick it, lads! We're making history!'

The colonel offered me a ride on his horse, but I refused, and then wished I hadn't, as anything was preferable to the continuous marching. We got back that afternoon among the refugees again. They were even worse off than we were – or, at least, they looked it. We gave the kids our biscuits and 'bully', hoping that would help them a little; but they looked so dazed and tired there did not seem to be much hope for them.

At 8 pm we bivouacked in a field and slept till dawn. Ye gods, what a relief!

September 4

I was sent with six men on outpost to a small wood on our left front and I had not posted the sentries more than half an hour before an officer found two of them asleep. The poor fellows were afterwards tried by courts-martial and shot. [These men were sentenced to death but this was commuted to two years' hard labour. One man was a private in the Dragoon Guards and the other a driver in the Army Service Corps.]

About 3 pm we all moved off again and came into action almost immediately, although I believe it was a food convoy that was mistaken for German artillery by our artillery. Anyway, no one I knew was hurt. It was said, however, that Jerry rushed his troops along after us in lorries.

All through the night we marched, rocking about on our feet from the want of sleep and falling fast asleep even if the halt lasted only a minute. Towards dawn we turned into a farm and for about two hours I slept in a pigsty.

September 5

Early on this morning reinforcements from England joined us and the difference in their appearance and ours was amazing. They looked plump, clean, tidy, and very wide-awake. Whereas we were filthy, thin, and haggard. Most of us had beards; what equipment was left was torn; instead of boots we had puttees, rags old shoes, field boots – anything and everything wrapped round our feet. Our hats were in the same state: women's hats, peasants' hats, caps, any old covering; while our trousers were mostly in ribbons. The officers were in a similar condition.

After the reserves joined we marched about twenty miles to a place called Chaume-en-Brie. It was crowded with staff officers. We bivouacked in a park, and then had an order read to us that the men who had kept their overcoats were to dump them as we were to advance at any moment. Strangely, a considerable amount of cheering took place. I discovered that the company I was in covered 251 miles in the Retreat from Mons, which finished on 5 September 1914.

A Scottish battalion falling back in good order through a French village during the Retreat. These pipers still have sufficient breath to pipe their comrades through the cobbled streets.

25-28 August, 1914

ABOUT TO BE SHOT
FOR A SPY
by Paul Maze

The author of this narrative was for four and a half years one of the most remarkable figures on the Western Front. A French artist and a fluent English speaker, he attached himself to the Scots Greys on their landing at Le Havre and acted as an informal interpreter and liaison officer. Afterwards he was on the staff of Sir Hubert Gough. During the retreat from Mons he was almost shot as a spy.

I woke up suddenly – it was daylight. I didn't know where I was. I only felt the weight of my boots. I looked at my watch – I had slept five hours. Not a sound came from the village. I peeped through the window – the street was deserted. I slipped down the stairs into the kitchen, shouting for madame. Her bread and coffee lay on the table. I got no response. Full of apprehension, I ran up the stairs, and as I seized my cap and revolver belt I heard the clatter of horses' hoofs – the square tops of Uhlan helmets were passing right under my window! I paused, breathless, then a motor-car rushed through the streets, carrying a party of Germans, revolvers in hand. I had to push the window open gently to see if anyone else was coming. The two riders I had seen turned off to the right were now out of sight.

I had to act quickly. Fortunately the village was small. Each farm opened onto a yard. I knew I had to avoid the roads. The kitchen door was locked; it opened onto a small garden. Jumping out of the window I climbed a wall covered with pears, crossed over a lane into a farmyard, then slipped through some stables and out into open space where I made for another farm, disturbing some hens pecking at a manure heap. They took off with much fluttering and clucking. At the next farm, looking through a window, I saw some people. They all talked at once. One little fellow, a hunchback, caught hold of my arm and said *'Suivez-moi'*, and I followed him. After much dodging about we came to a wall which I peeped over and viewed an expanse of countryside that looked like the whole of France spread out in the sunlight. The trees of two main roads divided the landscape; one led to the town of St. Quentin. I shook the hand of my guide, who said: *'Bonne chance, sauvez-vous vite'*. Hiding the best way I could, I crept towards the road, shuffling noisily through a wet cabbage patch that soaked me to the

Key men in the Alliance between England and France – members of the French Army who could speak fluent English. Paul Maze is the central figure in this group of seven Frenchmen. The group are still wearing the uniforms of their individual units prior to changing to British Army khaki.

skin. After a short run I flung myself headlong into the ditch bordering the road.

Carefully I looked around – not a soul could be seen anywhere. Putting my ear to the ground I could detect no sound of movement. I ran dodging from tree to tree which, happily, were thick trunked and not far apart, stopping only to recover my breath. I watched every haystack, keeping my eye on a village to my right. I had just paused for a moment and was on the verge of rushing forward again when there, standing against a high red brick wall, were three mounted Uhlans, their shadows sharply cast against the wall. My eyes were glued to them, I dared not move. A cold shiver ran down my spine as one of them rode his horse across the open towards a group of small hay-stacks about 200 yards from where I was crouched.

Stopping suddenly, he stood up in his stirrups and looked through his field-glasses. He took his time, concentrating on certain places. I could see his dark horse lashing the air with its tail. Nothing, however, had arrested his attention in my direction, but when he waved to the others and they promptly joined him at a quick trot, I thought I was finished. They stood a while conversing, then looked round and, to my relief, turned their horses and started at an easy trot, moving back towards the village, their lances with folded pennants swinging above their heads.

As I had my eyes fixed on them I heard coming up from behind a kind of flapping sound. It was a dog running straight at me. I gave a sudden jerk, swinging at it as it neared, which frightened it off. With suppressed yelps it swerved round me and ran on, with its tail between its legs, trailing a lead. Meanwhile, the Uhlans had neared the village and were disappearing behind farm buildings.

There was nothing for me to do but run. I looked in every direction first, before crouching and darting across to the other side of the road; noting as I did the dog, away ahead, still running for all it was worth. What hid me from sight was the depth of the ditch and the bank on both sides of the road. By keeping my head down I could run along, confident that I could not be seen from the fields. What distance I covered along that ditch I do not know.

Suddenly two shots rang out ahead and over to my right, echoing from wood to wood. I dropped down and lay still, my faced pressed against the damp earth. Cautiously, I raised myself and began moving very slowly along the ditch towards a crossroads. The light from the sun was blinding as I approached a bunch of road-side trees. More shots caused me to drop to the ground. Over by a small wood I could just make out what appeared to be men wearing the familiar khaki uniforms of the British. Inwardly I breathed a sigh of relief as I saw what was unmistakably two dismounted cavalrymen. With hopes raised I waited; there among the leaves I could see red faces – I was becoming more confident. Having advanced a little more, I cleared the bank and, waving for all I was worth, I shot in amongst them like a football between goal posts.

They were our cavalry, dismounted; their horses were just at hand, a few paces away. For a moment I could hardly talk I was so out of breath. The officer in command told me I was lucky, for German patrols were everywhere and they had been firing at anyone who showed himself.

'You were lucky they didn't see you. Your unit must be somewhere close by as it passed through here earlier in the morning. Brigade headquarters is about two miles away in that direction. They will be able to direct you. You had better begin walking – and keep your head down.'

Setting off in the direction indicated I joined up with an infantryman belonging to the Highland Light Infantry who was going the same way. Red-haired, tall, as brown as a berry, with a broad Border accent, he looked the picture of health, in spite of his long weary march. He told me the

Officers of the British High Command discussing the situation during the
retreat from Mons. On the left, leaning on his stick, is Lieutenant General Sir
Douglas Haig, commanding I Corps, he is talking with Major General C. C.
Monro, commanding the 1st Division. On the right are two members of Haig's
staff, Brigadier General J. Gough and Colonel Percival. It was to such a group,
which included Major General Monro, that Paul Maze approached directly to
offer information and was promptly arrested on suspicion of being a spy.

details of a severe scrap in which he had been engaged. His haversack was full of unripe apples, which he kept munching and spitting out as we trudged along.

The village we next walked into was occupied by British infantry and in the middle of the market square there stood a throng of officers obviously engaged in deep conversation. Among them was a stoutish man with a grey moustache, General Sir Charles Monro, who commanded the 2nd Division. As I was still new to the army, the sight of red tabs had not the sobering effect on me that it had on a regular private soldier.

Rashly I imagined that those staff officers would welcome any information that I might be able to supply. Approaching the group I saluted and asked the whereabouts of the Greys or of their transport with which I had lost touch. I was about to say where I had come from and what I had seen, when the General cut me short, looked me up and down from head to toe before informing me that the Greys had passed through the village earlier that day, but that he had no idea where their transport had gone. Suddenly his manner changed, with his face twitching, he sharply asked my name; there was a look of suspicion in his stare. 'Where have you come from?' I mentioned the village. 'That place has been occupied by the enemy since earlier this morning.' he replied. I felt a stir among the officers who were suddenly listening – one officer walked away quickly.

'What village did you say you were in?'
I could not remember the name.
'What is the name of your colonel?'
My memory failed me entirely.
'What squadron are you in?'
My mind was a blank.

Suddenly the ground disappeared from under my feet as I was lifted up and my belt and revolver taken from me. I was immediately searched, right down to my puttees. Hand-cuffed, my legs trembling under me, I was marched off to join a party of German prisoners and Belgian civilians who were tied to one another and standing by the headquarters' baggage cart. Suddenly we were marched off, escorted by men with fixed bayonets. It all happened so fast I had barely time to realize what was happening. A soldier called out 'Here is another blasted spy!' It was no use my appealing. It made me realize the dangerous situation I was in.

As the group marched along bound together the General and his staff drove past in a staff car without even giving us a glance. It was useless trying to get a hearing from those guards escorting us. I could not talk to the German prisoners, who all the time were mumbling to me, *'Bist du Deutsch?'* I dared not answer – it would look worse for me if I was seen talking to them in their tongue. I heard them discuss me – they could not make out what I was. The three Belgians looked such ruffians I thought it wise not to address them at all. We were made to step out, to keep up with the rear of the transport wagons. All around there was a general sign of urgency – riders were driving their heels into their horses; infantry alongside us were marching at a fast pace. Earlier the dew had kept the dust down, but now, even though it was still early morning, clouds of dust were rising. Staring at the wagon before me I followed the sound of its squealing as one does a tune. It was as though I was in a dream, not realising yet the full extent of the trouble I was in. A loud rumble of guns on our right grew nearer and nearer.

In a village where we rested later in the day, things livened up as the villagers caught sight of the *espions*. They spat at the captured spies and threw stones at us. One French Territorial soldier, for some unknown reason alone in that village, came up to us seething with rage and foaming at the mouth waving his bayonet. One of our guards became furious and handled him very roughly.

We resumed our weary march, picking up as we went along a considerable number of stragglers belonging to all sorts of regiments. From their appearance it was evident that they had had a bad time – but they looked determined and walked on, keeping in rank. Motor-cyclists and staff cars would rush past, raising a cloud of dust. Artillery would cut across fields, leaving the road free for the infantry, everybody was bent on pushing on. Every sound and sight I witnessed of the situation all around sharpened my apprehension.

UNHAPPY RECOGNITION

We overtook a halted wagon line and as ill luck would have it three German prisoners who had been with the transport the day before recognised me and waved. As they had been with us for a whole day I had chatted with them a good deal so as to try to get some information out of them so, of course, they knew me. How could I explain to the guards, who had witnessed their greeting, the circumstances of my acquaintance with enemy soldiers? The incident was at once reported to the military police and nothing I could say made things any better.

When night came I was led to a small shrine by the side of the road. Tired out, I lay down, a simple statue of the Virgin Mary above my head. I remembered what a nun had said on my way north as she had pressed a crucifix into my hands, saying that it would help me. Indeed, I now needed all the help in the world, even hers.

The night was very cold. Troops went by incessantly. Above the shuffling of feet I heard my sentry solemnly remark: 'Why don't they just shoot the bastard and be done with him, instead of keeping us shivering out here all night guarding him?' Somewhere in the darkness a fierce engagement was taking place, not too many miles away.

August 27 – I was taken out of the shrine at an early hour and into a thick fog. Artillery, transport and infantry seemed to be all mixed up. An officer was shouting out instructions as units extricated themselves from all the confusion and got on to the road. The three German prisoners from the day before were brought up and I joined them; we became part of a long column of infantry. We were given biscuits and a tin of bully beef.

Something serious had happened during the night – I did not know what it was, but I sensed it by the way the horses pulled and the chains strained and by the urgent voices of the drivers and increased pace of the marching men – all indicated the gravity of the situation. The enemy was obviously pressing in on all sides. In all this I wondered what eventually would happen to me.

After we had been on the march for some hours, the day cleared brilliantly. Suddenly, as I marched alongside some kilted men, I caught sight of a French soldier who happened to be a friend of mine. I hailed him and we walked along together. He had fought at Charleroi and lost touch with his regiment. As he knew no English it was difficult for him to explain that I was an old friend, but he eventually found an officer who understood French. Unfortunately, this turned out to be no help as the troops became split up and I even lost touch with my friend.

After a day-long march my feet were beginning to hurt and the pain took over from the predicament I was in. Over to the left a fierce battle was being fought and I could make out the quick bark of French 75 mm field guns. As darkness fell I was taken into a large modern house.

There were two beds in the room – we were three – I was assigned one of them. For the first time since leaving Mons my two guards were able to remove their boots. I could not recall when I had last had my boots off. The feeling immediately was not one of relief as I had expected.

One of my guards was a Cockney and he seemed marginally more sympathetic to my plight. The other was a Scot, whose only words to me when I tried to talk about my plight was: 'Dinna worry, if yr're a spy ye'll be shot alrecht, and if you're no, ye wilna be.' Which seemed logical enough. The Cockney confided, when we were alone, that he knew they had got it all wrong – and that I was not a spy.

READY FOR THE WORST

After a brief rest the Provost Marshal walked in with my haversack. He produced serveral of my possessions and asked if the razor was mine. Yes it was – a great German razor bought in Hamburg years before. I pointed out that if he had had any experience of either German or Swedish razors he would have one himself. He left smiling. After he left I couldn't sleep. I listened to the guns booming to the east and west of us, the sounds of which seemed to be increasing in an alarming way. The very air became heavy with tension.

As the grey light of dawn filtered into the room there was the sound of the clattering of bayonets on the wall and heavy steps on the stairs. The

'Cavalry to the rescue!' A party of Scots Greys on a road in France. Paul Maze was about to be taken away and shot out of hand as a traitor and a spy when a squadron of Scots Greys almost rode the party down. Leading the Greys was Major Swetenham, who immediately recognized him and was able to vouch for him.

door was flung open and the Provost Marshal stood framed in the doorway. Behind him was a sergeant major, who was calling for the prisoner to be marched out. This is it, I thought, as I was marched down into the street, which bustled with activity created by baggage wagons and infantry hurrying through the village street. Then I heard a voice yelling 'Make way for the cavalry!'

Suddenly I saw him – it was Major Collins riding ahead of a squadron of Scots Greys.

I shouted his name at the top of my voice – but he never saw me. In desperation I continued yelling his name as the squadron rode past. The clamour in the street drowned out my desperate cries.

'There you are, none of the Greys recognized him,' said one of my guards, and I was pushed on to where I assumed I was to be shot.

With leaden heart I stumbled on toward whatever fate awaited me.

'What the hell are you doing here?' It was Major Swetenham.

We had walked in front of his horse. He was leading the next squadron and had reigned back at the sight of me. With his arm raised to halt his men he repeated the question, puzzled as to why I was under arrest. He swung down from his horse and I was able to gabble a quick explanation.

'Sergeant Major – where is the Provost-Marshal?' Major Swetenham demanded. 'Lead me to him.'

We were told to wait and soon Mr Swetenham and the Provost Marshal were walking back towards us with smiles on their faces.

Major Seligman, who commanded J Battery, Royal Horse Artillery. Paul Maze was assured that he would be in good hands with the Battery.

'You had best come along with me sharpish – they were about to bally well shoot you.'

He stopped a limber of J Battery of the Royal Horse Artillery and had me jump up on to it. 'I have no horse to spare so you will have to make do with riding on this,' he said.

No words can express the feeling that came over me – I had been reprieved when minutes away from death at the hands of men of my own side.

After bouncing along for some time we came within sight of a small village called Cerizy on the St. Quentin – La Fère road, it was here we caught up with part of the Greys halted in the middle of a cup-shaped plain. J Battery drew up and I immediately found Colonel Bulkeley-Johnson, who was talking to Major Swetenham. On seeing me the colonel appeared pleased as he had concluded, after missing me for the last two days, that I had been taken prisoner. He expressed, in his charming way, a deal of sympathy for what I had gone through.

'You must remember that the 2nd Infantry Division have had a very bad time and they have been very nervy about spies. One can hardly trust one's brother these days, such odd things have happened.'

He told me to remain with J Battery in the meantime, as I would be in good hands with Major Seligman, who commanded the Battery.

28 August – 5 September, 1914

INFANTRY SUBALTERN ON THE RETREAT

Captain E. J. Needham

In 1906 Captain Needham Joined the Militia, afterwards converted into the Special Reserve, and on the outbreak of war he went to France with the 1st Battalion Northamptonshire Regiment as an 'amateur infantry subaltern'. During the retreat from Mons he and his men were reeling drunk with fatigue. His story ends with orders on 5 September to advance again towards the Marne in pursuit of a retiring enemy.

After five days of continual retreating, having scarcely fired a shot at or seen the enemy, everybody's nerves were on edge and it was becoming increasingly difficult to keep the men, and ourselves too for that matter, cheery. They kept asking why we were retiring; why we did not turn and wipe the Huns off the earth; what was the French Army doing, etc., etc. We, knowing no more than they did, could only tell them that it was a strategical retirement and that we were retreating to a prearranged and already fortified position – that our retirement would last only one day more, etc. Talk about the 'fog of war'!

I shall never forget the last halt we were to have that night. As usual, everybody – officers and men – threw themselves down just at the edge of the road. When the whistle blew for 'Fall in' many of the men lay where they were, not in any mutinous spirit but just because they were physically incapable of getting up. My platoon was the rear platoon of the company, which was the rear company of the Battalion. 'Payker' (a fellow officer) and I went round actually kicking the men till they got up and threatening, with our revolvers drawn, to shoot any man who did not fall in at once. We were reeling about like drunken men ourselves, past hoping for any rest, but knowing we had to go on.

At last we got them all on the move, and struggled along in the rear to prevent any men from falling out. About two miles on, at about 1.30 am, we found the Battalion was wheeling to the left through a gateway. The Brigade Staff Captain was standing by it and told us as we went through that we were to bivouac in the field and were to stay there the whole of the next day. I do not remember much about getting into that field or what happened afterwards, except that another officer, Joe Farrar, and myself lost ourselves trying to find out where the rest of the officers had to go and, seeing a water-cart, threw ourselves under it and went to sleep at once.

When we woke up in the morning we found we were under one of the 60th's carts, that the whole brigade was bivouacked in the field, quite a small one, and that all the units were hopelessly mixed up together. It had been absolutely pitch dark when we had got in, and nobody had been able to find anyone else, but everyone had more or less dropped down where he was. How lucky we were that the Germans were not close on our tracks that night and did not attack.

FIRST SHAVE IN EIGHT DAYS

The next morning, Sunday, 29 August, we sorted ourselves out generally, the officers got their valises and managed to get a good wash, shave and general clean-up, the first we had had since the 21st at Étroeungt. It was a lovely hot day and we spent it lazing about in the sun, sleeping and eating. It was a real joy to have a day off and especially enjoyable to be able to shave and have a really good wash. All day long we could hear the sullen roaring of the French and German guns behind us. It was very pretty where we were and, except for the aforesaid noise of battle afar, very peaceful.

The next day we were off again. I note that the Regimental War History states that we marched before dawn, but according to my diary we departed at 5.30 am. We marched through lovely wooded and hilly country, but it was again terribly hot and our feet were, if anything, more tender than ever after our day's rest, though in other respects all ranks

A detachment of the Scots Greys (2nd Dragoons), which operated as a part of the rearguard in the Retreat.

were much fresher for it. We were very pleased when we arrived at Anizy-le-Chateau, which was a very pretty place with an enormous chateau and park, the former having been turned hastily into a hospital. The officers of the 48th were extremely lucky in being billeted in the chateau and had a very comfortable night. The men, too, were all under cover and comfortable. Many of them bathed in a stream that ran through the grounds of the chateau, but personally I did not fancy it, as the water looked very muddy and was also somewhat smelly. However, they seemed to enjoy it.

During the march that day, while we were resting at the side of the road in a wood, during a ten minute break the Scots Greys came along and the 12th Lancers. They had had a very hard day of almost continuous rear-guard fighting about three days before, including a fine and very effective charge, and our men lined the road and cheered them lustily. Men and horses looked as hard as nails, but fine-drawn and worn-out. The Greys' horses had all been painted with iodine or some such substance to make them less conspicuous, and they were all a dirty sort of khaki colour. There were many empty saddles amongst their ranks. I asked what had happened to my cousin, Archie Seymour, and was told that he had been sent down to the base, as his ankle had been giving him a lot of trouble and was too painful to allow him to ride. We saw the Greys and also the 20th Hussars frequently during the retreat, as their cavalry brigade were working with the I Corps all the time.

The next morning we marched again at 5.30 am, very sorry to leave our comfortable quarters again, it was very hot, and we had a very trying and exhausting march. We marched through the town of Soissons, coming

down to it off the hills to the north through some very pretty woods. On the south side of the town we were faced with a long and very steep hill, which proved a most severe test for the wretched transport horses.

There were several dead horses lying at the side of the road, having been shot, as they were too far gone with exhaustion to get up the hill, or even to be led. Poor beasts, mostly heavy draught horses, which only a few weeks before had probably been leading a more or less peaceful life down on some farm.

We finally bivouacked for the night in a field, as usual all pretty well worn out. We started off again on 1 September at the crack of dawn. We halted for some time during the afternoon and listened to very heavy firing going on behind us and to our right. This, it afterwards transpired, was a severe rearguard action by 4 (Guards) Brigade of the 2nd Division, in which they had suffered heavy casualties.

Towards evening we marched through Mareuil-sur-Ourcq, and took up a defensive position in the woods on the high ground to the south of the river, while the Engineers were busily employed blowing up the various bridges over the River Ourcq. It was a pitch-dark night, heavy firing was going on apparently all round us, and everybody was expecting something exciting to happen at any moment. Motor-cyclist despatch riders were going up and down the road through the woods, which ran through a deep cutting on the slopes of which we were. It was an eerie feeling to sit there, hearing the booming of the guns all round and to hear the motor-cyclists tearing up and down the road with no lights and being challenged by sentries posted on the road. At one moment we heard one tearing by and then a terrific crash and then silence. It transpired that one of them had crashed head-on into a barricade placed across the road. Oddly enough, years later I was speaking to a friend of mine, one Jim Brocklebank, who had been a despatch rider at the beginning of the war, and I was telling him of this particular occurrence, he said, 'Yes, and I was that unfortunate devil!' It appeared that he had been blinding up the road, all out, and had never heard the sentry's challenge above the roar of his engine and the noise of the guns, and had run smack into the barricade. The next thing he remembered was hearing an English voice saying, 'Gor blimey! The b......
is alive!' which told him he was, amongst friends. He was pretty badly smashed up and his machine was in little bits.

The next morning, the 2nd, we were off again at 2.20 am – another very hot and dusty march and the air thick with rumours as well as dust. This continued marching in the wrong direction was beginning to get on everybody's nerves, and it was getting increasingly difficult to keep the men cheerful. They could not understand it, and neither could we for that matter. But otherwise they were simply splendid. No one who did not go through that retreat can possibly imagine what it was like. Up and away at dawn, marching all day in a tropical sun and amidst clouds of dust,

French cavalry riding past the 1st Cameronians, bivouacked under the cover of a heavily wooded area during a pause in the long march.

generally on the terribly rough pavé roads or pushed down into the equally rough and very stony gutter by other columns of troops on the same road, or by Staff cars rushing past and making the dust worse than ever. Never any proper meals, never a wash or a shave, never out of one's clothes, carrying a terrific weight of arms and equipment, and, as regards 2 Brigade, never getting a chance of a shot at the enemy, except that one day at Wassigny to cheer one up a bit.

An additional difficulty on the road and one very corruptible to the morale of the troop, was the continuous stream of refugees going along the same roads as ourselves. The terrible tragedy of those poor people: hobbling along the road with all their worldly goods piled up, layer on layer, on crazy handcarts, perambulators, wheelbarrows, farm-carts, etc., with usually the old grandfather and grandmother on top of all the goods, and all the rest of the family, women and children that is (as all the younger men were with the forces), trailing along in the dust as best they could. Needless to say, the men insisted on sharing their meagre rations of bully beef and biscuits with them, and often, if they got the chance, took a hand to push along their nondescript vehicles. But it was terrible and it was demoralizing. One felt all the time that they were cursing us – the wonderful British Army that they had greeted so marvellously when we had gone up the line, and which was now in full retreat, compelling them to leave their homes like this, or fall into the hands of the hated Germans. Some of them did curse us too, and spat at us; but the majority plodded painfully on, thankful for any little help we could give them, and apparently oblivious to their future or fate. Nobody knew what happened to them at night, but there they were every day, plodding, plodding, plodding; and the farther south we went the larger grew this other ghastly army – the 'Refugee Army'.

'Red tape' took a hand at this time, too, in what seemed to us the most

Part of the 'Refugee Army' retreating along with the Allies before the German invasion. Belgian civilians resting by the roadside.

unnecessary manner. All along these roads of France grew fruit trees, mostly apple, now in full fruit. Naturally all of us, officers and men, picked this fruit as we halted; it was nourishing and refreshing to our dust-parched throats and palates. What possible harm could this have done to anybody but the pursuing Hun? The inhabitants had all left the countryside and anything and everything edible left was food for the enemy. The same applied to food, bread, chocolate, etc., left behind in the shops, the owners of which had fled. Why should we not have been allowed to eke out our rations with them, and why must they be left to feed the enemy? Yet day after day I saw Staff officers riding down the road giving orders for this and that man's name to be taken for 'stealing fruit'. What utter rot.

The same thing applied to the herds of cattle left grazing in the fields, to a certain extent. In one case, some regiment, I forget which, did drive a large herd before them for days, and these were, I believe, eventually sent down by train to the base to be turned into beef for the troops. But I expect they got into trouble for it. If the cattle could not be driven by us, why

could they not be shot, instead of being left behind to feed the Germans? I can now tell the powers-that-were-then that the P.B.I. officers and men had many hard things to say about these things and felt this show of useless 'red tape' very bitterly.

On this day it was, I think, that the remnant of the 2nd Battalion the Royal Munster Fusiliers, about two officers and seventy-odd other ranks, came through us. They had been cut to pieces that day on the River Oise when C Company had so nearly been cut off themselves at Thenelles. The messengers who were sent to them with orders to retire were killed before getting to them, with the consequence they they never got their orders, were surrounded by the Germans and had to cut their way out, with appalling casualties. This remnant of a fine battalion had to be sent to the base and their place in 1 Brigade was taken by the 1st Battalion the Cameron Highlanders, who had, up to then, been on lines of communication.

We got into bivouac at about 5.30 that evening in a field just north of Meaux, only some twenty-odd miles north of Paris. And, joy of joys, there was a mail in – the first we had had since we left Esqueherries. I had some welcome letters, but none of the cigarettes and tabacco which I was longing for, or of the money which my letters told me had all been sent. I was now down to my last fifteen francs. Our bivouac this night was fairly buzzing with rumours, the chief and most popular being that we had finished foot-slogging for the time being and were to entrain the next morning for Paris, to form part of its defence. The Staff Captain of the Brigade told us he had heard this and believed it was true, which sounded fairly 'straight from the horse's mouth.' I thoroughly enjoyed my letters and papers. It was good to hear from the outside world after all this long time. But I missed my cigarettes. However, after some food and a final look through my letters and papers, I was not sorry to turn in and sleep the sleep of the just on the hard ground.

We started the next morning at 4.30 am, but instead of entraining for Paris as we had been led to suppose we were going to go, we marched east to La Ferté-sous-Jouarre, where we took up a position on some hills on the north bank of the river and town. This position had a very good field of fire, but we did not at all fancy it as, if attacked in force, we should have to retire down the hill, through the town and over the one bridge across the River Marne. It was reported that large formations of Germans had been seen marching west to east.

On our march from Meaux to La Ferté we had seen rather a fine sight: the entire 5 Cavalry Brigade (Scots Greys, 12th Lancers and 20th Hussars) riding in open country parallel to and on the left of our line of march. They made a very inspiring sight. They were acting as flank guard to I Corps and had their flanking patrols out to the left front. After we had been on our hilltop above La Ferté for some hours, we had orders to retire and

Commanding Officer of the 1st Battalion Cameronians, Lieutenant Colonel Robertson (centre), looking for signs of the pursuing Germans. This battalion had been on the lines of communications but were ordered to take the place of the 2nd Battalion the Royal Munster Fusiliers, who had suffered heavy losses during a fighting retreat at Étreux.

recross the river, which we were very pleased to do. The town of La Ferté seemed full of inhabitants, who gave us fruit and chocolate and who were most anxious to know if the Germans were coming behind us or not. We

British Lancers acting as shepherds during the retreat of the British Expeditionary Force to the Marne.

said not, which seemed to me an awful shame, but it was necessary to prevent a panic and prevent the roads by which the British Army was retiring being completely blocked with still more refugees.

As we were going through the town, my old friends the 12th Lancers came past, and Jack Eden (who was one of my oldest and best friends at Eton, and the eldest brother of Mr. Anthony Eden; he was killed at Amerika in October 1914) reported that they had been almost into Chateau Thierry and had not seen a German, though the latter town appeared to be in flames. As we marched over the bridge the Sappers were busy preparing their demolition charges, and I, for one, felt very sorry for the inhabitants of La Ferté, who were to be cut off from retreat to the south. We went into billets at a tiny village called Romeny, about one and a half miles south of the river, and shortly after we were settled in we heard the terrific reports of the bridge being blown up.

The next day, the 4th, we paraded at 3 am, but we had – marvel of marvels – a very easy day. We marched across country for a bit and then halted for some time at the junction of our track with the route nationale. At this juncture we had the edifying spectacle of about half a dozen Staff cars with their gilded Staff and their drivers all busy washing. After a while we pushed on, and about four miles farther on we were marched through a gateway on the right of the road, up a long track to a delightful old farmhouse, with a lot of outbuildings and an enormous walled fruit garden. We were told we should be here for the rest of the day, and that officers would have their valises. There was a little rustic stream running through the grounds, and in this we bathed to our joy. Also, to our joy, we got our valises and were able to have a really proper wash and shave (the first for five days), and to put on clean shirts, socks, etc.

The walled garden was full of fruit, pears, peaches, plums, apricots, apples, etc., in perfect eating condition and, the owners having left the farm, we were actually allowed to help ourselves, which we most certainly did. Never had fruit tasted better than that fruit. For the next two hours the garden was full of all ranks fully occupied in picking and eating.

Then everybody lay about in the shade and slept. It was another scorching day and it was most pleasant lying there with nothing to do but

A village in northern France, with British transport carts clogging the street during the withdrawal to the River Marne.

laze and watch the aeroplanes, our own and hostile, busy with their reconnoitring.

We did make an early start the next morning, at 2.30 am and marched off in a south-westerly direction. As we turned out of the gate on to the main road we saw eight or ten dead Germans and horses lying on the grass at the side of the road. It appeared that a squad on sentry duty of, I think, either the Black Watch or Cameron Highlanders of 1 Brigade, had heard a cavalry patrol riding towards them on the grass at the side of the road. It was a very dark night and they had let them get close up and then let fly with their machine guns and had also given them fifteen rounds rapid fire with their rifles. They had wiped out the entire mounted patrol.

We marched on through the town of Coulommiers, a biggish place, where the usual hurried departure of the inhabitants was, as always these sad days, taking place. 'Galway' Warren, our Transport Officer, managed to buy or 'win' – I am not sure which – a hooded two-wheel cart into which 'Uhlan' our captured enemy war-horse, was harnessed and which, I believe, he afterwards drew for years. 'Galway' had done awfully well with the horses throughout the retreat, and I do not think we lost more than two at the most, if that. He had 'won' a good-looking blood chestnut which had strayed to us from some cavalry regiment and which he annexed for himself.

I found I was for night outpost, which did not please me at all, as I was feeling very rotten with the most awful pain in my middle, and also felt very sick. In addition, the village was full of rumours of a likely attack by the Hun that night.

I got my men told off and in position, and, as it happened, we had a very quiet night, with no alarms or excursions whatever, for which I was truly thankful. During the early part of the night, 'Payker' came round to see me and told me that Guy Robinson had been to Divisional HQ that evening to get orders for the Brigade, and had been told that the retreat was over and that, on the morrow, we were to advance. Great news!

So ended our Retreat from Mons.

1 September, 1914

THE ACCOUNT OF L BATTERY

An Epic of the Great Retreat

by Gunner Darbyshire

The story of one of the outstanding actions of the early days of the war, the artillery and cavalry stand at Néry, 1 September, 1914, is told by Gunner Darbyshire, of L Battery. Of the characters in this story Captain Bradbury was awarded a posthumous VC; Sergeant Nelson and Battery Sergeant-Major Dorrell were awarded VCs, and the author of this narrative and Driver Osborne received the highest French decoration for bravery in the field, the Médaille Militaire.

Driver Drane, in the 1930s, who was at Néry serving with L Battery, RHA, is seen here placing a wreath on one of the battery's guns at the Imperial War Museum to commemorate the anniversary of the action.

All through the retreat we had been fighting heavily, and throughout the day on 31 August we fought till four o'clock in the afternoon; then we were ordered to retire to Compiègne. It was a long march, and when we got to Néry, near Compiègne, early in the evening, both horses and men were utterly exhausted.

Outposts were put out by the officers, and the cavalry who were with us, the 2nd Dragoon Guards (Queen's Bays), were in a small field on the side of a road which was opposite to us. That road was really a deep cutting, and I want you to bear it in mind, because it largely proved the salvation of the few survivors at the end of the fight.

Having made all our dispositions, we went to sleep and rested till half-past three in the morning, when we were roused and told to get ready to march at a moment's notice. We breakfasted and fed the horses and expected to be off again, but the battery was ordered to stand fast until further notice.

2nd Dragoon Guards (Queen's Bays).

Sergeant Major Dorrell thought that this would be a good opportunity to water the horses, so he ordered

British 13 pdr gun crew during the Retreat.

the right half-battery to water, and the horses were taken behind a sugar factory which was a little distance away. The horses were watered and brought back and hooked into the guns and wagons; then the left half-battery went to water. Everything was well, it seemed, and we were now expecting to move off. A ridge about 600 yards away was, we supposed, occupied by French cavalry, and a general and orderly retreat was going on in our rear. Then, without the slightest warning, a ranging shot was dropped into the battery, and we knew instantly that the German gunners were on us.

Immediately after this round was fired the whole place was alive with shrapnel and machine-gun bullets, and it was clear that the battery was almost surrounded by German artillery and infantry. As a matter of fact the French cavalry had left their position on the ridge before daybreak, and a strong German force, with ten guns and two machine guns, had

A German battery about to open fire.

Under fire: an air burst rains shrapnel down on these British troops. One man, centre, receives a shrapnel wound to the head.

advanced under cover of the mist and occupied the position, which was an uncommonly good one for artillery.

The very beginning of the German fire caused havoc amongst the battery and the Bays, and the losses amongst the horses were terrible and crippling. 'Who'll volunteer to get the guns into action?' shouted Captain Bradbury.

Every man who could stand and fight said 'Me!' and there was an instant rush for the guns. Owing to heavy losses in our battery I had become limber gunner, and it was part of my special duty to see to the ammunition in the limbers. But special duties at a time like that don't count for much; the chief thing is to keep the guns going, and it was now a case of everyone striving his best to save the battery.

The guns were ready for marching not for fighting, which we were not expecting; half the horses were away, many at the guns were killed or wounded, and officers and men had suffered fearfully, in the course literally of a few seconds, after the ranging shot dropped among us.

The first gun came to grief through the terrified horses bolting and over-turning it on the steep bank of the road in front of us; the

Captain E.K. Bradbury was awarded the Victoria Cross posthumously for his actions at Néry.

British 13 pdr gun crews, men and horses, cut down during the withdrawal from Mons.

second gun had the spokes of a wheel blown out by one of the very first of the German shells; the third was disabled by a direct hit by a shell which killed the crew; the fourth was left standing, though the wheels got knocked about and several holes were made in the limber and all the horses were shot down. The fifth gun was brought into action, but was silenced by the crew being killed, and the sixth gun, our own, remained the whole time, though the side of the limber was blown away, the wheels were severely damaged, holes were blown in the shield, and the buffer was badly peppered by shrapnel shards.

In a shell fire that was incessant and terrific, accompanied by the hail of bullets from the Maxims, we got to work.

German Maxim 08 gun team in action.

The 13-pounders of the Royal Horse Artillery can be fired at the rate of fifteen rounds a minute, and though we were not perhaps doing that because we were short-handed and the limbers were about thirty yards away, still we were making splendid practice, and it was telling heavily on the Germans. As the mist melted away we could see them plainly – and they made a target which we took care not to miss.

As soon as we got No. 6 gun into action I jumped into the seat and began firing, but so awful was the concussion of our own explosions and the bursting German shells that I could not bear it for long. I kept it up for about twenty minutes, then my nose and ears were bleeding because of the concussion, and I could not fire any more, So I left the seat and got a change by fetching ammunition.

Immediately after I left the seat, Lieutenant Campbell, who had been helping with the ammunition, took it, and kept the firing up without the loss of a second of time. But he had not fired more than a couple of rounds when a shell burst under the shield. The explosion was awful, and the brave young officer was hurled about six yards away from the very seat in which I had been sitting a few seconds earlier. He lived for only a few minutes.

When I felt a little better I began to help Driver Osborne to fetch ammunition from the wagons. I had just managed to get back to the gun, with an armful of ammunition, when a lyddite shell exploded behind me, threw me to the ground and partly stunned me.

When I came round I got up and found that I was uninjured. On looking round, however, I saw that Captain Bradbury, who had played a splendid

In this painting by Matania, Captain Bradury, Sergeant Major Dorell and Sergeant Nelson are depicted operating F Gun during the fighting.

part in getting the guns into action, had been knocked down by the same shell that floored me and was mortally wounded. Though the captain knew that death was very near, he thought of his men to the last, and begged to be carried away so that they should not be upset by seeing him, or hearing the cries which he could not restrain.

By this time our little camp was an utter wreck. Horses and men were lying everywhere, some of the horses absolutely blown to pieces; wagons and guns were turned upside down, and all around was ruin caused by the German shells. Nearly all the officers and men were either dead or wounded.

The Germans had ten of their guns and two machine guns going, and it is simply marvellous that every man and horse in our battery was not destroyed. Not all the German artillery consisted of field guns: they had big guns with them, and they fired into us with the simple object of wiping us out.

Sergeant Major
G. Dorrell VC.

It was not many minutes after the fight began in the mist when only No. 6 gun was left in the battery, and four of us survived to serve it – the Sergeant-Major (who had taken command), Sergeant Nelson, myself and Driver Osborne – and we fired as fast as we could in a noise that was now more terrible than ever, and in a little camp that was utter wreckage. It was not long before we managed to silence several German guns. But very soon Sergeant Nelson was severely wounded by a bursting shell, and that left only three of us.

CAVALRY'S FINEST WORK

The Bays' horses, like our own, had been either killed or wounded or had bolted, but the men had managed to get down on the right of us and take cover under the steep bank of the road; from that position, which was really a natural trench, they fired destructively.

Sergeant D.
Nelson VC.

British cavalry, dismounted, did some glorious work in the Great War, but they did nothing finer, I think, than their work near Compiègne on that

September morning. And of all the splendid work there was none more splendid than the performance of a lance-corporal who actually planted a machine gun on his own knees and rattled into the Germans with it. There was plenty of kick in the job, but he held on gamely, and he must have done heavy execution with his six hundred bullets a minute.

By the time we had practically silenced the German guns, the three of us who were surviving were utterly exhausted. Osborne, who was kneeling beside a wagon wheel, had a narrow escape from being killed. A shell burst between the wheel and the wagon body, tore the wheel off and sent the

Following the destruction of the British guns of L Battery at Néry the British cavalry counter-attacked driving the Germans back. Here men of the 2nd Dragoon Guards (Queen's Bays) have just captured some prisoners.

A captured horse belonging to the 9th Uhlans is inspected by a British officer. The 9th Uhlan Regiment (2nd Pomeranian) was on the right flank of the German attack at Néry.

spokes flying all over the place. One of the spokes caught Osborne just over the ribs and knocked him over.

The three of us had served the gun and kept it in action till it was almost too hot to work, and we were nearly worn out. But we went on firing, and with a good heart, for we knew that the Germans had been badly pounded, that the Bays had them in a grip, and that another battery of horse-gunners was dashing to the rescue. On they came in glorious style. There is no finer sight than a horse battery galloping into action.

Two or three miles away from us, I Battery had heard the heavy firing and knew that something must be happening to us. Round they turned, and on they dashed, taking everything before them and stopping for nothing till they reached a ridge about 2,000 yards away; then they unlimbered and got into action, and never was there grander music heard than that which greeted the three of us who were left in L Battery when the saving shells of I screamed over us and put the finish to the German rout.

By September 5, 1914, the agonizing retreat from Mons was at an end. The Germans had missed their objectives of encircling Paris and forcing an easy surrender. Conforming to the forward movement of the French armies, the British Expeditionary Force now took part in the advance, which involved the crossing of five rivers, the chief of which were the Marne and the Aisne. The battles which ensued are here described by writers who were on the spot when these historic events took place.

5-10 September, 1914

WOUNDED, CAPTURED, THEN RESCUED
The Diary of a Casualty

by Aubrey Herbert

Aubrey Nigel Henry Molyneux Herbert MP, son of the 4th Earl of Carnarvon, served as a captain in the Irish Guards. In 1915 he joined Military Intelligence and served in Gallipoli, where his ability to speak Turkish was vital in negotiations with the Turkish forces for a truce to bury the dead. He spoke French, Italian, German, Arabic, Greek and Albanian. He also served in Mesopotamia and was involved in the siege of Kut. He ended the war as head of the British mission to the Italian army in Albania, with the rank of lieutenant colonel. He died in September 1923.

As I swung into the saddle a shot came from behind, just missing me. I rode back as fast as my horse, *Moonshine*, would go. The lull in the firing had ceased, and the Germans were all round us. One could see them in the wood, and they were shooting quite close. The man who finally got me was about 15 to 20 yards away; his bullet came into my side broken up. It was like a tremendous punch. I galloped straight on to my regiment and told the Colonel. He said: 'I am sorry that you are hit – I am going to charge.' He had told me earlier that he meant to if he got the chance.

I got off and asked them to take over my horse. Then I lay down on the ground and a Royal Army Medical Corps (RAMC) man dressed me. The Red Cross men uttered a loud whistle when they saw my wound, and said

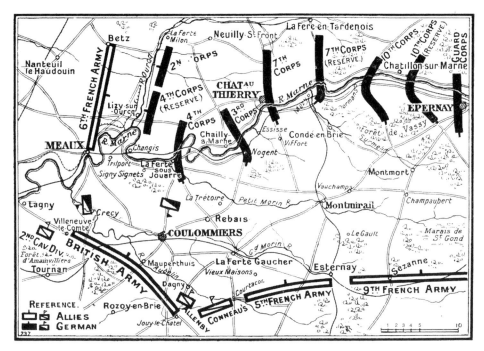

The German advance into France was stalled as they were halted before Paris.

the bullet had passed right through me. The firing was still frightfully hot. The men who were dressing my wounds were crouched down or lying on the ground. While one of them was dressing me a horse – his, I suppose – was shot just behind. I asked them to go, as they could do me no good and would only get killed or captured themselves. The doctor gave me some morphine and I gave them my revolver. They put me on a stretcher, leaving another empty stretcher beside me. This was hit several times by bullets. Shots came from all directions, although the firing seemed to be less than earlier in the day. The bullets were passing just above me and my stretcher. I lost consciousness for a bit; then I heard my regiment charging. There were loud cries and little spurts of spasmodic shooting: then everything went quiet and peace fell upon the wood. It was very dreamlike.

As I lay on the stretcher a jarring thought occured to me. I had in my pocket the flat-nosed bullets which the War Office had served out to us as revolver ammunition. They are not dum-dum bullets, but would naturally not make as pleasant a wound as the sharp-nosed rounds, and it occurred to me that those having them might well be shot. I searched my pockets and flung my snubbed-nosed revolver rounds away. It was first hearing German voices close by that jogged my memory about these bullets. The same idea must have occurred to others, for I heard the Germans speaking angrily about the flat bullets they had picked up in the wood, and saying how they would deal with anyone in whose possession they were found. The glades became resonant with loud, raucous German commands and occasional cries from wounded men.

After about an hour and a half a German with a red beard, and with the sun shining on his helmet and bayonet, came up looking like an angel of death. He walked round from behind, and put his serrated bayonet on the empty stretcher by me, so close that it all but touched me. The stretcher broke and his bayonet poked me.

In broken, yet polite German, I asked what he proposed to do next. This was prompted by what I had been reading in the English newspapers concerning atrocities being carried out by the German forces.

He was extraordinarily kind and polite. He put something under my head; offered me wine, water and cigarettes. '*Wir sind kamaraden*,' he said

Another soldier came up and said:

'Why didn't you stay in England – you who made war upon the Boers.'

'We obey orders, just as you do,' I replied. 'As for the Boers, they were our enemies and are now our friends. And it is not your business to insult wounded men.'

My first German friend then cursed him heartily, and he moved on.

A sunny day in early Autumn and men ot the 2nd Cavalry Division are halted for a rest on their way to take part in the Battle of the Aisne.

During the second day of the Battle of the Marne an important part was played by l9 Infantry Brigade in the operations which resulted in the British and French recrossing the river and driving the Germans back. Here elements of l9 Brigade are seen going into action at Signy Signets, and the capture of that place carried the British to the high ground over-looking the Marne. Guns of 29 Brigade Royal Field Artillery are seen on the right, coming into action to support the infantry.

Below, Royal Engineers have thrown a bridge across the Marne at La Ferté-sous-Jouarre and British troops begin to pour across to help push the Germans back to the River Aisne.

The Germans passed in crowds. They seemed like steel locusts. Every now and then I would hear 'Here is an officer who speaks German,' and the crowd would swerve in like a steel eddy. Then, '*Schnell Kinder!*' and they would be off. They gave an impression of lightness and iron.

After some hours, when my wound was beginning to hurt, some carriers came up to take me to a collecting place for the wounded. These men were rather rough. They dropped me and my stretcher once, but were cursed by an officer for it. They then carried me some distance, and took me off the stretcher, leaving me on the ground. The Germans continued to pass in an uninterrupted stream.

One motor cyclist who came to look at me was very unpleasant, he carried a bayonet in his hand, 'I would like to stick this in your throat and turn it round and round,' he said thrusting his bayonet in front of my nose.

That sort of thing happened more than once or twice, but there were always more friendly among the enemy than nasty. As night fell the chance of being left without the more friendly inclined captors increased.

As it grew dark. I began to feel rather cold. One of the Germans saw this, covered me with his coat 'Wait a moment, I will bring you something else,' he said as he went off and, I suppose, stripped a dead Englishman and a dead German. The German's jersey which he gave me had no holes in it; the Englishman's coat had two bayonet cuts.

The wounded began to cry dreadfully in the darkness. I found myself beside a fellow officer named Robin, who was very badly wounded in the leg. The Germans gave me water when I asked for it but every time I drank it made me sick. At, I suppose, 9.30 or 10 pm, they took us off into an ambulance and carried us to a house that had been turned into a hospital. I was left outside, talking to a Dane, who was very anti-German, though he was serving with them as a Red Cross man. He cursed them loudly in German. He said it was monstrous that I had not been attended to and that the Germans had had a defeat and would be beaten. I said, 'Yes, it's all true, but please stop talking like that because they'll hear you and punish me.'

Just before mid night they carried me into the make-shift hospital and on to the operating table where my wounds were dressed. Then I was helped out to an outhouse and I was laid beside Robin. It was full of English and German wounded. They gave us one drink of water and then shut and locked the door and left us for the night. One man cried and cried for water until he died. It was a horrible night. The straw was covered with blood, and there was never a moment when men were not groaning and calling for help. In the morning the man next to Robin went off his head and became like an animal with pain. I got the Germans to do what was possible for him. I asked the Germans to let me out, and they helped me outside into a chair, and I talked to an officer called Brandt. He sent a telegram to the German authorities to say that Robin and I were lightly wounded, and asking them to let our families know. He would not let me pay. I would have liked to have done it for everyone, but that wasn't possible.

They took us away in an ambulance at about 11 o'clock. It was a beautiful September day, very hot indeed. The heat in the covered ambulance was suffocating and Robin must have suffered horribly. He asked me the German word for 'quick,' and when I told him, he urged the Germans on.

At the town of Viviéres I found fellow officer Shields, who said to me, 'Hello, you wounded, and you a volunteer, at that,' as if a volunteer ought to be immune from wounds. We were carried upstairs and told that Valentine and Buddy [fellow officers], whom I had last met under the cedars, were in the same hospital. Valentine had the point of his elbow shot away just after I had left him. He had raised his hand to brush a wasp off his neck, and could only remember pitching forward when a bullet struck his elbow. He woke up in a pool of blood. A German came up and took the flask of brandy that I had given him after my visit to Soissons. He gave Valentine a drink and then, when Valentine had said he did not want any more, swigged the whole of the rest off. It was enough to make two men drunk, solidly, for hours. Later, five Germans came up to Valentine and ragged him. One of them kicked him, but an officer arrived, took all their names, promised Valentine they would be punished and assigned an orderly to stay with him for the night. Buddy was badly wounded in the back and arm. He found his servant in the church at Viviéres.

It was there in the house at Viviéres that we all met up. The doctors gave Robin and me a strong dose of morphia. That afternoon a German doctor, whose name was Hillsparck, came in and woke me. He gave me a gold watch with a crest on it, and a silver watch and a purse of gold (£8 in it). He said that a colonel to whom the watch belonged had been buried close by in the village of Haraman, and asked me if I knew who he was. We heard that our Colonel had been killed, and I imagined it must have been his. We could not tell for sure, as apparently every single man of the seventy odd who had charged with him had been killed. The doctor left that watch with me.

Our experiences on the field were all the same. We were all well treated, though occasionally we were insulted. In hospital an old *oberstadt* was in command of the doctors. He was very good to us. The English doctors were named Rankin and Shields. They were both good doctors. Rankin and Shields were excellent fellows. Rankin was later killed while dressing a wounded man on the field of battle and was recommended for the VC. Shields was killed in the same way [in October 1914], and I believe would also have been recommended for the decoration but his CO was also killed. They were both the best sort of man you could find.

After a couple of days I moved into Buddy and Valentine's room. A little way down the street there was the chateau, full of wounded Germans. Our men were carried there to be operated upon. Our doctors who went to help discovered that there were 311 wounded Germans as against 92 of our own, so we didn't do badly.

German and Allied wounded soldiers lie side by side in this make-shift hospital.

Every morning the German sentries used to come in and talk to us. Our German was very weak, but we managed to get along all right. Downstairs those who were lightly wounded sat outside in the chairs they took from the house in the sunny garden. It was a fairly luxurious house, with notepaper marked 'F.H.' I thought it was a girls' school, for the only books we could find were the *Berger de Valence* and Jules Verne.

My side was painful the first few days. Then they cut me open and took out the fragments of the bullet, which was in bits. It was rather hard lines on the others to have operations performed in the room, but I felt much better after it. The food difficulty was rather acute. There was very little of it and what there was was badly cooked. We lived principally on thick, un-leavened biscuits.

Some among the captured wounded men began to give trouble. There was, of course, nobody in command of them. There was an ex-comedian who was particularly tiresome. We even had to ask the Germans to punish one particular man for us. About the fourth day one of the orderlies escaped, a man called Drummer McCoy. He passed for four days through the German lines, and on one occasion watched a whole Army Corps go by

German infantry prepare to meet a French attack in the fighting at the Marne. Note the German skirmish line out in front; the French are almost upon them.

from the boughs of a tree. Then he found the French, who passed him on to the English, where he went to the Staff and told them of us. That is how we were picked up so quickly on the 11 September.

There follows a some entries made in my diary.

Wednesday 9 September:
The people are beginning to return, but not the priest, who is with the army. We want him for the regiment. Up till this time only six of the wounded have died. The Germans tell us every kind of story – the United States are declaring war on Japan; Italy on France; Denmark on England, etc., etc. Also that Paris has been given twelve hours to accept or reject the German terms, and if the French Government is obdurate the city will be bombarded. We are told that we are to be taken as prisoners to Madgeburg. It is a week since I have had a cigarette.

Thursday, 10 September:
We are all very anxious to get news home, but there is no chance. Last night S. Herbert died. I had a Testament, and Valentine and I found verses which Valentine read over his grave. Valentine has bad pain. Three bones broken in his arm and the point of his elbow gone. Buddy is better, but hit cruel hard. Robin has a bad wound, and is very restless. They don't like giving us

morphia. Luckily. I have got my own medicine chest, which is a good thing for all of us, as I can give the others sleeping draughts. Last night a French cavalry patrol came within two miles of us. Early this morning there was rifle fire close by. It sounded to be coming from the wood that we supposed was Haraman.

We think the Germans may evacuate this place any time. The bandages have been given out. Stores are not coming in. There is a big aeroplane depot quite close by and the whole air is full of aeroplanes. It looks and feels as if there might be a big battle round here soon. They have shot an old man wandering about the aerodrome. But he was asking for it.

9 am
The aeroplanes are being shifted from the depot. Last night we heard that arms were issued to all the wounded Germans in hospital who could carry them. This morning the Germans are digging trenches hard. There are Red Crosses everywhere. The doctors want us to go down to the cellars if we are shelled. The French women in the village say that the French are coming; firing is increasing.

9.15 am
The German Hospital across the way is ordered to be ready to move at once.

10.25 am
An order has come for all prisoners to parade at the church at 12 o'clock. The German lightly wounded are being sent on. We are very anxious as to whether they mean to take us too. More of our wounded who have died are being buried.

11.10 am
A German doctor has arrived. He said: They are leaving and taking all of the British prisoners; 18 of our lightly wounded, and leaving 25 of their badly wounded.

French wounded are now coming in. We have no more bandages at all. A German sentry with whom I had talked has just come in. I asked him some days ago to buy some handkerchiefs. He said: 'I have not been able to buy you any handkerchiefs, or to get the cigarettes you wanted, but here is one of my own handkerchiefs, which I have washed. We have got to go.'

8 pm
The last order is that the previous orders are countermanded and the Germans are to stay on ten more days.

Friday, 11 September
Our English prisoners were marched off this morning. We are full of speculation as to what has really happened. Valentine, Buddy and I are well.

10.10 am
There are machine guns firing about four miles away.

10.30 am
There is heavy rifle fire within a mile. It is very trying lying here in bed. We have nothing to read except The Rajah's Heir, *which V. sent to me, and which has become known as the treasure-house of fun. It's a sort of mixture of* Hymns Ancient and Modern *and the* Fairchild Family.

2 pm
There is a Maxim within a few hundred yards of the house. Rifle volleys outside in the garden. A rising wind and rain threatening.
3 pm
Heavy rain. The French are visible, advancing.

3.10 pm
The French are here. They came in in fine style, like conquerors; one man first, riding, his hand on his hip. The German sentries who had been posted to protect us wounded walked down and surrendered their bayonets. The German doctors came to us for help. I offered to go, but W. went. The French infantry and cavalry came streaming through. Our wounded went out into the pouring rain to cheer them. They got water from our men, whose hands they kissed. The German guns are on the skyline. The Germans are in full retreat, and said to be cut off by the English.

The French attacking to drive the invader out of their country.

5 pm
A heavy bombardment of the German guns began from here. I have come upstairs to a long, low garret with skylights, in order to leave Valentine and Buddy more room. Through the skylight one can see every flash of the French and German guns. The doctors all came up here to watch with their field glasses through my skylights.

Saturday, 12 September
Yesterday when W. went down he found the German doctors receiving cavalier treatment from the French. He explained to the French that they had treated us with the greatest kindness; after that the French treated with courtesy the old oberstadt. *Shields carved a great wooden tombstone for the thirteen men who had died up to date. It is a month today since I left England.*

This afternoon Colonel Thompson, the English Staff Officer attached to General Menmry, who had been attached to the Serbian Army through Balkan War, came in. McCoy, who had escaped, had found him and told him about us at Viviers. He said he would take me into Villers-Cotterêts after he had done some other business. We talked a lot about the Balkans, but I finally went back and lay down in my garret and shall not get up again today.

Sunday, 13 September
I went off with Thompson this morning. We passed through the wood where we had had the fight and a long grave of 120 men was shown to me by McCoy.

A British officer's grave, with its rough cross, on the field of the Marne.

10 September, 1914

THE CROSSING of the RIVER MARNE

A.A. Martin, MC, ChB, FRCS (Ed.).

Dr Martin, who had seen active service in The Boer War in 1901, was in 1914 attached to a Field Ambulance of the 5th Division. This account shows his experiences on the day when the British army crossed the Marne. He had an unequalled opportunity of watching the historic advance.

Coulommiers looked to be clear of Germans. It had been occupied some days previously, and now the British had it. The French inhabitants were in Paris. The narrow old streets looked very cheerful and inviting when I passed through, for our Army Service men had several fires merrily blazing at the side of the pavé, and the smell of frying bacon and roasting coffee beans was inviting and appetizing. Signs of the German occupation were everywhere apparent. Round the ashes of their fires in the side streets and square were the charred remains of old and valuable furniture – a carved leg of an old chair, a piece of the frame of a big mirror, a bit of a door and so on. I think the German soldier enjoyed the novel sensation of cooking his food over burning cabinets and tables and chairs made in the times of the Louis of France. Our men were extremely careful to avoid damage to French property, and made their fires of chopped wood logs. Tommy has good feelings and is always a gentleman, and he genuinely pitied the French in their despoiled towns.

My orders were to report to the Principal Medical Officer of the 5th Division of the Second Corps. The headquarters of General Smith-Dorrien, the Commander of the Second Corps, was a little cluster of houses by the roadside, and when we arrived the whole staff were standing by the road, while the grooms stood near holding their horses. Smith-Dorrien, with another staff officer, was poring over a map and indicating some spot on it with his finger.

The Principal Medical Officer, Colonel Porter of the Army Medical Staff, was just coming out of a cottage and I walked up, saluted, and reported my arrival. The Colonel gave me a cheery greeting, asked if I had breakfasted, and, noticing the South African War ribbon on my tunic, said that as I had seen service before I would soon be quite at home.

I was then ordered to report to the officer commanding a section of the 15th Field Ambulance, which was situated about 500 yards further down

Men of the 18th Field Ambulance, 6th Division, seen here halted for a midday rest at Hartennes, south of Soissons, during the retreat from Mons.

the road. I reported to a major of the Royal Army Medical Corps, who told me that he was waiting to evacuate some wounded to Coulommiers before moving up to rejoin the headquarters of the ambulance which was advancing with 15 Infantry Brigade. There were sixteen wounded British in a small farmhouse beside the road. They were lying on straw on the floor and the wounds of all of them had been dressed. When I entered they were drinking milk supplied by the old farmer and his wife.

This old farmhouse had been occupied by the Germans two days previously, and the old farmer brought me through the house to show what the Huns had done. His two wooden bedsteads had been smashed; his wife's clothes had been taken out of a chest of drawers and torn up, and the chest had been battered with an axe; the windows were broken and two legs of the kitchen table had been chopped off; an old family clock lay battered in a corner and an ancient sporting gun was broken in two. The farmer showed me one of his wife's old bonnets which had been thrown into the fire by those lovely Germans and partially burned. Fancy burning an old woman's bonnet! Two German soldiers got into the hen coup and stuck all the birds with their bayonets. A fine Normandy dog lay dead at the garden gate, shot by a German non-commissioned officer because the poor beast barked at him.

The old-fashioned furniture and adornments of the house had been destroyed. All the pictures were broken except two – one of these was a framed picture of Pope Leo XIII, and the other was one representing the Crucifixion. We guessed that the German troops must have been Bavarians, who are mostly Catholic.

I have described this wrecked home in some detail as it was typical of hundreds of others that I have seen in France. It all seemed so stupid, so senseless, so paltry and mean. Imagine the pointlessness of burning an old lady's bonnet and smashing an old clock that had been in the family's possession for three generations, and had ticked the minutes to the farmer's folk and whose face had been looked at by those long since dead. The old farmer was in tears and miserable. He said that the German soldiers had been very drunk and had brought a lot of bottles of champagne with them, round which they spent a very hilarious night. One of the men had a very fine voice and sang a German drinking song, while the others hiccupped the chorus. There were certainly a lot of empty champagne bottles scattered about, and I do not think the old farmer's beverage would have soared above *vin rouge*, so the bottles must have been German loot.

About eleven o'clock, while we were still waiting for returning empty supply wagons to take off our wounded, when we heard that some German prisoners were being marched in. This caused some excitement, and, speaking for myself, I was consumed with curiosity to see some specimens of this great German army and observe what manner of men they were. Under a strong guard of cavalry three hundred prisoners with about ten officers were marched into a field close to our farmhouse. It was laughable to see our old farmer. He rushed up the road, his eyes blazing with excitement and joy. He just stood gazing at his country's enemies with an expression of malicious pleasure and delight.

I was struck with the appearance of these prisoners. They were very tired, absolutely done in, and marched along the road with a most bedraggled and weary step. Were these the men who had goose-stepped through Belgium's stately capital and had pushed the united armies of France and England before them in one of the most rapid marches in history?

They were utterly broken down with fatigue and their famished expression and wolfish eyes betokened the hardships they had recently undergone. When they were halted in the field they simply slumped to the ground in sheer exhaustion. On looking closer, however, one could see that they were fine soldiers: athletic well-built, lean, wiry fellows with shaven heads and prominent features, slim-waisted and broad-shouldered, clothed in smart, well-fitting bluish grey uniforms, well shod with good serviceable boots, each with a light waterbottle clipped to his belt and a haversack over the shoulder; certainly no fault could be found with them as specimens of muscular and active soldiery.

Officers, disdaining to show any signs of fatigue, sat by themselves smoking pipes and cigarettes. Bully beef and biscuits and buckets of water were brought to them for drink. They at once threw off their exhaustion and simply rushed the food. We realized that they had been marched to a standstill, and that the commissariat of that particular Army Corps must have broken down. This was a good sign.

Some empty motor supply wagons returning from the front were stopped. We packed plenty of straw on them and put our wounded British and Germans comfortably on top, and sent them all on to the hospital train at Coulommiers. Then our commanding officer gave the order to our ambulance drivers to harness up the horses and prepare to trek. We knew that our army was making a stand at last, and that the long retreat was over.

All the morning heavy firing was heard on our front towards the River Marne, and we were not sure what was happening. We knew that our cavalry was at work somewhere, for the captured Guard *Jägers* had been bagged by our cavalry, but more than that we did not know. However, we were soon on the road, and following Napoleon's maxim to his generals – always to march towards the firing. The roads were terribly dusty, and the day was hot and sultry, and a blazing sun beat mercilessly down upon us. We all cursed our caps, and certainly the khaki cap supplied to our officers and men deserved a curse. It gave no protection to the back of the neck in summer, and in rainy weather it was soon soaked.

Marching on foot behind lumbering ambulance wagons on a dusty road and under a hot sun is no picnic. Eyes get full of dust, throats get parched, feet get hot, and the khaki uniform wraps round one like a sticky blanket. So for many miles we marched, and all the time the sound of the guns became more and more distinct and intense. We passed St. Ouen and by St. Cyr, and at 4.30 o'clock we seemed to be in the centre of the artillery thunder area. Great guns were screeching and roaring all round us, and some of the enemy's shells were bursting to our left front near the road along which we were moving. We were then ordered to pull our wagons off the road and bivouac them under a clump of trees near at hand in order to conceal them from enemy aeroplanes, which were hovering high up in the blue.

The reason for at times to concealing a Field Ambulance is that when a column is on the march the Field Ambulance has a definite position in the column; generally it is behind the ammunition column. The ambulance wagons, with their big white tented covers and conspicuous red crosses, are often the most prominent features on the road. The enemy airman

The main street of Braine after the Germans had been driven out and the wounded were being evacuated. The Germans were falling back to the River Aisne, with the French and British in hot pursuit.

when he spots a Field Ambulance knows that there is at least a brigade consisting of four battalions and an ammunition column in front of it, and he can then direct his gunners to plant their shells in front of the ambulance and so get the ammunition column and the brigade. Hence the necessity for sometimes hiding the whereabouts of a Field Ambulance.

After we had bivouacked, our section cook managed to light a fire in a hollow among a clump of trees, and soon brought us a much desired mess of fried mutton, good bread and marmalade, and a can of tea. We rushed this down as eagerly as the German prisoners had done the bully beef earlier in that morning.

In a battle one really sees very little and knows very little of what is going on, except in the near neighbourhood. The broad perspective, the great view of a battle, cannot be seen by one pair of eyes. This can only be

Army cooks producing a fine meal once the retreating has stopped. The Germans are back across the Marne and once more the field kitchens send up their savoury smells to tempt the hungry Tommy.

understood and appreciated afterwards when facts and events are gathered together and dovetailed to form the battle story.

When I was sitting by the roadside on that September afternoon, amidst the crashing and shrieking of the guns, the bursting of the shells, the curious crackling of the rifles, and the snarling notes of the machine guns, I guessed that a battle was in progress and that we were blazing furiously at an enemy who was blazing furiously back at us. Beyond that, I did not know very much. During the night I learned a good deal more of the day's events. But the whole story was not connected up till many days afterwards. I am quite sure that the people of London knew more about the Battle of the Marne from the war bulletins than I did, although I was in one of the humble units present in the actual fighting.

On this sultry summer day our ambulance section was resting by the side of the dusty road that stretched to our rear towards Paris and on our front towards a lovely green valley, at the bottom of which meandered the River Marne. It wound its sinuous way from our far right to our near left. Directly before us, and on the distant side of the river, was a steep ridge, part of a low chain of uplands which rolled hazily away to the right and stopped abruptly in clear-cut lines in our front. The road beside which we sat dipped into the valley and crossed the river on a fine stone bridge and continued through the undulating country beyond to the north.

Small villages were scattered about – Méry to the right, Sacey at the bridgehead, and small clusters of houses and farms on the countryside over the river. Some squadrons of dismounted cavalrymen were standing by their horses in a meadow near the bank of the river. These horsemen had been busy earlier in the day, and had done some hard riding, cutting off stragglers from the retreating German Army Corps. Infantry were hidden from view in the depths of the valley. Batteries on our left were sending a plunging fire of shot and shell on to the ridge and dips beyond the river, and the road leading from the bridge. With a field-glass, moving dots, and what looked like wagons, could be made out on the road and the field alongside. It was on these moving dots that our guns played, and cloud-bursts of earth and dust showed that our gunners had the range beautifully.

General French passed us twice in his limousine car. General Smith-Dorrien passed twice – General Sir Charles Ferguson passed – all in motorcars travelling like mad. Gallopers with messages spurred up and down the road. Guns thundered into position, unlimbered and were quickly in action. Infantry marching rapidly passed down the road into the valley where a tornado of rifle-fire was going on. One could make out the distinct note from our own rifles and the muffled one from the more distant German Mausers. Two German shells burst short of the battery on our left and uncomfortably close to us. We were in an odd position for an ambulance – in front of our own battery, which was pelting shot into the

This French château is in use as an Advanced Dressing Station. As wounded are being carried out to take them by ambulance to a Base Hospital, fresh straw is being taken in as floor covering.

Germans and which a German battery was trying to locate. When the enemy shells fell short they fell near us. Our position, however, was a dress circle box seat as a view-point, so we stopped where we were. It was not every day that one could look on at a real live battle.

Before dusk came on an aeroplane appeared over the ridge flying towards us, and was shot at by enemy anti aircraft guns. The shells burst all round it, but it flew through them all, and landed safely in our lines, likely with some valuable formation.

When the action was at its hottist and every gun was busy, a car raced up from the valley in a swirling cloud of dust. The brakes were jammed hard down opposite us, the side door opened. Out stepped a well-knit, muscular, lithe figure, looking physically fit, smart and cool in a well-made khaki uniform and red-banded cap. The face was a burnt-brick red, the moustache white, the eyes alert, wide open and 'knowing'. A savage, obstinate, determined chin dominated the face. It was the chin of a strong, stubborn nature, the chin of a prize-fighter. This was Smith-Dorrien, the Commander of the Second Army Corps, and at this moment the Second Corps was at grips with the enemy.

With a few rapid strides he had reached the battery on our left, asked some question of the battery commander, and at once clapped field glasses to his eyes and gazed long and intently at a spot on the other side of the valley pointed out to him by the battery commander. Our party of officers, filled with curiosity, also got out field glasses and focussed in the same

Former goods wagons converted to carry wounded being unloaded by men of the RAMC.

direction. Our shells could be seen bursting on a far ridge, and after a long stare we managed to make out what we thought were some guns, but we were not sure. A few more words to the battery commander, a careless salute, and Smith-Dorrien was back in his car, which rapidly turned and disappeared down the dusty road up which it had just come. As the car disappeared a tremendous rifle fire broke out all along the valley beyond the stream. It made one's pulses beat with excitement. The Second Army Corp was fighting hard in the valley at our feet, and Smith-Dorrien was down in the valley with his men.

When the devil's din was at its loudest, another powerful limousine coming from the rear pulled up opposite us. 'Go on, go on,' shouted a voice from the inside, and the car again sped on. Inside was Field Marshal Sir John French poring over a map held out with both hands over his knees.

His car also disappeared into the valley and we again surmised that there must be some big thing going on down below to draw a Field Marshal, Corps Commanders, and Divisional Generals.

An hour elapsed; all of the batteries except one had ceased firing. The cracking of rifles was still heavy but more distant; two cars were seen coming slowly out of the valley. In the front car were French and Smith-Dorrien. We augured that all was well, for the car was proceeding slowly, and the Field-Marshal was placidly smoking a cigar. Our augury was correct. We had forced the passage of the Marne, and were grimly in pursuit of the retreating foe.

13-14 September, 1914

DEATH in a WOOD
on the RIVER AISNE

by Corporal John Lucy

When the British reached the River Aisne they crossed at several points and fierce battles ensued. Corporal (later Captain) Lucy, earlier wrote a description of the Battle of Mons (see page 43), endured the hardships of the retreat and was amongst the first to come into action on the Aisne. He relates, incident by incident his experiences of a day of fighting and records the loss of his brother in the same battalion of the Royal Irish Rifles.

Our advance continued steadily as the Germans were driven back from the Marne. Their rearguards showed some resistance every day, and occasionally, we picked up stragglers and wounded from the enemy army. Although we took our turn in our brigade as advanced guard and outpost duties, our battalion did not really cross swords with the enemy again until 14 September. On that day, and on the few days preceding it, rain fell, and we were not very comfortable either in bivouac or on the line of march. The weather began to get cold.

On the evening of 13 September a British aeroplane, one of the few the British Army possessed, approached us from the German side and, wheeling around, alighted in a field to the right of our marching columns. The flying officer climbed slowly out of his heavy kit, did not wait to find an officer, but shouted to us all, 'There they are, waiting for you up there, thousands of them.' And he waved his right arm towards the wooded heights, across the river Aisne, some three miles away.

Then he composed himself and asked for the nearest battalion commander. We showed him the mounted figure of our colonel at the head of our unit. But we did not fight that day. We went into bivouac on the south side of the river and had a meal before resting for the night.

Early next morning a battery of our field guns came into action near our bivouac. They were camouflaged with green branches of trees, and appeared to be firing across the river at some target in the woods on the other side. The tone of the orders given us, the close inspection of our ammunition, and our rapid fall-in showed that there was immediate work ahead. We marched on quickly down the sloping south side of the river valley to the River Aisne, passing close to other guns in action and making

Battalion HQ of the 11th Hussars on the Aisne.

British heavy artillery moving up on the Aisne.

way for the ammunition wagons which were feeding the batteries.

It was a fine, fresh morning, and we moved on, exhilarated by a feeling of the unexpected, down a wet leafy lane, until we came to an open space between the woods and the southern bank of the river, where we made our first deployment.

We gripped our rifles hard. We felt to be on the edge of a fresh battlefield, with the curtain about to go up, and looked all about our front for the direction of the first threat of danger. Our shells swished close overhead on their way to the dominating heights on the far bank, and presently enemy shrapnel whipped and cracked above us. A curse or two expressed the nausea which every man with a stomach experiences when he feels helpless under a rain of slivers of steel and bullets hurled at him by an enemy two miles or so out of rifle shot.

My Company turned right on gaining the river and moved section by section in single file east along the river bank, and from time to time we halted a moment to crouch or lie flat behind tussocks of grass lining the bank, as the enemy shell-fire increased. We were making for the railway bridge east of Vailly, which was at that moment being crossed by an English battalion withdrawing out of action from the northern side of the river. The bridge had been blown up by the Germans and was now under steady observed shrapnel fire – also rather heavy stuff, too, judging by the sounds of the bursts and the dense rolling clouds from the explosions above and about it.

As we approached the bridge we saw that it was completely wrecked; a tangled mass of ironwork, most of which was submerged, with a dead horse held against it by the current and only a line of single planks, which sagged in the middle, as a means of getting over. This line of single planks was hastily and precariously rigged against what was left of the iron supports of the railway bridge. Crossing was a particularly nasty proposition.

We did not wait to contemplate it. A fresh English battalion crossed over as we drew nearer, and we scrambled across it, section by section, close under the bursting shells. No casualties occurred near me but shouts of alarm from behind showed that the following company had caught it. We did not turn to see. We heard that some of those hit had fallen into the river. Our commanding officer, with his usual bravery, stood upon a height on the south bank, just close to the bridge, during the whole time taken by his battalion to cross.

On gaining the other side we found the regiment which had preceded us disappearing towards our right front as it worked up the hill through the trees and undergrowth. We deployed rapidly into attack formations. A shrapnel bullet penetrated my haversack and tore into the middle of a folded towel inside it. I felt startled and angry at the tug it gave and at my narrow escape, and I pushed on with the others. The Germans had seen us

British infantry taking shelter in the lee of a bank, with shallow fox holes providing primitive protection. The Aisne marked the beginning of trench warfare.

The German Army had been pushed back from the River Marne and had halted at the River Aisne, where they dug in to stop the British and French advance.

cross over, and were now firing salvos at us. Our company commander was hit in the arm.

Two or three other officers of the following companies were also hit and a good many men were knocked out, but we did not miss them in the excitement.

We went on steadily uphill, seeing nothing of the enemy. We had hardly cleared the shelled area near the bridge when bullets began whistling about us. We must have been within a couple of hundred yards of enemy riflemen, but though we looked hard through the undergrowth we could not see them. We cursed them, and relying on the luck of soldiers we bowed our heads a little, clenched our jaws and stubbornly went on. Quicker we went – on to our toes and crouching lower. In for a penny, in for a pound, quicker and quicker to get it over. Their rifles cracked sharply now, and the whistle and whine of bullets passing wide changed to the startling bangs of bullets just missing one. The near rattle of machine guns set our hearts thumping, until we saw them on the line frontage of the English on our right. They were getting it hotter. The rifle-fire in front ceased gradually, and we pushed on harder still.

Our own shells were now bursting a short distance ahead, just beyond a crest line clearly visible to us. This line marked the near edge of a large plateau, and as we made it in a rush we found this plateau edge forming a small continuous cliff of chalk varying from two to four feet high, giving good protection from bullets and fair cover from shell-fire. There were caves in the chalk banking. Automatically we halted here and our officers ordered us to improve the position by digging.

We missed some of our number when we had a look round after taking a breather. They had fallen quietly in battle, almost unnoticed, for in the attack the dead and wounded soon drop out of sight to the rear. On the whole the enemy riflemen had been rotten shots.

Our company had been forward in the attack which gained the plateau, and was now called into reserve. Another company took our place in the front, and we went underground into conveniently situated large caves, a little distance in rear of the line.

The medical officer had opened up his dressing station at the mouth of one cave, and was already busy attending to the wounded and the dead. He went along the line of those who had been hit, and his preliminary test for life in each lying figure seemed to be a pinch under the jaw. Those he found to be dead he ordered to be taken out into the open, and waved the most dangerously wounded towards his assistants for immediate attention. He wasted no words.

We had hardly entered the caves when the Germans counter-attacked, and we were at once ordered to stand up and fall in ready to go to help our people outside. The sound of the battle heard from the caves was awe-inspiring. Clouds of smoke from bursting shells obscured the already dim

A group of officers sheltering in one of the many caves to be found on the Aisne.

light which filtered through the cave mouth. Heavy shells crumpled into the earth roof of our shelter and shook us.

Projectiles whined and crashed at varying distances, and machine guns rat-tat-tatted. The indistinct figures of stretcher-bearers collecting dead and wounded moved unceasingly in the cloudy light of the cave mouth.

We felt trapped, and wished ourselves outside fighting, instead of standing restless in the semi-darkness.

The appalling noise of the conflict outside made all very anxious as to the progress of the enemy counter-attack, We got nervy and fidgeted and avoided each other's eyes. One interested soldier at the cave mouth morbidly occupied himself by passing in the names of the latest dead and wounded. I did not want to hear them, and though I listened with strained ears my mind could not cope with the situation. Each fresh name bludgeoned my brain.

I had hardly envisaged one strong man lifeless and gone when another name followed. The casualties appeared to be very numerous. A great sense of misery and loss began to possess me as the litany of familiar names continued, and I moved over to my brother's platoon to be near him. He appeared to be absolutely calm and his bearing had the effect of putting me at ease, so I went back to my own section very soon.

The German attack ceased. It had been beaten back with heavy loss, and all became quiet again. On examination we found that the casualties were not at all as bad as we had thought. We were now to learn a bitter lesson.

We were ordered to fall in outside the caves and out we went, shying a bit at the sight of blood-dripping stretchers propped against the wall of the cave mouth. Outside we saw some of our dead lying in grotesque positions. A few of these had previously cut their long trousers into shorts during the hot August weather; now they looked like slain schoolboys. This impression was enhanced by the peaceful and youthful looks on their dead faces. A hollow in the ground about ten yards from the caves was filled with bandaged wounded, with whom we conversed.

They did not seem very much distressed; one or two groaned in low voices, others had dilated pupils, and looked surprised in a rather silly fashion, wondering about their wounds, I supposed, while a few unimpressed ones smoked casually.

I was looking keenly at this picture of our wounded, and thinking how good and brave they were, and also envying those with slight wounds who would go away back to England, or, with luck, to Ireland, when the scene suddenly changed. A rising tearing noise like that of an approaching train heralded the arrival of a heavy shell. Nearer and nearer it came and we all crouched down where we were. The wounded squirmed lower down in their hollow.

We clenched our teeth to the shattering burst, which seemed right on top of us, and then after a pause and a deep breath I slowly raised my head to see that the shell had exploded precisely over the hollow and killed every one of the wounded.

'Lead on, A Company,' and we moved forward to the front line in answer to the order, glad to get off at once from the immediate scene of that awful tragedy. We halted on familiar ground, under cover of that little cliff of chalk which we had occupied yesterday. An occasional shell burst behind in the woods and some very large ones were sighing over our heads, high up on their way to Vailly, a mile below us on the river bank. Just as we came to the little cliff, the officer commanding a company on our right came striding towards us, a tall, gaunt captain with the light of battle in his eye. A very religious man he was, too, always talking about duty, and a great Bible reader. Tall, sinewy, with pale face and pale-blue eyes, colourless hair, and a large, untidy, colourless moustache, he came at us looking for blood. He reminded me of a grisly Don Quixote.

'All the Germans have gone away, except about one platoon, which I have located in that wood to our left front. I intend to capture that enemy platoon with my Company, but I want volunteers from A Company to move across the open to support me, while I work forward through the wood, which enters the left of my Company line. Now, who will volunteer?'

I suppose he knew very well that the native pride of Irish troops could be depended on. Anyway, the whole of A Company immediately volunteered to assist. The officer selected the two nearest platoons, which happened to be mine and my brother's. He then sent Muldoon, one of my platoon, up a tree to look across the plateau at the wood, in order to confirm the presence of the enemy for our edification. 'Mul', as we called him, shinned up, and presently shouted down,

'Yes, there they are, I can see them in the woods.'

'Good' said the officer. A Company's two platoons will move forward in line from here, keeping parallel to the right edge of the wood, as soon as my company gets going,' and Don Quixote went off rapidly to launch his attack.

A rifle shot aimed at Mul cut short that lad's curiosity, and he slid grinning and safe to the ground. We fixed our bayonets, as the enemy were close, and sorted ourselves by sections along the plateau edge, searching for easy places to surmount so as to get on to the level of the plateau.

It cannot be said that the operation was very well organized. It was all too rapid, and we got no definite objective, our task being to engage any enemy on our front by advancing to find him and attack him. My brother's platoon suddenly got the order, unheard by me, and up went the men on to the open grassland led by their officer. Denis went ahead, abreast with his officer, too far in front of his section I thought. He carried his rifle with the bayonot fixed threateningly at the high port, and presented a good picture of a young leader going into battle, not quite necessary for a lance-corporal, he was exposing himself unnecessarily and would be one of the first to be shot at. I raised myself high over the parapet of our cliff, and shouted to him, 'Take care of yourself,' and I blushed at such a display of anxiety in the presence of my comrades. My brother steadied a moment in a stride which was beginning to break into a steady run forward, and looking back over his shoulder winked re-assuringly at me. The beggar would wink.

Forward he went and out of my sight for ever. I had to forget him then, because Lieutenant Waters drew his sword and signalled us. We rose from cover and doubled forward over the grass to the right of my brother's platoon. There was an uncanny silence. We could see fairly level wooded country and some cottages to our immediate front, backed by more broken landscape. With a sinking heart I realized that our extended line made an excellent target, as we topped a slight rise, and went on fully exposed across flat country without the slightest cover. The Germans were waiting for us, holding fire.

As we cleared the crest a murderous hail of missiles raked us from an invisible enemy. The line staggered under this smash of machine-gun, rifle and shell-fire, and I would saythat fully half our men fell over forward on to their faces, either killed or wounded.

Some turned over on to their backs, and others churned about convulsively. With hot throats the remainder of us went on, as there is no halt in the attack without an order.

The wood on our left, through which the other company was advancing, seemed on fire, as it sparkled with bursting enemy shells, and then became almost hidden under a pall of rolling smoke. The wood was a shell-trap, and the company had 'bought it', has the troops curtly say. More men fell, but my section still went strongly. Two men of the nearest-section to our left fell and both immediately sat up and began to tear open, their First Field Dressings. They had been hit low, in the legs.

A bullet ripped through the sole of my right boot as I ran on and jerked my own leg aside. For the next few paces 1 kept stamping my right foot on the ground, testing it and half expecting to see blood spurt from the lace holes. This low fire was a bloody business, and most efficient – the kind of stuff we were taught ourselves. I believe I was now beginning to get really afraid of these Germans. The high rate of concentrated fire continued, and the men were now advancing in a very thin line, with most of their number scattered on the grass behind. No officer remained.

A sergeant on the left shouted and the men nearest him got down into the prone position. We followed suit and hastily threw ourselves flat on the grass. Hardly had we done so when a machine gun raked the whole line – a weak and feeble line now and shot accurately home into it. Some of the lying men flapped about. Others, shot through the head, jerked their faces forward rapidly and lay still. I trembled with fear and horror. This was a holocaust. The relentless spray of the deadly machine gun traversed back along the line from the left towards us. The Catholic soldiers blessed themselves in a final act of resignation. But the curve of the traverse came luckily short as it swept across my section, and it traced the ground in front. Little spurts of earth showed the strike of each group of bullets, a few yards before our faces. This was more perilous than shots going over our heads because the bullets ricochetted, shrieking like some infernal cat-fight all about us, but it was better than being hit direct.

By lucky chance or instinct I saw the enemy machine gun. There it was, mounted daringly on the roof of a cottage, close to the left side of a chimney, about six hundred yards away, and directly to my front. With all my strength I shrieked the range, described the target, and ordered five rounds rapid fire. There was a heartening response as we opened fire at the first and only target we had seen in this terrible attack. In about four seconds some thirty bullets were whistling about that dark spot near the chimney as we slammed in our rapid fire, glad to have work to do, and gloriously, insanely, and incredibly the German gun stopped firing, and then it disappeared as it was quickly withdrawn behind the roof. 'Fire at the roof below the ridge of the house, about three feet down,' I ordered exultantly, and I could have whooped for joy, I was now commanding effectively. Damn the rest of the enemy fire. Their rifle-fire was always poor, anyway, and blow the shells, they might hit you and they might not, there was none of the deadly accuracy of the machine gun in other weapons of the enemy.

I breathed a long breath of relief and looked about. I looked right and left at my section to see that all were firing. Bugler Tymble had been wounded in the right arm and, having discarded his equipment, was moving away back. Others on the left were firing well and steadily. On my right, the nearest lay still with his face in the grass. I roared, 'Are you hit'? and he raised his head to show a grinning face. I got angry and shouted at the scrimshanker: 'Why the hell don't you fire?' The man began to laugh. I did not know him well. He had arrived with the first reinforcement only about ten days before. He laughed and laughed and dug his face back in the grass. It was no grim joke, as I then suspected. The man was hysterical with fear. I did not know hysteria, and could not understand him. Some wounded had bandaged themselves and had continued to fight. The sight of them made me madder, and I edged towards the laugher, swearing at him, and I struck him twice in the ribs with my rifle butt. That steadied him, though his grin turned to a look of terror. I threatened him with a court martial and told him to pull his socks up. This sounded damn silly in the circumstances, even to myself, so I crept back to my central position to supervise the actions of more useful men.

Muldoon rose some yards to my left with his face covered in blood, which poured down on to his jacket and equipment. He had been shot through the top of the head. He came, to me and asked for the platoon sergeant. I said 'What for ? Go back,' and he said, 'No, got to report first.' And report he did, going down that awful line, under heavy fire, spurred by a most soldierly but ridiculous conscience to ask permission to fall out. He got back safe, with a peculiar wound, not at all fatal, for the bullet had hit him near the top of the head and passed under his scalp and out at the back, without injuring his skull.

We were still in great jeopardy, losing men every moment. Nine officers of the two companies – all we had – were knocked out. They fell forward in the advance waving their naked swords. The Germans, aided by the flashes of these outdated weapons, had concentrated their fire with success on our leaders. Two officers had been killed and seven wounded. From this date swords went out of fashion. Our attack had been a fiasco.

Without officers and sorely stricken, we still held on until a sergeant waved us back, so we rose and returned to where we had started, exhausted and disappointed. Some of the men walked back to Vailly. The Germans followed up our short retreat with shells, and worried us with more casualties among the few survivors. This was very harassing, almost the last straw. Our casualties had already amounted to one hundred and fifty, more than half the strength of the two unfortunate companies.

A sliver of shell hit the hysterical laugher of the front line and sent him all diddery. It struck him in the foot and, completely out of control, he rushed limping for sympathy to me, shouting 'Oh, oh, Corporal, what shall I do?' Someone seized him, disarmed him, took off his boots, and led him away, still groaning, 'Oh, Corporal, Corporal, Corporal'. My vials of sympathy were emptied and I was glad to see the last of him.

A young Cork man named Lane came smiling towards me with his arm

A German photograph of British dead on the Aisne battlefield.

in a sling. He was of my brother's platoon. I asked him about Denis, and he gave me the glad news that he, too, was slightly wounded in the arm, and had gone down to the village of Vailly with some other wounded. I was pleased and relieved. The next few minutes reminded me of the artist Butler's picture of the Crimean roll-call, when the senior N.C.O.s listed our casualties from information given by the survivors:

'08 Corrigan?'

'Dead, Sergeant.'

'I saw him too.'

'Right, killed in action. Any one seen 23 Murphy?' No answer.

'Right, missing.'

'What about MacRory? Anyone see MacRory coming back after he was hit? 'No answer.

'Right, wounded and missing,' and the sergeant's stubby pencil scribbled on. The depleted company moved back the short distance to reserve and grouped in little parties to discuss their experiences. I left them, to seek the orderly-room clerk, who verified that my brother's name had been submitted in the list of wounded of his platoon. The clerk would not tell me the total casualties. He had been forbidden to speak about them.

Actually my brother was lying dead out in front, about three hundred yards away, all this time, and I did not get to know this for days. Only one man of his section had come back alive. That I did not know either. After some days this survivor told me that my brother was killed with the rest of the section by shell fire. He also confirmed that he had been wounded first. Volunteers from other companies were called for and these went out, when darkness fell, to bring in the wounded They worked all night and suffered casualties themselves.

The company on the left had got a bad hammering. Their wood was now a shambles of wrecked trees and human bodies. Men had fallen in heaps under the intense shell concentration, yet the stout fellows had pushed on and actually entered and captured a German trench, and brought back several enemy prisoners, among whom were some gunner observers.

These gunners had a knob instead of a spike on the top of their helmets The strange enemy field-grey uniforms made some of us feel bitter, but as we continued to look at them cold reason told us that they were only troops like ourselves, and not so straight-backed either. They looked pale and scared.

The warlike commander of the left company, bleeding from several wounds in various parts of his body, and looking more fanatical than ever, would not have any of his hurts dressed until he had interrogated his prisoners. He questioned them in German, and was removed from them with difficulty and made to lie on a stretcher.

Some of our wounded lying out did not wait for rescue. They crawled and hobbled in of their own accord. One man presented a wild appearance, coming in half naked. He had been peppered with shrapnel, and had stripped himself under fire out there to look at his wounds. A man is always urgently curious about his wounds. Blotches of blood showed up startlingly on the white body of this half-naked fellow, who was a man who had knocked me out with bare fists in what already seemed the far-off days of peace. A ghastly sight, and he was simply full of abuse. He cursed us for not trying harder, and told us we had disgraced ourselves. A hardy fighter indeed, but we had had our bellyful and were in no mood to listen to his recriminations.

He was soundly cursed at in turn, and left us with a bitter twist on his thin lips, still reviling us with the vituperation of Belfast's back streets, while his red hands wandered unconsciously from wound to wound.

He repelled us, and as he looked strong on his legs, we left him to his own devices.

An inquisitive corporal from one of the companies that had remained behind approached one Cordwain, asking him what the attack was like and the strength of the opposition we met with.

'Hell's bells!' said tall Cordwain, as he remembered the intensity and variety of fire we had endured. 'We met the whole of Von Kluck's lousy army and the bloody German navy as well!'

And he spat reflectively over the hot muzzle of his rifle.

17 September, 1914

GERMAN WHITE FLAG TREACHERY

by Captain E. J. Needham

During the confused fighting on the Aisne, Captain Needham of the Northamptonshire Regiment had the shattering experience of seeing a fellow officer shot down while parleying with Germans who were showing the white flag. Was the outrage deliberate? He answers: 'We shall never know !'

Thursday, 17 September, was a stormy one for the Northamptonshires, as many more days were to be during the next four years. G Company was in reserve, the three other companies being in the front line. The morning passed fairly quietly except for the usual shelling of the village allotments. But at about 1.30 p.m. the Germans launched an attack on our line in pouring rain and in considerable strength. C Company were ordered up to reinforce the right of the line, and to launch a counter-attack. We fell in quickly and doubled along the terrace to a point where the high bank between us and the front line levelled off, just opposite the right flank of A Company, the flank company of the battalion. Here we turned to the left and advanced, still at the double, in extended order. We reached the road (Chemin des Dames) and lay down there for a few minutes to get our breath. Then 'Payker' (Officer Commanding C Company) gave the order to fix bayonets and a few minutes later to charge. Over the low bank we went, Payker shouting 'Come on, the Cobblers!' and the men, cheering like hell. I ran as hard and as best I could over the roots, with my drawn sword in one hand and my revolver in the other, stumbling over and cursing the roots and expecting any moment to be tripped up by my sword scabbard. We charged through heavy rifle and machine-gun fire and men were dropping off in every direction.

We got to about thirty yards from the trench which we had passed over on Monday, 14 September and which was now strongly held. Everyone was pretty well blown, and I was thankful when I saw the whole line to my right throwing themselves down flat. I shouted out 'Down!' to my men, and suited my action to the word; in any case, nobody could have heard me over the appalling din.

We lay where we were for some considerable time, keeping up a steady fire at the trench ahead of us. We were being well sprinkled with shrapnel all this time, and again, owing to the rain and misty conditions, were getting practically no artillery support from our guns. I remember vividly a man immediately behind me letting off his rifle in my right ear and deafening me for a long time. He must have just missed blowing my head off. Now it was, and for the next hour or so, that I found how very difficult it was to command one's men under active service conditions. To control fire with an extended firing line was absolutely impossible. I shouted until I was hoarse and just could not make myself heard above the firing.

The line was now at a standstill and looked like remaining so; the only thing to do appeared to be to keep up our fire and take what cover we could in the tree roots. After what seemed hours, I saw young Gordon (a fellow subaltern) crawling along on his tummy towards me from the right flank of the company; he eventually reached me and told me that poor, dear old Payker had been killed leading the charge and that I was in command of the company and also of the company of the 60th Rifles [King's Royal Rifle Corps] on our right, all of whose officers had been either killed or wounded.

I was horrified to hear of Parker's ['Payker'] death and also at my position. Gordon and I lay down together for some time debating as to what on earth we should do. We decided to try to get the line organized and rush at the trench. We passed messages down to each flank to tell everyone to be prepared to renew the charge when we blew our whistles and started.

But when we did blow them as loud and long as we could, and started forward with the men next to us, who had got the message correctly, the hostile fire broke out again stronger than ever; and as the rest of the line had not budged an inch, down we had to go again. We could see a group of people back in the road in the direction from which we had come, and I asked for a volunteer to take a message back to the Commanding Officer. A man next to me volunteered and I wrote out a message in my field-service notebook to say that Parker had been killed, that I understood all officers of the 60th were casualties, and that we were held up; and asked for orders. The man crawled off, and presently we saw him running down the hill to the road. After about ten minutes he came back with a written message for me telling me to hold on till further orders and to keep up my fire as much as possible. This we continued to do for another hour or so.

Then suddenly I heard the men shouting, 'They're surrendering!' and, looking up, I saw a line of white flags (or rather white handkerchiefs or something of the kind tied to the muzzles of rifles) held up all along the German trench from in front of us right away to the left. I shouted out to the men to cease fire and stop where they were.

After a few minutes I saw a large number of Germans, two or three hundred at least, moving forward from their trench towards A Company on the road, some with their rifles, but many with white flags tied to them,

British soldiers setting up a machine gun position.

and many with their hands up. They got down to A Company's trench and stood there for some time apparently conversing. All this time the white flags in front of us continued up and many Germans were standing with their hands raised.

All of a sudden a burst of heavy firing broke out down by A Company's trench and we saw the Germans and our men engaged in a hand-to-hand fight. Still the white flags in front of us remained up. Just as Gordon and myself had decided to reopen fire and to chance whether we were right or wrong, I saw Captain J. A. Savage, of D Company, and Lieutenant J. H. S. Dimmer, of the 60th, walk through the left of C Company and on up to the German trench in front of us. Apparently they could speak German. Anyway, they stayed there talking for about five minutes and then started to walk back to us, the white flags still being up.

To our horror, after they had got about halfway to us, the Germans opened fire on them, and we saw Savage pitch forward dead, shot in the back.

Dimmer threw himself down and started to crawl back to us, eventually reaching our line all right. (Dimmer won the Victoria Cross later in the war, and was eventually killed in March 1918.)

During all this white-flag episode, Gordon and I had been kneeling up, trying to make out what was going on, and were still doing so when the guns opened fire on Savage and Dimmer. Gordon, who was not a foot away from me, suddenly pitched forward on his face and yelled out, 'Oh, my God, I'm hit!' He writhed about on the ground in agony, and I tried to keep him quiet, while at the same time trying to watch Dimmer and what was going on down the line. He assured me again and again that he was shot through the stomach and that he was going to die. Poor devil; it was hell, not being able to do anything for him and to see him in such agony. I could only try to reassure him. The scrap down by A Company was still going on, and by now we also were firing at the Germans opposite as hard as we could, having reopened fire as soon as Dimmer got back safely to us.

Then, to our joy, we heard the tap-tap of a machine-gun behind us, and saw a machine-gun detachment (that of the 1st Queen's, as we afterwards learned) fairly lacing into the Germans in front of A Company, who started to bolt back into their own trench, Very few got back, however, those who were not mown down by the machine-gun fire (firing at about 150 yards' range) being finished off by the infuriated remnants (about seventy men) of A Company.

We redoubled our own fire and about a quarter of an hour later up went the white flag again in front of us, to which we paid no attention whatsoever.

Young Gordon's batman had volunteered to go back and get some stretcher-bearers up and presently these arrived and we got poor Gordon on to the stretcher. He made me promise to see that his sword was sent back to his family, and his batman took it. They carried him off, and I never saw him again. Poor boy he died at the casualty clearing station the next day, as he said he was going to, having suffered terribly, and was buried there. A typical cheery, plucky boy, straight from Sandhurst, gazetted only that January, to whom everybody had taken a great liking and whom I had particularly warmed to.

TRENCH FULL OF DEAD

By now all firing from the German trench had stopped, though intermittent shrapnel still continued and it was getting pretty dark. Dimmer, who had taken over command of the company of the 60th, and who was senior to me, now passed word along to advance, take the trench and any Germans still in it.

Men of a Scottish regiment are holding a trench as yet little more than knee deep.

Accordingly we advanced and found the trench full of dead and dying Germans. Three or four badly wounded men got up and put their hands up. I went up to them and, pointing my revolver at them, signalled to them to go down towards the road. They shambled off quickly enough, and I sent some men down with them. We then, with the men of the 60th, proceeded to fill in the German trench, burying the dead, all of us furious and embittered at having seen Savage and Gordon killed under the white flag like that. Having finished this unpleasant job, we got orders to retire to the road, which we proceeded to do. On arriving there we found the Colonel, Major Norman and Guy Robinson. Guy came up to me and said, 'You poor old devil! You must have had the hell of a time of it out there, but you did well.'

This kind greeting cheered me up no end, as I was feeling just about all

British infantry prepared to repel an attack.

in, being wet through to the skin, chilled to the bone and nerve-racked, after having one of my very best friends in Parker killed; in having poor young Gordon practically killed beside me, and in seeing poor old Savage butchered in that foul style. Also the whole show had been such an awful muddle and I was terrified of having done the wrong thing. I shall never forget that afternoon till my dying day, the horror and uncertainty of it.

I can remember quite clearly today every incident connected with it, and I always shall: the white-flag incident, as I have related it, is as I saw it and can see it now. To this day it is a mystery to me. Did the Germans really mean to surrender, but on getting down to A Company to do so and finding so few men there, changed their minds and tried to reverse the proceedings and take them prisoner? Or was the whole thing a put-up job? We shall never know.

I give also hereafter the version of Second Lieutenant L. H. B. Burlton, who commanded the detachment of A Company concerned, as given in the Regimental War History, which fully bears out the appalling muddle that ensued:

'To our outstanding joy, we saw the enemy in front of us making signs of surrender by putting their hands up. Their fire stopped, and I ordered my men to do likewise. I stood up on the parapet and called for an officer to meet me. An individual, I think a private, who spoke English, responded to the call, and I went out some forty yards ahead of my trench to make the necessary arrangements. On finding out that he was not an officer, I ordered him to return and tell his officer to replace him, A sergeant or under-officer next turned up, but was also returned as 'not wanted', after which an officer did materialize. He appeared to find great difficulty in understanding me. I agreed to accept surrender, but, as a preliminary thereto, naturally ordered him to make his men lay down their arms. Our conversation took place half-way between the opposing trenches, and, to my annoyance, I saw a large number of the enemy detach from their trenches before my arrangements were completed. Most of them had their rifles, but many had not and many had their hands up. I tried to make the Boche officer understand that I would order my men to fire if his men continued to advance with their arms. All this time the enemy continued to advance and the officer appeared quite willing to surrender but unable to grasp my idea of his men putting their rifles down as a preliminary. I found myself being surrounded by the advancing Germans, and as there was no officer in our trench (Second-Lieutenant Jarvis was in a state of concussion and non-effective), I could not afford to remain out in No Man's Land, which was rapidly being overwhelmed by the advancing Huns. I was, at the time, quite sure of their *bona fidos* as to surrender, and did not want to open fire for two reasons. (I do not know how far I calculated these reasons at the time, but their validity was certainly in my mind.)

'Firstly, I thought it was a *bona fides* surrender, as many of the enemy came without arms and with their hands up; and, to make that illusion complete, some of them who were armed handed their rifles over to some of our Tommies who had come out to meet them on their own. It would have been a dirty business to have opened fire on men who were advancing still carrying their arms because they did not understand English.

'Secondly, I had a message, delivered verbally to me by one of my men from the General, not to fire.

'I remember that message most distinctly: its incongruity did not strike me at the time and I thought it a genuine one. It came down from the right of our line from a quarter in front of which the enemy had also put up their hands. By this time I was back on the top of my trench with the Boche officers and the under-officer. The Huns, about four hundred strong, already amongst us, and in many cases surrendering their arms to Thomas Atkins and being warmly shaken by the hand. This situation however, passed very quickly, for a German quite, close to me shot one of my men dead, and the officer on my saying that if he did not order an immediate cessation of fire I would order mine to open fire, informed me I was his prisoner. We then all got to in earnest, so to speak, and at point-blank range, of course, no accuracy of shooting was necessary – the men used their butts and bayonets lustily. We were, however, far out-numbered, being but some seventy-odd against, I believe, four hundred. Then the most wonderful thing happened.

'The Queen's (I think) on our right, seeing we were in trouble, and seeing that the Boches were, for the most part, standing on our parapet and firing down on us in the road, turned on their machine gun, and the spectacle was one never to be forgotten. They fairly enfiladed the Huns on our parapet and the execution can only be compared to that of a harvesting machine as it mows down wheat. A regular lane was cut – those Boches on their side of the lane (perhaps some hundred strong) made their best pace back to their trenches: those on our side of the lane threw down arms and surrendered; but we declined their offer, and, in fact, I think only kept one prisoner – a souvenir no doubt!'

Germans infantry crossing open ground.

4-8 October, 1914

DOOM OVER ANTWERP
Witness to a Nation's Exodus

by J.M.N. Jeffries
Dally Mail *Correspondent, 1914-1933*

The harrowing scenes which accompany the flight of a civilian population is described by Mr. Jeffries, who was representing his paper in Antwerp during the city's last hours. In the words of a journalist, he tells of the final attacks of the Germans, of Winston Churchill's effort to save the city; and of the despairing trek towards a hoped-for safety by the inhabitants of a city.

Everything altered for Antwerp on the 6 October: the Royal Navy Brigade had been reinforced by 6,000 men of the Royal Naval Volunteer Reserve which, although full of courage, were hardly trained. Winston Churchill's comment on them was that they 'were incapable of manoeuvre'. They had been rushed from England to the front in Belgium where, in the phraseology of communiqués, 'they were briskly engaged'. How wonderful are these military expressions – 'briskly' – you would imagine the British and the Germans had an alert wash-and-brush-up together.

Although some of the RNVR personnel had, until then, never discharged a rifle, they proceeded to make good enough use of them. However, despite their efforts the advancing Germans forced their way into the town of Lierre only to be driven out briefly again by the Belgians and British counter-attacking.

As the hours advanced there were signs of breaking and disorder among the Allied troops and the roads back towards Antwerp became clogged. Motor vehicles travelling to and from the Front became snarled up with rearing horses – ambulances and ammunition wagons honked and their drivers screamed at each other, with the prospect of enemy shells landing at any moment in the midst of the disorder, and no one to direct, no one to disentangle the jumble which grew worse by the minute. No one, that is to say, till a man jumped from a car and, hoisting himself to vantage upon some unseen pedestal or other, began to cry out at the mob in Anglo-French, and to point with vigorous, imperative gestures to this or that centre of the maelstrom. He was a remarkable, and in that place, an inexplicable figure, clad in a flowing dark blue cloak, clasped at the neck with silver lionheads or something of that sort, after the fashion of the cloaks worn by prelates in Rome, and this cloak fell in great folds from his stretched oratorical arm. But there was purpose in his gestures, and power in his voice, and under his direction cars and carts were unlocked from each other, and the traffic gradually sorted into streams.

The car in which I was, fell into its own channel and flowed on with the others, but as I looked back he was still at his post, poised like a statue, watching till the order he had created became instilled with durable momentum.

It was Winston Churchill.

In my telegram that evening I did not fail to mention this characteristic and valuable little piece of work, for valuable it was. But all was forbidden by the censors in London, even my description in harmless pleasantry of the blue cloak (and I seem to remember there was a dark yachting-cap) as the active-service uniform of an Elder Brother of Trinity House. Its wearer must have been on his way there to confer, if he could reach him, with General Paris, who commanded the Naval Brigade, and was somewhere in action down Lierre way.

This brigade of Paris's held stubbornly to its rough-made positions. You could scarcely call these trenches; they were only defensive troughs. The British Brigade, too, was in continual danger of being  outflanked and being cut off, owing to the weakening of resistance on its left. Resistance, indeed, was ebbing most definitely. As I crossed the fields again, I was aware of troops dropping back.

Uncertain of my own situation, and obliged to keep away from the roads which were not places to linger. I skulked about close to the railway line behind hedges. Suddenly there came the blast of resounding fire from near at hand and, looking for the cause I saw an armoured train, with guns blazing steaming towards me. It halted, fired again. I ran towards it, and was obligingly hauled aboard by a couple, of Belgian officers who were

British sailors of the Royal Naval Division march out to take up position for the defence of the port of Antwerp.

standing at its open door into a goods van or horse van which formed the wooden tail of the metal train.

As I struggled in I saw the forms of some of our own sailors at the guns in the armoured trucks ahead. This train was an improvisation of an officer of the Royal Navy, ever at its most effective when ruling over difficulties. It had been assembled with the help of the Cockerill workshops in

Antwerp. It was one of a pair, each bearing 4.7-inch naval guns in steel-plated trucks, with a couple of magazine-trucks attached, drawn by two engines. Lieutenant Commander Littlejohns was its deviser and presided over one of his trains. The other was in charge of a Belgian, Captain Servais. Naval gunners manned both trains, assisted by Belgian volunteers.

These trains were, to say the least of it, widely known in defence circles, and had all sorts of names from *Le Rapide Leet-le-jaw* (Littlejohns in Flemish) to *le Wagon-lit*. Somehow they maintained a seafaring character cruising all over the threatened Lierre hinterland, firing away indefatigably at the enemy. What is more, they eluded him persistently; despite all his kite-balloons, Zeppelins and aircraft. As soon as the Germans had got their range either Littlejohns or Servais would tack up the railway-line and watch interestedly the shells detonating over their recent berth. If any instrument of war can be light-hearted this train was.

When I was dragged on board to the grins of the watching seamen, I found that its Belgian officers and men had absorbed the communicative naval manner.

ARMY THAT WAS TOO LATE

I stayed up most of that night. Earlier in the evening there had been another Council of War at the Royal Palace, and the determination had been reached to fight on. King Albert, Churchill records, 'preserved an unalterable majesty' in the face of untoward fortune. Hope endured still that an Anglo-French force would reach Antwerp from the coast within three days, in time to raise the siege. Some of our troops had already massed for the purpose in maritime Flanders, but the decision, or perhaps the opportunity, to form this army had come just too late. Time was lost in the passage of notes between England and France in the technical preparations of transport and in various facings and frontings soon made necessary by the German army's movement at the northward end of its line.

So the situation rushed into crisis at Antwerp. Our last offensive was taken that afternoon by two Belgian regiments, who, at the bayonet's point drove the Germans established on the near bank back across the Nèthe. Part of the newly arrived Naval Brigade attacked at their side. But there was much confusion and a lack of co-ordination. I cull from the official history of the Marines during the war the acid statement that 'there appear to have been present a number of un-official staff-officers and politicians who attached themselves to the staff and gave orders to the troops.' I do not think this is intended for Mr. Churchill, who as First Lord of the Admiralty could hardly be described as unofficial.

If it were so intended it would be unjust, for he only gave orders when it was a question of his orders or of none at all and after he had conferred with General Deguise and had obtained his agreement and his leave.

Belgian troops defending a canal bridge as the main force falls back on Antwerp.

In any case, this effort of the Belgians could not be renewed. The sweet fibre of Allied support drew out, thinned to spun-sugar and melted in the flames of burning Lierre, which I stood and watched from the roof of a hotel or some such eyrie. Towards midnight the Germans re-established themselves over the Nèthe, crossing near the town of Duffel, at many points.

They swam over; they came with machine guns in pontoons; it was the swarm of definite occupation this time. The exhausted defenders fell back, and fell away. Yet I remember that even in that final hour Antwerp showed a brave face. Some vain few hundred reinforcements marched that night through the streets; I met them on my way to the 'Pilotage' where headquarters were. They passed through the dark, unlit, blinded city to the sound of fifes, and thousands of cheering shadows came out to greet them.

I had returned before then towards Contich, to encounter wounded,

German troops marching through Belgian town receive water from local women.

stragglers and whole sections of fugitives. Artillery were cantering in with caissons and such equipment, but officerless and gunless, having lost commanders and pieces, answering enquiry about them, 'Sais pas... ils sont allés' [Don't know, they've gone missing] It was a sort of rout.

The Germans were getting cavalry over the river [the river Nethe]. Another fort, Broechem, fell. When its commander had taken it over he had found that if he were to open rapid fire, with- out intermission, there was but a quarter of an hour's supply of ammunition for his main armament and six minutes' supply for his flanking! The outer defence was non-existent now, and the Germans were attacking strongly at Termonde, to cut off all retreat over the Scheldt from the forces in Antwerp. The inner forts still remained, but they could do no more than the outer had done, and now Termonde in its need began to cry out for reinforcements.

King Albert held a last council and gave orders for the field-army to evacuate the city while the bridges over the Scheldt were still intact at Tamise and Hoboken, before the enemy could bring up his guns. He acted in the nick of time. Termonde was taken next day. But the army already had begun to withdraw through the corridor between Termonde and the Dutch frontier, and most of it made good its with- drawal before the Germans advanced across the three roads and two railway lines of the corridor which led to Bruges or to Ghent. That night the members of the Government took ship for Ostend. Mr. Churchill went by motor through the corridor to the same town.

Civilians left the city by the western roads or by the northern towards

Holland in steady, melancholy streams. The First Lord had to withstand, soon afterwards in England, very bitter attacks for his intervention, for his optimistic endeavour to save a hopeless situation, for his risking of British prestige. But he knew more about prestige than the whole pack of his critics. Their idea was to preserve prestige in a showcase, as though it were a museum-piece; he saw that prestige must be brought into use instantly, the moment the first great risk appears. The silk colours of regiments are placed in the cathedrals; prestige is the one banner left to the nation that can lead its soldiers into action.

THE ONLY MAN WHO TRIED

It is true that Mr. Churchill told the Burgomaster of Antwerp: 'We are going to save the city,' and failed to save it. But in Belgium he is remembered not as the man who failed but as the only man who tried to succeed. As for practical results, since the German forces did not occupy Antwerp till the 9th, six days were gained by his stand as against the earlier intended evacuation on the 3rd, during which time the western end of Belgium was sealed, Dunkirk protected from enemy occupation, and the sea was secured as the left flank of the Allied armies.

We quitted Antwerp between ten and eleven, a little group of five persons in the end. I had had to abandon my luggage, naturally, and it

A Belgian machine gunner prepares to cover the withdrawal to Antwerp.

perished when later in the day the bombardment was resumed and my hotel was struck and set on fire.

We walked past the shipping at our slow gait as though officially inspecting all that we owned there before it passed out of our possession. It was melancholy to see the quantity of vessels lying so trimly at their moorings, ready filed, as it were, for insertion in the prize-lists of the invader.

Away before us a stream of fugitives stretched to the village of Eeckeren, three miles beyond. To the right, over more bare country, flowed another great stream of mankind. Seen from afar this was so sombre and moved so little that it had the likeness of something cut deep into the soil of some vast drain. From where we stood I could judge the hours which must pass before we ourselves joined up with it.

The day would be growing dark before our united ooze of forlorn mankind could gain the woods next to Eeckeren, whence I could perceive even now, a further area of flight stretching to the region which lay near the frontier.

The number of those departing was so great that I gave no thought to estimating how many. If huge crowds had fled the city I might have tried to reckon how many they were. But what I perceived now was not a mere escape or withdrawal of huge crowds. Departure was widespread; Antwerp was like a box which had been opened, tipped up and its population had flooded out of it.

Alexander Powell, the American correspondent, who saw the German entry into the abandoned city, describes that extraordinary scene, taken as from legend, with the regiments tramping in step and the bands playing through streets where there was no one left to watch or to listen, and the glass from the broken windows lay on the deserted footways.

Another writer at the time declared that only five thousand persons, were left in Antwerp. Suppose he exaggerated and ten times that number remained, what were they out of three hundred thousand? The composition of the long array ot fugitives, in the middle-distance, as I watched, where the outlines could just be distinguished of men and women, of laden vehicles and of animals, gave it the appearance of a nation upon the move. That appearance, too, answered to the fact of the continual shrinking of Belgian territory because of the advance of the foe had forced the population from town to town, till in Antwerp to its own inhabitants there had come an influx drawn from all the sources of that small but thickly settled land. These were mostly those peasants and humble townsfolk who are their country's fundamental stock, and all unknowingly hold the recipe of its character. In Antwerp, more than in the capital Brussels, the race had taken refuge. Now it was driven forth again and with its primitive belongings was plodding into exile. No wonder then that the unbroken press before me, wherein old-style chariots and

Terrified Belgians seeking escape through the port of Antwerp.

improvised litters and herds were all mingled, made me think of the Israelites and of Exodus. These thoughts soon were chased by my own difficulties of the moment.

With the over-recurring recollection in my mind of the telegram which I must somehow send to London, I tried, with my companions, to progress through the throng about us. This was a scarcely a conceivable task.

TRUDGING, SHAMBLING MOB

If there had been an ordinary large crowd on this road it would have been excessively fatiguing to slip through it, veering about, changing level all the time, swerving under elbows, cutting in and out, knocking against the kerb or the iron rails – and to go on doing this for miles. But now that the road was filled with the flight, to penetrate it became exhausting in ten minutes, and after as much time I would abandon the effort and would drop into the step-by-step trudge of the throng, and would jerk, shamble and halt with everyone else, till again I felt equal to pushing through quarter-made gaps, to stumbling between cows and crooking at an angle round tree-trunks, only to be beaten once more by the exertion, to fall into my uneasy socket, and then to begin again and to fail and to re-begin.

All the time the afflictions of the route encompassed me. Most of the fugitives paced along sadly, their gaze on the ground or lost in the distance. Here and there were riders, bareback or on rough farm-saddles, limp-

A baby is handed down to the last boat to leave Antwerp.

shouldered from their eternal jog, their heads as bent as their horses. Enormous wagons occupied half the road, bearing twenty, twenty-five, thirty persons pent in a heap, girls huddled listlessly together upon heaps of bedding, aged brown women like shrunk walnuts, buried in shawls, children fitfully asleep, shaken and querulous, and babies crying interminably. There were no cars; no car could have stood the rate of progress without its driver going mad; and it was a poor people's march.

But there were bicycles with shapeless, angular or bloated bundles fixed to them, protruding on either side of the wheels, lolloping insecurely, or else slung and over slipping and calling for adjustment and some had a little child tied to the saddle, pushed by its patient father on and on, stop and go, stop and go, endlessly. Perambulators, too, were filled with children and with children on whom clothes and linen had been piled because of need of space, or who were a little older and could manage to carry clocks or boxes in their arms. Sons wheeled old fathers along in wheelbarrows, and strong men were carrying (for how long?) chairs slung from their shoulders in which daughters or wives, ill or with child, sat gripping the arms of the chair rigidly. Led horses with household goods strapped to their backs or even bearing hen-coops as panniers made their heavy way along.

All such issued from the mass of plodders, of men leaning on sticks, of couples arm-linked for support, of families irregularly strung out; mixed with whom again was a surf and an undersurf of domestic beasts, clogging every pore of progress; bevies of wretched hoof-weary baa-ing sheep; dogs barking distractedly; bellowing cattle in droves. To their din was joined the exasperating, ceaseless jingle and twang of the bells of city cyclists, who, until towards dark they learned sense or learned hopelessness, were for ever making yard-starts, turning a pedal once, ringing violently – as though there were any chance of way being made for them there – subsiding awkwardly on to one leg, colliding with walkers, or with dogs which yelped at the impact.

WEEPING AS THEY WALKED

Some of the legions of dogs dragged little carts; others trotted cowed between the wheels of a wagon; still others were bunched upon its straw-piled top with cats and goats and with three or as many as four generations of a family.

Numbers of women cradled cats in their arms, and I walked awhile alongside two who carried between them a sort of laundry-bundle out of the top of which peeped the head of a pathetic little wastrel of a pup. The bundle swung back and forth; the women cried silently as they walked. A couple of others had a cat, swinging similarly, but in a curtain tied or sewn about it, from which the miaowing cat kept trying to wriggle away.

The awful slowness of movement wore out the soul. Hundreds upon hundreds gave up, flung themselves down by the roadside or formed camps amid the trees by the border, so that the roadway became twice congested and the moving flood was dammed in long delays.

As I had reckoned only too well evening came on while we were still in its midst. The campers pulled boughs from the trees and kindled fires, and as we came up out of the darkness and approached each fire I saw the sleepers lying side by side and over upon each other, stacked near the warmth; in their midst a seated figure or two, hands collapsed in lap, face dumb with perplexity and with the wrong of everything, gazing unregardfully at the multitude which went swaying into the further darkness beyond. About then individuals here and there began to light lanterns, and candles also, both because of the failing light and because many had brought the blessed candles which they kept in their homes to be lit on feast-days, or in any emergency. Now, therefore, with their candles held in their hands, they passed on twinkling like a pilgrimage, as though in this extremity they had turned their steps finally towards the abode of God.

Their state, of course, had worsened with the lengthening day, through growth of fatigue and through want of food. Perhaps half of them had brought food with them, but what they had brought they had generally shared lavishly, so that no one had eaten much at all. Water to quench the thirst occasioned by the heat of the morning and by the turmoil and the dust was still harder to come by.

An extraordinary sight stays in my mind still, seen when I had struggled forward to learn the cause of a long halt in the ranks. In mid-roadway was a group of women, all clothed in black, leaning humped together, as the old masters draw women at the foot of the Cross, and moaning in unison like Jews under the walls of Jerusalem, crying: *Donnez-nous à boire! Sainte Vierge, donnez nous à boire!'* [Give us a drink! Madonna, give us a drink!]

Sometime in the evening we reached the frontier of Holland, ten miles away. I dispatched my telegram, an outline of the day's events.

In flight before a pitiless foe – the face of the child tells the tragedy of war.

4-8 October, 1914

AN ANTWERP ADVENTURE
Shells and Burning Oil

by Rev. Canon H. Clapham Foster, M.A.

Temporary Chaplain in the Royal Navy, the author of this account tells of the stand made by the British Naval Division in the defence of Antwerp. He was a padre attached to the 2nd Naval Brigade. As such he shared the adventures of the men, and most graphically describes the fighting defence which ended in inevitable retirement.

The news that we were to leave immediately for France spread very quickly round the camp, and among the men there was a scene of boundless enthusiasm; loud cheers were raised as they hastily dressed and got their kits together. There was no time to lose. Breakfast was at seven am, and at eight we were told the transport would be ready to convey our baggage to Dover.

The Second Royal Naval Brigade started on the march to the pier at about nine am, amid scenes of great enthusiasm, two brass bands and a drum and fife band accompanying them. The men selected some curious words for their own special 'marching songs', and these are, as a rule, set to familiar melodies. It would have astonished, not to say shocked, the Salvation Army had they heard the following words sung to a hymn tune when passing a public-house:

There's a man selling beer over there
There's a man selling beer over there
Over there, over there, over there, over there—
There's a man selling beer over there.

Another favourite ditty with men on the march is a song with a somewhat unsavoury refrain:

Wash me in the water
Where you wash your dirty daughter
And I shall be whiter than the white-wash on the wall.

This song is sung by all regiments, and it would be interesting to find out who originally invented it.

Singing such ditties as these, we marched from Betteshanger to Dover. We were accorded a magnificent reception in the streets by crowds of people who cheered lustily and waved flags and handkerchiefs as we made our way to the pier. At about five o'clock our men commenced the somewhat dreary task of getting the baggage on board. We took with us, besides 'field kit,' our base kit, and first-line-of-transport kit. At about 9.30 we were ready to sail, so well had the men worked. In a short time we were underway and slowly sailing out of Dover Harbour. It was a strange, not to say uncanny, sensation to be leaving one's native land on active service for the first time.

Our escort, consisting of two destroyers, kept close to us during the whole of the night. The voyage however, proved to be uneventful, and at about one am on Monday, 5 October, we anchored off Dunkerque.

For eight weary hours we lay off Dunkerque, awaiting orders, in a choppy sea. At last a French destroyer came alongside and a somewhat portly French naval officer shouted through a megaphone that we were 'to proceed into harbour' and moor at the quay. It was just about noon when we entered.

Those were stirring days – the 'Tipperary' days we might call them – and the war was but two months old. The cheers from troops and civilians on shore, re-echoed by a thousand throats as our transport stirred the emotions, and will live in the memories of those who heard them to the end of life. But the most moving incident of all was when our brass band came up on deck and played the 'Marseillaise'; nothing delighted the French more than this little compliment, and they cheered again and again as the ship moored at the quay.

Our actual destination, so far, had been unknown, but on getting to the quay we were told that we were to entrain for Antwerp immediately, to

Men of the Eastbourne (Sussex) Division RNVR, D Company, Howe Battalion, 2nd Brigade, Royal Naval Division, seen here in the Belgian street in Vieux Dieu, an eastern suburb of Antwerp.

take part in the defence of the city. The first train did not leave the quay until 10.45 pm, with the Nelson and Howe battalions. We had but little food, and that consisted of bully beef and biscuits, with nothing to drink.

Each man received 120 rounds of ammunition before getting into the train, and our Commandant, Lieutenant Colonel George Cornwallis West, addressed us. He said there was a possibility of the train being attacked in the night, that it was uncertain as to whether or not the railway line had been cut by the Germans. 'Remember you are British', he said in conclusion, 'and I am sure you will give a good account of yourselves.' A tremendous cheer greeted this remark, and it echoed and re-echoed through the lofty sheds on the quay.

The men, weary with their labours and the long wait, tumbled into the troop train with evident joy, in spite of the fact that the journey might be fraught with danger and uncertainty. At about 2 am on Tuesday, 6 October we crossed the Belgian frontier.

At all the smaller stations on the line, in spite of the early hour, crowds had turned out to greet us. At the more important stations, such as Dixmude and Thielt, large numbers of people brought the men presents of fruit and cakes. Sometimes the train would stop out in the country, where there was no station near, but from a small cottage an old peasant woman would come tripping out with a monstrous jug of hot coffee, with which she regaled the men. All along the line we received the same royal reception.

There were signs about 9 am that we were drawing near to a large and important town. So far our journey had been passed amidst peaceful surroundings, but now, as we looked out of the carriage windows, we saw quite plainly the first signs that a war was really being waged. Shrapnel could be seen bursting quite distinctly in the vicinity of Antwerp, and two captive balloons were up in the sky directing the German fire. Hundreds of Belgians were busily engaged, on both sides of the line, in constructing entrenchments, and many fields had been flooded to put a check on the German advance.

The Marine Brigade of the Royal Naval Division, composed almost entirely of regular troops, had reached Antwerp on the night of 3 October. Never have war-worn warriors been more delighted to be relieved than were the Belgians when the Marines took over the trenches facing Lierre, and enabled them to get a much-needed and well-deserved rest. Armoured trains, with gun crews formed of British bluejackets, got into action on 4 October and did excellent work. We of the 1st and 2nd Naval Brigades were due to enter Antwerp on the evening of 5 October, but the unfortunate delay at Dunkerque meant that we arrived some twelve hours late.

The very day on which we arrived in Antwerp, 6 October, was a momentous day in the history of 'the second strongest fortress in Europe' and what happened then really brought about the fall of the city earlier than the Belgians expected.

During the day, after a fluctuating night engagement, the exhausted Belgians were driven back by the enemy in a furious assault from the direction of Lierre, backed by powerful artillery. The Marine Brigade, which had continued to hold its position most gallantly and against overwhelming odds, was unable to do anything else but follow suit.

It will be seen, therefore, that the 1st and 2nd Naval Brigades really arrived too late to attempt to save Antwerp, because the Germans had now established themselves on ground from which they were able to bombard the city with their powerful howitzers with the greatest ease, to meet which we had only the few naval guns at our disposal and the small guns on the forts in the inner ring.

We arrived in Antwerp shortly before 10 am on Tuesday, 6 October. We were met at a suburban station by the civic guard and several important officials and then came our march through the streets. It is impossible to say whether or not the people looked upon us as the saviours of their city, but we shall never forget the reception they gave us. Charming Belgian maidens pinned little flags made of silk on to our tunics and attempted to embrace two of our officers, greatly to their embarrassment and confusion.

Large jugs of light beer were brought out of houses, from which the men filled anything that would hold liquid. The scene was one of indescribable enthusiasm, but all the time the distant boom of guns sounded on our ears,

Enthusiastic crowds gather around the British sailors, convinced that these troops would repel the advancing Germans.

and seemed to strike a warning note, telling us that, though it was fine then, the storm might burst at any moment. We marched about four miles to a place on the outskirts of the city, where we had a most welcome rest. The officers were billeted out for their meals to various houses.

I found myself in a house where the only occupants appeared to be three old ladies, who could not speak a word of English. I made them understand, however, that I was ravenously hungry; the table was quickly set, and I was provided with a delicious omelette and some fried ham, with a bottle of light beer to wash it down. Afterwards, feeling in need of a sleep, I went upstairs to a bedroom and was soon in peaceful slumber, in spite of the boom of guns, which every hour seemed to be drawing nearer.

After a glorious sleep of about two hours, I was suddenly awakened by a loud knocking at the door and a voice shouting something in Flemish. The voice sounded rather agitated, and I expected at least that the enemy had broken through, and that a German officer was about to walk upstairs and demand my instant surrender. It transpired, however, that the Brigade had fallen in and was about to move off. Rested and refreshed, we marched away, amidst renewed cheering, to further excitement.

A march of some five miles brought us to the village of Vieux-Dieu, a quaint spot on the confines of the city. Here we halted and were told that we were to rest a short time before going up to the firing line.

We were told that we were to be quartered for the night in an old château, standing in its own grounds and surrounded by trees. There was abundant evidence that its occupants had been wealthy people, and that they had fled away in haste. There was a quantity of valuable furniture, and we found everything just as its late owner had left it.

We ascertained that one of the servants belonging to the house was still at her home in the village, and after a good deal of persuasion we succeeded in getting her to come and cook some supper for us. Those of us who are still alive will not readily forget the scene in that old room of the château. There we sat round the table, a light being supplied by a candle stuck securely in the neck of an empty bottle, eating like the gourmands who haunt Simpson's in the Strand and other famous London eating houses. Plates and forks were scarce, but pocket-knives came in exeedingly handy. The windows had been plastered up with brown paper so as not to let

Men of the Royal Naval Division constructing defences near Antwerp.

'Bluejackets' of the Royal Naval Division preparing to meet the German invaders at Antwerp.

out a single streak of light. There sat such well-known personages as Lieutenant-Colonel George Cornwallis West, Arthur Asquith, Denis Browne and Rupert Brooke, eating pieces ot veal with their fingers and drinking coffee out of tumblers and milk jugs.

At the bottom of the garden which surrounded this château was one of the Antwerp forts, and so sleep was practically impossible, as the guns were cracking out every few minutes, shaking the house to its very foundations. Not far off the six-inch naval guns were also speaking with no uncertain voice, while every now and then the whistle of the enemy's shells was distinctly heard, followed by the sound of distant explosions.

USELESS TRENCHES AND FORTS

At 2 am next day (Wednesday, 7 October) we were awakened by a Belgian officer and were told to fall in at once and leave for the front trenches. We had a most romantic march in the darkness to Fort No. 7, one of the forts on the inner ring. It was a calm, still night, and the men marched along quietly, having been warned of the serious nature of the task in front of them. At dawn we reached our destination and for the first time saw the trenches that were to be our home for only two days. Those open trenches had been cleverly constructed by the Belgians, but they would have proved utterly useless had they been subjected to a violent bombardment. They linked up the forts of the inner ring, which were fifty years old and mounted with inferior Krupp guns.

Our trenches were at the end of a large turnip field, and about 150 yards behind them there was a modem villa, surrounded by a pretty garden. It was empty and devoid of furniture, and in this house the doctor and I were installed and were told to transform it into a hospital. A meal was just about to be prepared in the kitchen of our new home, when the Fleet Surgeon came to tell us to clear out of it immediately, because as a hospital it was quite unsafe, and might be shelled at any moment.

We took up our abode finally in a bomb-proof shelter, or dug-out, some twelve feet long by six feet wide, the roof being formed of steel plates an inch thick laid on strong iron girders.

It was a pitch dark night and very cold. Suddenly the alarm was given and our men opened fire. I went out into the open and watched. There were our men blazing away and peering into the inky blackness of the night. Shells began to burst all round us. I only just had time to run under cover when a shrapnel shell burst over us.

No one can say definitely what happened, except that some Deutschers had evidently crossed the river and were detected while making a reconnaissance. There were several other alarms along the line held by the Naval Division during the night, but the fighting never actually got to close quarters.

During the first surprise attack, seven Belgian gunners in the fort close to us were killed. We were fortunate in having very few casualties, and they were mainly slight shrapnel wounds. The men had kept remarkably cool during a trying experience, and were only disappointed that no opportunity for using their bayonets had come their way. The brunt, of the Antwerp fighting undoubtedly fell on the Marines, and it is impossible to speak too highly of the courage and bravery they displayed while holding their part of the line against the repeated onslaughts of the enemy. They were called upon to stand and face heavier shelling than either of the two Naval brigades, and their grit and devotion to duty set us all a noble example.

When Thursday, 8 October dawned, both officers and men looked exhausted and fagged out. Stores were getting somewhat low, and for breakfast we had each a tin mug of coffee, one biscuit, a piece of bread, and a small bit of cheese.

It was evident that the German artillery had advanced considerably nearer during the night. I went up into an observation post and saw quite distinctly, with the aid of field-glasses, German gunners getting a heavy gun into position. The scream of shells overhead never ceased, and we got so accustomed to it as not to notice it.

Shortly after midday dense clouds of black smoke began to ascend into the sky, darkening the sun and the whole horizon for miles, until it began to be more like evening than noonday. Enquiry elicited the fact that those huge columns of smoke came from the petroleum tanks at Hoboken that had been set ablaze by the Belgians themselves in order to prevent the Germans getting hold of one of the largest stores of petroleum in the world.

DAYS OF DESPAIR

Meanwhile, the sound of the German guns seemed to have come closer, and shells began to burst unpleasantly near. Some parts of the line held by the Naval Division suffered heavier bombardment than others, but so far, luckily for us, most of the shells were, as the men put it, 'bound non-stop for Antwerp'. It is, perhaps, somewhat difficult for those who were not there to imagine the utter hopelessness and despair of the men who had been sent with the intention of defending Antwerp. Unknown to us, the fate of Antwerp was decided before we arrived.

We had absolutely nothing with which we could reply to the German siege batteries. All that we could do seemed to be to wait as calmly as we could for the end.

About five o'clock darkness was setting in. Antwerp was seen to be on fire in some quarters. Our baggage party arrived and said that the railway station at Wilryck, in which our baggage had been stored, was in flames. This tragic piece of news made many an officer draw a long face as he proceeded to enumerate the various articles of value he had tucked away in his valise which he was never to see again.

A British Naval Armoured Train defending Antwerp.

The doctor and I had been sitting in our dug-out for a time, wondering what would happen next, when the drum-major put his head in at one of the openings and exclaimed in a low tone:

'We have to clear out immediately, sir, as we are almost cut off on all sides and they intend using their heavy guns against us tonight.'

Our men loathed the idea of a retreat, but the majority realized that every minute the position was becoming more critical and that immediate retreat was our only hope of escaping capture. Almost all the Belgians had gone, except those in the forts, and in our covering fort only one Belgian gunner remained. One of our naval gun crews gallantly offered to remain and work the guns in order to cover our retreat, which they did up until the very last minute.

In order to cross the Scheldt we were forced to pass the burning petroleum tanks at Hoboken. The road was narrow but it was the only road left. The fumes wore overpowering and the intense heat proved too much for some of the men. The flames at times blew right across the road, and large German shells were falling in amongst the storage tanks at the rate of four a minute. Sometimes a shell would burst with a terrific report in the boiling oil, and flames shot up to the height of two hundred feet.

As we approached the blazing tanks it was like entering the infernal regions. The burning oil had flooded a field on one side of the road and dead horses and cattle were frizzling in it.

'Now, boys,' shouted an officer, 'keep your heads and run through it!' And we did – but I don't know how we did it. Once we had got past the oil tanks we were in comparative safety for a hundred yards because the road was sheltered, but then for some thousand yards it was exposed again to the enemy's fire.

We were ordered to run at the double over this bit of road, and most of us were fortunate enough to reach the pontoon bridge over the river. A spy was caught by one of our battalions in the act of trying to blow up this bridge, but his designs were frustrated just in time and a bayonet thrust ended his career.

Sentries were posted at intervals while we went across and shouted to us to change our step every few yards. This was so as not to cause the bridge to begin vibrating to the measured tread of those crossing. At least we were safe on the other side and could breath again. The relief felt by the ranks on crossing the river can hardly be imagined and, although even there we were by no means out of danger, yet we knew that an important step had been taken.

The petrol storage tanks at Hoboken on fire after the Belgians destroyed them to save the fuel from falling into the hands of the Germans.

WHEN THEY LOST ZONNEBEKE

by The Hon. Ralph G. A. Hamilton
The Master of Belhaven

Lieutenant Colonel Hamilton was generally known as the Master of Belhaven, 'Master' being the courtesy title of the eldest son of a Scottish viscount or baron. He was an officer of the Royal Artillery during the First Battle of Ypres. His diary was written from day to day in the field. Here is an extract which describes the fierce fighting that led to the fall of Zonnebeke near Ypres, in October 1914, and a spy hunt in which Lieutenant Colonel Hamilton took part. The only son of the 10th Lord Belhaven and Stenton, he was killed in action 31 March, 1918, whilst in command of a Brigade of Field Artillery

All that night the population of the country streamed through the town (Zonnebeke) and by next morning (19 October) the streets were fairly clear. Our infantry, after falling back, took up the entrenched line which they had providentially prepared two days before. At daylight the guns also took up positions immediately in the rear of the infantry brigade. From that moment the battle of Ypres began.

All that day we were bombarded by the Germans, but so far they confined their attentions to the trenches and did not drop shells in the town. Also, they had evidently not yet got up their heavy guns, as we were only under shrapnel fire. The German infantry did not make any attempt to assault.

I spent most of the morning with Bolster, who commanded the 106th Battery, in his dug-out immediately in the rear of the infantry trenches. (He was killed two days later.) We were on the crest of a small rise, and thirty or forty yards in front of us, on the forward slope, was the line of our infantry trenches, at that point held by the South Staffordshire Regiment. We had an excellent view of the country to our front, which much resembled Essex or Suffolk, being greatly enclosed and with many hedges and small woods.

Standing in the trench with nothing but my eyes showing, I watched, with Bolster, the enemy's infantry trickling over the skyline in very open order and come on in short rushes. They did not present much of a target for artillery; and, owing to the farms, woods and hedges, we could only see them here and there as they crossed open patches. This ridge they were crossing was under fire of our guns, and whenever we saw enough of them bunched together, we let off a few rounds at them. I shall never forget seeing some thirty or forty Germans running across a green field which was divided in two by a wire fence, probably barbed, as I noticed that on reaching the wire fence they all concentrated and ran through a gate in it. Our lines of fire were already laid out, and from the map we were able to get the range to a yard.

ONE SHELL – FIFTEEN DIED

The next time we saw a party crossing the fields and making for the gate Bolster ordered a round of gun-fire. At this short range (2,300 yards), with my Zeiss glasses I could almost see the faces of the Germans, it being a gloriously fine, sunny day.

Just before they reached the gate, he gave the order to fire. The guns, which were hidden behind us, loosed off and we heard the shells whining away. As the Germans clustered in the gate, a shell from No. 1 gun burst immediately in front of them, The whole lot at once lay down, and at first I thought that they were taking cover until our fire stopped. However, I watched them for some hours, and not one of them moved again. I counted fifteen in a circle of some twenty yards diameter.

By now a good many of the German infantry had crossed the ridge, not only immediately in front of us, but all along the front. Owing to their

being so close, and the fact that our guns were behind the crest of our hill, we were unable to reach them. We continued, however, to pour shrapnel on their supports as they crossed the skyline, doing considerable damage.

At one time I was leaning against the wall of a little house, some twenty yards from Bolster, who was in his hole, and I pointed out to him that the enemy were bunching behind a certain clump of bushes. My head was eight or nine feet higher than his, and he could not see them. He, therefore, asked me to range the battery for him, and so one of the ambitions of my life was realized in that I ranged a battery of guns in action. Measuring off the angle between the place at which we were then firing, and the place where I had seen the Germans bunching, with the graticule calibration of my glasses. I gave the necessary switch of some five degrees, and ordered a round of battery fire. The ground sloped away from left to right. The range on the left was about right, but the right section were short.

This was owing to the angle-of-sight being different for the two flanks of the battery. However, as I did not wish to upset the battery angle-of-sight, I increased the range in the right section by fifty yards, and then ordered a round of gun-fire. This was completely successful, two shells bursting in the clump of bushes in which I had seen the Germans collecting. I think that some twenty or thirty of them must have been in these bushes, and when the shells burst I saw only two or three run out. One ran away altogether; the other two, after staggering a few yards, collapsed. The remainder, I think, must have been knocked out at once.

Meanwhile, the German infantry, who were now too close and too much in the hollow below us for our guns to reach, were coming on, and we soon saw their scouts emerge from a pheasant cover not 200 yards in front of us.

As the guns were only 200 yards behind us, this was getting uncomfortably close for artillery. However, we did not feel any anxiety, as our own infantry were well dug in between us and them. As soon as those German scouts appeared our infantry opened fire on them at 200 yards, and the wretched Germans, who evidently did not know of the existence of this branch, began to fall thickly. They at once retired into their pheasant cover, and, being reinforced in considerable strength, opened fire on us.

Things were now very lively, and Bolster could neither leave his observation hole, nor could I leave the wall against which I had flattened myself. At the same time the German field artillery discovered the position of our trenches and the shrapnel began to arrive. Every time one put one's head out it was immediately saluted with half a dozen bullets, which made a noise like very loud and angry mosquitoes as they passed. I stopped at this place for some time, but in the lull of the firing I managed to run back to the gun-line.

In the course of the afternoon General Lawford asked me to take a message to the colonel of the Staffordshires in his trench. With some difficulty I got there, crawling the last twenty yards, perfectly flat. I found

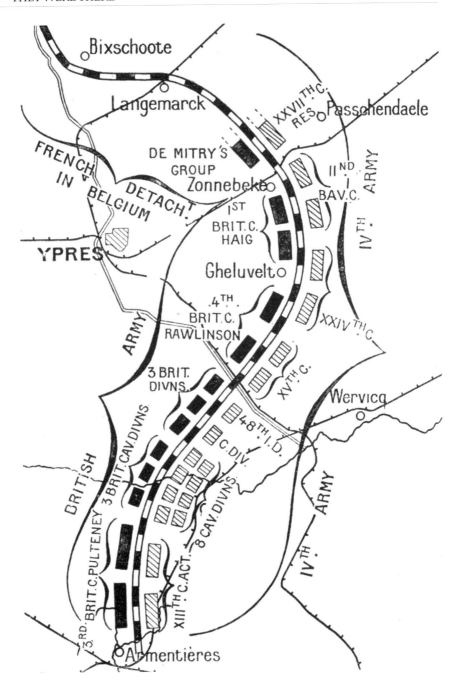

British positions in front of Ypres after 24 October, 1914, before the onslaught on Gheluvelt.

that the Staffordshires headquarters had made themselves extremely comfortable in a very big bomb-proof, which one approached by going down several steps. The colonel told me that his pioneer sergeant was a coalminer, and I at once recognized the pitman's work by the way in which the roof and the bomb-proof had been 'propped'. I had tea with them down there, and a cigarette, and was quite sorry to leave these comfortable and perfectly safe quarters for the perilous journey of returning to Zonnebeke.

I had scarcely left the Staffordshires' bomb-proof when a shrapnel shell burst just behind me and on my right, the pieces striking the ground some ten yards to my right. Ten seconds later the second shell of the pair arrived, and burst ten or twenty yards away to my left. Had I been ten yards more to the right, or more to the left, one or other would have got me. I had the same luck all the way back, shrapnel bursting all round, but none touching me. That night we again stayed in Zonnebeke, the guns being withdrawn at dusk.

All the next day (20 October) the Germans continued to shell our trenches. The loss among the infantry was very heavy, but the guns, being well concealed, and not having been located by the hostile aeroplanes, scarcely suffered at all. As usual, the batteries were withdrawn at nightfall, and went into billets round Frezenberg, some two miles west of Zonnebeke. Our headquarters were in a dirty little inn on the crossroads in Frezenberg. We occupied our old positions before dawn (21 October) and the battle continued. The Germans had, however, been very heavily reinforced and the attack was much heavier.

About midday the enemy began to bombard the town itself for some hours, but only with shrapnel. This did not do very much damage, but was very alarming, as the bullets from the shrapnel and pieces of the shells flew about the streets like hail. They were firing in bursts – that is to say, six shells arriving at a time. The air was thick with the flying lead, fragments of steel, slates from the roofs, glass and bricks. The noise was appalling: one could hardly hear oneself speak. One really wondered how anything could live in such an inferno, the more so as the main street of Zonnebeke was a prolongation of the German line of fire, and rifle bullets were continuously whining down the street.

About 3 o'clock in the afternoon the 'Black Marias' (high-explosive shells) started. Zonnebeke has a church standing in a small square, with a very high steeple, and evidently the German gunners, knowing that our headquarters were in the centre of the town, were using the church steeple as a target.

This bombardment in the streets of a town by high-explosive shells was, I think, the most alarming part of the experience. Everything in the town shook when one of those shells burst. The whole ground appeared to tromble as if in an earthquake even when the explosion was 100 yards away. About 5 o'clock news came down that Major Malony, who commanded the 104th Battery, in action near the level crossing, had been seriously wounded. He was observing from the infantry trenches some 800 yards in front of his guns and at the foot of the windmill by Zonnebeke Station. The medical officer at once went off to try to find a motor ambulance, and I rode up to the station.

The fire was so hot in the street that I decided to leave my horse *Bucephalus* under a large porch, and I continued my way to the windmill on foot, keeping close into the walls of the houses on the side from which the shells were coming. So long as the houses in the street were continuous, they afforded me complete protection from shrapnel or rifle bullets, and I was hit only by bricks and mortar from the walls of the houses; but as I neared the outskirts of the town the houses became detached one from another, and then it was very unpleasant having to cross the spaces between them. The shrapnel was bursting at intervals of ten or fifteen seconds, and it was impossible to judge when they would come. However, I found that by waiting until a shell had just burst, I usually had time to run like a hare to the next house. The rifle bullets, of course, could not be legislated for at all.

ONE IN TWELVE ALIVE

I eventually reached the windmill close to Malony's observation post. Here I found a young officer of, I think, the Queen's, who was sheltering under the mound of the windmill with some twenty men. He told me that he and his men were all that were left of a company of 250. He also told me that Malony had been dragged out of his trench and was lying behind a cottage on the other side of the road. On reaching this, I found that he had already been moved back towards his battery. I could see him being carried on a stretcher. He was now under, cover from rifle-fire and it was much better to let them continue across the 800 yards intervening between where he was hit and the battery, than to take him all the way round through the streets of the town, which were being heavily shelled. I therefore started back down the street towards where I had left my horse, and was met by the motor ambulance which the doctor had sent up. I stopped it, made the man turn round and got in beside him,

telling him to drop me when we passed my horse. The motor was a Daimler with the well-known scuttle-dash. I sat on the floor and stuck my head well under cover of the dash. I thought that if I was going to be hit I might as well avoid getting it in the head.

In spite of the shells bursting in front and behind us the ambulance was not hit, and the driver certainly exceeded the speed limit. I found *Bucephalus* happily munching some hay, and re-mounted him. I sent the ambulance on to the level-crossing.

By this time the Germans had got the range of the church accurately; the open place I had to cross was thick with white smoke from bursting shrapnel. I never expected to cross it alive. The street was paved with round cobbles and covered with slimy mud – a place, under ordinary circum-stances, I should have hesitated along at a walk. However, on this occasion we negotiated it, including a right-angle corner, at as fast a gallop as poor old *Bucephalus* was capable of, and regained the cover of the narrow streets untouched.

I found the ambulance at the level-crossing, and took it up to the farm, where we were joined by the medical officer. Malony had just arrived at the farm and was lying on some straw in the kitchen, with several other wounded men. At first I thought

The early months of the war the many windmills dotting the plains of Flanders became observation posts, field dressing stations and machine gun emplacements. These easy targets were progressively reduced to piles of blasted rubble.

he was dead, the bullet having struck him on the side of the head and apparently had passed through the brain. He had been looking through his range director when hit. He was breathing very heavily and the doctor thought he was in a very bad way. I was, however, able to tell him that only an hour or two before, Malony had told me that he had a bad attack of asthma, and this probably accounted for the breathing.

We got him into the motor ambulance and sent him off to Ypres. The doctor and I trotted along the road leading from the farm to the main road, immediately behind the ambulance.

It was now just dark. The wagon-line of Malony's battery was in a field beside us. The battery had not been shelled all day, but suddenly a single shrapnel burst twenty feet above our heads in the darkness. It must have been a chance shot. The ambulance put on speed and the doctor and I galloped after it. At the time we had no idea that the shell had done any damage. However, the next morning, we heard that it had flattened out two complete teams. Our infantry were all this time being subjected to appalling fire both by shrapnel and 'Black Marias', the trenches in many parts being completely blown in, and the men in them buried. They dug out as many as they could, but when the cover was gone the survivors were exposed to view, and as nothing can live under fire unless

British infantry moving through unspoiled fields in Flanders, 1914.

entrenched, I fear that many of the men were buried alive.

By nightfall it was obvious to General Lawford that our position was becoming untenable, and it was decided to withdraw as soon as it was dark.

By this time we had no supports, the supports and reserves having long ago been sent up into the trenches. Even the General's own headquarter guard had gone up, too. The only men available were some belonging to a company of the Royal Engineers. These hastily threw up a little shelter trench at the level crossing, and if the worst came to the worst we hoped to be able to hold the crossing until the remains of the infantry got through.

Unfortunately, we had no position prepared in the rear, and it seemed quite likely that we should have no chance of digging in at a fresh place. The same thing had been happening on our right, and the other brigades were compelled to withdraw also. The remains of the brigades evacuated their trenches and retired in the course of the night in good order and without confusion.

At dawn the next morning (22 October) we took up a position extending roughly from the level-crossing west of Zonnebeke to the V of Veldhoek. This line, unfortunately, passed through a thick wood, and it was in this wood that on succeeding days our losses were most heavy.

The previous afternoon we had been much bothered by spies, who adopted every possible sort of trick to communicate with the enemy. At

one time it was noticed that the arms of a certain windmill were turning in a most erratic manner. The windmill was deserted, the sails furled, and there was apparently no one in it. It was, therefore, quite clear that someone was playing with it; and by the time we reached the windmill the spies had got away. We blew it up next day.

MOST DANGEROUS SPY HUNT

We also suspected that the Germans had adopted their usual trick, when evacuating a town, of leaving men behind, concealed usually in the cellars of the houses, with a telephone. General Lawford instructed me to go with the provost-sergeant and search the houses for spies. This was as unpleasant a task as one could well hope to perform.

By now the eastern part of the town, where I was searching, was being subjected to a heavy and continuous shrapnel fire. The street was also enfiladed by rifle fire. All the doors had been locked by their owners before leaving the town, and I think that this part of Belgium must make a peculiarly strong form of locks and bolts; never would I have believed it would have been so difficult to break in doors.

However, at last we found a forge, and in it a large bar of iron, so heavy that it was as much as two men could do to carry it. Our task now became quite easy. The sergeant and I would take up our positions, revolver in hand, on each side of the door, while two men charged across the street with the heavy bar of iron. One blow was almost invariably enough. The bar and its carriers would collapse on the pavement, while the sergeant and I rushed in.

We searched dozens of houses in this manner, but found them all empty. However, we came to one house where, on rushing in, we were met by a man in plain clothes with a rifle, who immediately fired and shot the provost-sergeant practically through the heart. He did not live many minutes, but our assailant did not survive to see the result of his treachery.

By now the roofs of the houses were coming in, and I withdrew my search-party to brigade headquarters and reported to General Lawford that I did not consider it possible to continue a house-to-house search until the fire moderated. He approved of my action and ordered the search to be discontinued.

The enemy captured Zonnebeke immediately after we left, but fortunately did not press their attack.

12-23 October, 1914

CABARET OF DEATH
Shelled by Friend and Foe

by Captain E. J. Needham

Captain Needham, of the Northamptonshire Regiment recounts a day and night of fierce fighting in the neighbourhood of the Kortekeer cabaret and of Langemarck and Poelcappelle. In October 1914 these villages still retained their red roofs and church steeples, but would later became mangled and unrecognizable.

I found the battalion lining a railway embankment about a quarter of a mile away out of the village of Langemarck. I asked what had happened, and was told that the Germans had attacked 1 Brigade, who were holding the line in front of the road running between Langemarck and Steenstraat, and the line to their left, which was held by dismounted French cavalry. These latter, having no entrenching tools of any description, had been unable to 'dig themselves in' and were soon driven out of their line.

German infantry attacking in the Autumn of 1914.

The Huns had occupied this and had enfiladed the left of 1 Brigade line, held by the Cameron Highlanders, who, in their turn, were driven out of their trenches. Heavy fighting in this neighbourhood was still going on.

We stayed on the railway bank for about an hour and then got orders to return to Pilckem, but to hold ourselves in readiness to move at very short notice. We marched back, and just as we arrived at the village the head of the battalion halted. We could see the brigade commander, General Bulfin, and his brigade-major in conversation with the colonel. Presently the colonel rode back to us and told us we had to return immediately and take back the trenches lost by the Camerons. C Company was to lead the way, and I was told, not at all to my satisfaction, that I was to go ahead with the 'point' of the advance guard, taking every possible precaution, as nobody knew just where the line was; just where the Camerons were; or indeed the enemy. It was now pitch dark; in fact, one of the darkest nights I have ever known in my life. It was impossible to see more than a yard in front. I think that for the next half hour or so I was more thoroughly frightened than at any other time during the war. Moving up a lane in the inky darkness, not knowing where one was going to, but only that somewhere ahead were the enemy, waiting for us. We moved along the ditches on each side of the road so as not to give away our advance by the sound of our feet tramping along the hard surface of the lane. After going about two kilometres, suddenly from the left-hand side of the road came a loud

A French infantryman on sentry duty, Autumn 1914.

'*Halte ! Qui va la?*'

As soon as I had recovered from the shock of this sudden challenge in the dark I called back,

'*Amis, anglais.*'

'*Passez vous, mes amis,*' called back the French sentry, who I could just make out was standing outside a small cottage. On we went, thankful to have been challenged instead of shot at first and challenged afterwards.

THE GERMANS WERE VERY NEAR

After another two kilometres or so we heard footsteps coming down the road. I promptly halted my men and passed the word back to halt the rest of the advance guard and main body, and waited till the footsteps sounded quite close. Then I called out,

'Halt! Who goes there?'

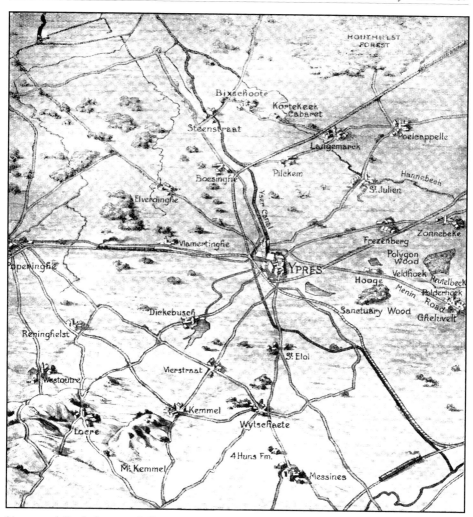

Ypres and the infamous Salient as it was in 1914 This sketch map shows the
country round Ypres as it was when the first battle of Ypres was fought
between 19 October and 22 November, 1914. It is impossible to indicate the
exact position occupied by the British Army, for the line was still fluid and
varied from day to day as the enemy made a succession of thrusts in an effort
to break through. The position did not become stabilized until after the Second
Battle of Ypres in April and May 1915.

A voice answered,

'Medical officer, Cameron Highlanders, with Captain Cameron, badly
wounded.'

'Who are you?'

I told him, and asked where the Camerons were and also the Germans.
He told me that about a kilometre farther on was a cross-road, and that if

British Army transport moving along the Menin Road in the Autumn of 1914.

we turned to the left there we should find the remnants of the Camerons about eight hundred yards up that road, and that the Germans were about four hundred yards beyond them again. I thanked him and on we went again.

Presently we heard the rumble and rattle of horse transport to our right, and shortly afterwards we reached the crossroads; and there, just arrived at them, was a whole lot of horse transport. I asked them who they were, and they replied they were 1 Brigade First Line Transport. I asked if they were aware that the Germans were only about a thousand yards away, and they said they had not the slightest idea of it. I told them they had better stay where they were and keep as quiet as possible until our colonel came up, and then ask him for orders. They were very lucky to arrive there just when they did and when we did, for otherwise they would have ridden right into the Germans, or, at any rate, to within a few hundred yards of them, and they must have been heard and fired upon with disastrous results, as the lane was much too narrow for them to have turned round and retired.

We marched on once more, still keeping to the ditches at the side of the road, and some minutes later we were suddenly challenged again – in a

very Scotch accent. This proved to be the sentry over the Camerons' headquarters – a farmhouse, in and around which were the remains of that battalion. I told him who we were and asked for an officer. One soon appeared, and told me that we must keep very quiet, as the enemy were quite close by, along a road running at right angles to the one we were on, about three or four hundred yards ahead. This officer went down the road to speak to Colonel Osborne Smith and to tell him the situation. In the meantime, we stayed where we were.

Very shortly afterwards we heard loud shouting, cheering and singing in front of us, which we gathered was the merry Hun disporting himself after his victory of the afternoon. After waiting about half an hour, Bentley (a company commander) came up to me and said that C Company were to extend across the field to the right of the road, advance towards the enemy and drive them out of their position, with D Company on our right. Shortly afterwards the rest of the company came filing up the ditch and then out to the right across the fields. They were followed by D Company, who carried out the same manoeuvre. Presently the word was passed down from the right for both companies to advance, and off we went, stumbling over turnips, trying to keep touch with the man on our right and left, and utterly unable to see anything.

Suddenly heavy firing broke out on our right and we heard cries of alarm, accompanied apparently by much guttural cursing, to our front. A few bullets started to come our way, so we lay down and fired five rounds rapid into the darkness to our immediate front and then charged, yelling at the tops of our voices. We arrived at the road to find the enemy gone, and promptly started to dig ourselves in as hard as we could. After a while, Bentley came along, and sent me back to try to find one platoon which had got lost in the dark. I wandered off, edging away to my right, and presently came to the lane we had left, in the ditch of which I found about half a company of Coldstream Guards.

During all this time, heavy fighting was going on on our right, where D Company were attacking a mill, in which were some German machine gunners. Just about the time Russell (a fellow subaltern) and I reached our line, the mill was captured and our machine guns were installed in place of the Germans' MG. Things now quieted down, and we were able to dig in peace. I spent the whole night walking up and down our line, very cold and very hungry. We had all gone supperless as we had moved out of Pilckem too early, and it was quite impossible for the cookers to come up anywhere near us, and even if they had, it would have been impossible for carrying parties to find our line in the intense darkness.

Just before dawn we were able to make out a small cottage immediately in front of C Company's line. We sent out a patrol under a sergeant to find out if it was occupied, and they presently returned to say they had found the dead body of a man, stark naked, but from his identity disk round his neck, a private in the Cameron Highlanders. The Huns had evidently made off with his kit and accoutrements, and no doubt some Hun had a wonderful souvenir to send home in the shape of the unfortunate man's kilt. We 'stood-to' for about a quarter of an hour and then C Company was ordered to occupy some trenches to our right front, about one hundred and fifty yards in front of the road which the Camerons had been driven out of the evening before. Just before we stood-to, a terrific outbreak of firing on our left broke out. I must explain that at the junction of the lane by which we had come up from Pilckem, and the Langemarck-Bixschoote road on which we now were stood an inn called the 'Kortokeok Kabaret' [sic] and this was strongly held by the enemy.

On the side of the road on which we had spent the night, and about four hundred yards east of the inn, stood the mill which D Company had attacked and captured during the night. This outbreak of firing heralded a strong attack by A Company, in conjunction with some of the Camerons, on the inn, which was successful in so far as they got right up to the inn, but the opposition was too strong for them, the Germans having a large number of men and many machine guns in it, so that our troops had to retire with heavy losses.

Shortly after C Company had moved without loss or trouble to its new position, the terrible news came along to us that poor old Russell had been killed in this attack. I was frightfully cut up about this, Russell having been one of my best friends in the old days at the Depot. He was one of the nicest fellows I have ever known.

CURSING OUR OWN GUNNERS

We all got busy trying to improve our new so-called trenches, which were really nothing more than a narrow ditch about two foot wide and a yard deep. We were now immediately in front of the mill, and very shortly after we took up our position – to our horror our guns started to shell it.

We sent back messages to battalion headquarters to ask them to let the gunners know that we were in front of the mill, but the shelling continued and presently the Germans started to shell it too.

So now we were in a lovely predicament: we were collecting all the

German 'shorts' and 'overs' from our own gunners and could not do anything but lie at the bottom of the ditch shivering and cursing with fear and rage, and sending back messages at intervals to try to get our gunners to give their attention elsewhere, where it was more needed. This double shelling continued off and on the whole day and we had several casualties from it.

About 9 or 10 o'clock the Queen's came up and, advancing through the Camerons and the remains of A Company, attacked the inn, with the 60th and Loyal North Lancashires attacking on their left. This time the attack was successful, the inn being captured together with about three hundred Germans, many more of them being killed. After this the morning dragged on, fine but coldish.

The mill continued to be bombarded by both sides and heavy firing was going on to our right all the time, where 1 Brigade was heavily engaged. In front of C Company the ground, a field of roots, sloped away down to the little stream of the Hannebeek, the banks of which were clearly defined by pollarded willows. Behind this stream again the ground sloped upwards gradually to a small wood stretching along a low ridge.

The stream was about three hundred and fifty yards in front of us, and the wood another four hundred yards behind that again. To our right front and about a mile away stood the church and red-roofed houses of Langemarck, and beyond that again and about the same distance away from it, the church and roofs of Poelcappelle.

No food had come up to us during the morning, not even our usual tea and rum, and we had to fall back on our iron rations of bully beef and

British artillery during the fighting east of Ypres October 1914.

biscuits. About 1 pm we could see large bodies of Germans collecting in the wood on the ridge opposite, and 'Jumbo' Bentley and I knelt up in our ditch so as to be able to see better what they were up to, and we both scanned the wood closely through our field-glasses.

Suddenly I felt a terrific blow on my right arm, just as If somebody had hit me on the funnybone as hard as he could with a sledge-hammer. It spun me round like a top and I collapsed in the bottom of the trench. The man next to me rolled over and said, 'You ain't 'alf bloody well got 'it in the 'and, sir, ' and on looking down I saw that my right hand was a mass of blood.

My arm still felt numb from the blow, and I could hardly realize that it was my hand that was hit, as it did not hurt at all. However, this man cut my field dressing out of my tunic, and after dousing my hand with iodine, which did hurt, he bound it up very well; he then made a sling out of my woollen scarf which I was wearing, insisted on giving me one of his own cigarettes and lighting it for me, and told me not to worry, I was 'for "Blighty" all right with that packet'. This sounded too good to be true, and I felt distinctly better.

He also said, and I then realized it for the first time, that I had been very lucky not to be killed, as I had my field-glasses up to my eyes and the bullet which had hit my right hand would have got me in the head if it had been one inch farther to the left. He told me my right collar badge was badly dented and the bullet must have hit this after hitting my hand. About five minutes after I was hit, a man two yards away from me on the left was kneeling up looking out towards the Germans when he was shot straight through the head. We came to the conclusion that there must be snipers lying in one of the pollarded willows by the stream, about three hundred and fifty yards in front of us, and that they must be pretty hot shots.

Anyhow, Bentley gave orders that no man was to expose himself from now onwards unless we were attacked.

All this time shells from both sides kept dropping all around the unfortunate mill, which was now on fire in several places. I suppose it was the after-effects of the shock of being hit, but anyhow my nerve went completely. I lay in the bottom of the trench expecting the Huns to come over and wipe me out, lying defenceless there. Or I began to panic that instead of going home with a nice wound, a shell would land in the trench and blow me up.

I SWEATED WITH FUNK

The farther the afternoon drew on, the worse my nerves got. It was impossible with that damned sniper in front to get out of the ditch and walk away over the open to find the dressing-station; the only thing to do was to lie where I was until night-fall, and then to make a bolt for it, and pray that the Hun did not attack us before that.

German sniper with his eye on British officers and NCOs.

About four o'clock we could hear much singing and cheering from the enemy's direction, and this continued for the next two hours. This did not cheer me up, as we all decided that it was the Hun cheering himself up before making an attack upon us. At last it started to get dark, and, at six o'clock, I said good-bye to Bentley, wished him all the best of luck in the world and, scrambling out of the ditch, ran across to the road behind us, where I found Cartwright and D Company in the ditch. I stopped for a minute to tell him what had happened to me, then said good-bye and bolted round the back of the mill on a short cut for where Cartwright told me battalion headquarters was, on the lane running to Pilckem.

The man who had bound up my hand insisted on coming back with me and carrying my pack and equipment. As we passed the mill the whole of the top of it fell in, and a huge column of smoke and flame shot up to the skies, illuminating the ground all around over a very big area and, of course, silhouetting us both clearly. Never before or since in my life have I run so fast. It seemed miles to the road, but at last we arrived there blowing and wheezing, and hurled ourselves into the ditch.

I found the colonel and Guy Robinson, reported myself wounded, and was most kindly spoken to by the colonel, who wished me the best of luck and was kind enough to say he should miss me very much. They were both most kind and considerate and told me I should find the dressing-station in the cottage along the lane where the French sentry had challenged us the night before.

While we were talking a terrific outburst of gun- and rifle-fire from the

Germans broke out all along the line, and was at once answered by our men. Shells started to burst all round, and spent bullets to ping their way past. The colonel told me I had better be off as quickly as I could go, as the Germans were evidently going to attack, so I said good-bye to them both and, accompanied by my faithful volunteer batman, fairly legged it down the lane and on we ran, expecting every minute to be our last, as shells were bursting all round, but at last we got to the crossroads, where we had stopped the transport of 1 Brigade the night before and, turning to the right, found ourselves out of the zone of fire. We arrived at the cottage and I went in, saw an open door on the left of the entrance passage where a medical officer attending to a wounded man. I told him my regiment, and that I was wounded, and asked him if Captain Lochrin, our M.O., was about. 'Oh, yes,' he said, 'you will find him in the room opposite.' I thanked him, crossed the passage and opened the door opposite. On going inside I found, to my horror, poor Lochrin stretched out on his back on the floor, dead. To this day I cannot imagine why the M.O., who must have known that he was dead, ever let me, wounded as I was, walk in on all that was left of poor Lochrin like that. It gave me an awful shock, and I fairly bolted out of the place and down the lane. We passed some Tommies at the entrance to the village and asked them if there was another dressing-station there, and they told us there was another in the village school.

We found this. Inside the schoolroom the floor was strewn with straw, and in the middle of it were two deal tables on trestles. On these were laid various badly wounded men being attended to by the doctors, who were working in their shirt-sleeves. All round the tables on the straw-covered floor lay wounded men. The room was stacked with them. An orderly found me a corner somewhere, and I lay down, feeling completely exhausted after all the panic, shocks, and excitements of the afternoon.

I lay there from about 7.15 pm till 10.30 pm. The whole time wounded men were being taken out and fresh wounded were coming in, and operations, including amputations of legs and arms, were being performed on the trestle tables. How different from the cleanliness and orderly organization and discipline of the operating theatre in a hospital was the scene in that schoolroom. On the walls, maps and pictures of animals and birds; easels and blackboards along the walls; at the tables stood R.A.M.C. orderlies holding candles stuck into wine bottles to light the shirt-sleeved surgeons at their task.

They worked quickly, noiselessly and efficiently, without fuss or bother about the awful conditions for such work; they were so kind and gentle to the unfortunate men on whom they worked, most of whom were in terrible agony.

31 October, 1914

STOPPING THE PRUSSIANS
The Day the War was Nearly Lost

by Private. H.J. Polley

The date 31 October, 1914, has been called by some the most critical day of the whole war. It was the day the Germans came within an ace of breaking the thin British line and smashing their way through to the Channel ports. The capture of these would have added immeasurably to the difficulties of the Allies. Private Polley, of the 2nd Battaliion, Bedfordshire Regiment, tells of his experience at that time. First there was the excitement of advance, then followed by the grim hours of defence.

The Germans tried to hack their way through to Calais, they were at first held and then hurled back. I am going to tell you something of the way in which this was done, for I belonged to the Bedfordshire Regiment, the old 16th Foot, and the Bedfords were part of the Glorious Seventh Division, and did their share in keeping back the German forces, which included the Prussian Guards, who at this time were being rushed up to this sector because it was thought that no troops could stand against them.

These idols of the German nation were picked men and brave fellows, and at that time had an absolute belief in their own invincibility; but events proved that they were no match for the British Guards and the rest of the British troops who fought them at Ypres.

For later these Prussian Guards from Berlin were literally mown down by our artillery, machine-gun and rifle fire, and were left lying dead in solid masses – walls of corpses. The Kaiser had planned to enter Ypres as a conqueror, at the head of his Guards; but he hurried off a beaten man, leaving his slaughtered Guards in heaps.

Originally in the 1st Battalion of the Bedfords, I later went into the 2nd, and I was serving with the 2nd in

A Prussian Guardsman – considered to be the élite of the German Army sweeping through Belgium in 1914.

South Africa when the European War broke out. It is an interesting fact that nearly all the battalions which formed the Seventh Division came from foreign service – India, Egypt, Africa and elsewhere – which meant that many of the men of the Seventh had seen active service and were veteran fighters. They had not learned their warfare at peace manoeuvres in England.

Our division consisted of the 1st Grenadier Guards, the 2nd Scots Guards, the 2nd Border, 2nd Gordon Highlanders, 2nd Bedfordshire, 2nd Yorkshire, 2nd Royal Scots Fusiliers, 2nd Wiltshire, 2nd Royal West Surrey, 2nd Royal Warwickshire, 1st Royal Welch Fusiliers, 1st South Staffordshire, and the Northumberland Hussars; and we had a pom-pom detachment and horse, field, and garrison artillery. We were under Major-General Sir T. Capper, D.S.O.

Major-General Sir Thompson Capper.

We had been sent to help the Naval Division at Antwerp, and early in October we landed at Zeebrugge – the only division to land at that port. But we were not there long, for we soon learned that we were too late, and that Antwerp had fallen. We were sorry, but there was no time for moping, and we were quickly on the move to the quaint old city of Bruges, where we were billeted for a night. Sir Harry Rawlinson had moved his headquarters from Bruges to Ostend, so next day we marched towards Ostend and took up outpost. Then we had a forced march back to Bruges, and from Bruges we started marching, but we did not know where we were going till we got to the city of Ypres.

So far we had not done any fighting.

We had been marching and marching, first to one place, then to another, constantly expecting to come into action, and very nearly doing so, for the Germans were swarming all over the countryside. We had to be content with being on outpost and guarding bridges, and so on – hard and necessary work, we knew; but we wanted something more thrilling, something bigger – and we eventually got it. There was practically only the Seventh Division available for anything that turned up. The Northumberland Hussars were able to give a very good account of themselves, and were, I believe, the first Yeomanry corps to go into action.

The few Uhlans I saw while I was at the Front had been taken prisoners by these Hussars, who brought them in, lances and all. But there is very little to say about cavalry work; it was mostly a matter for the infantry, and, of course, the artillery. While we were around Ypres, waiting for the Germans to come and break through, we heard a good deal, indirectly, of what was going to happen to us and to England.

The marketplace of Thielt, north east of Ypres, Belgium. The 2nd Battalion Scots Guards pack the square, 12 October 1914.

The Germans had all sorts of monster guns, and with these they were going to bombard England across the narrow Channel when they got to the French coast, and they were going to work all sorts of miracles with their airships and aeroplanes. We soon heard, too, that the Kaiser himself was in the field; but the only effect of that information was to make us more keen to show what we could do. Truth to tell, we were far from being impressed by the presence of either the Kaiser or his vaunted Guards. We were in the best of spirits, and had a sublime belief in Sir John French and all his staff and our own officers.

It was on October 31 – which has been called the decisive day of the fight for Ypres, and which was certainly a most terrible day in every way –

that the Seventh Division was ordered to attack the German position.

The weather was very fine, clear and sunny, and our spirits were in keeping with it. We were thankful to be on the move because we had had nearly three weeks in the trenches, and had been billeted in all sorts of queer places – above and below ground – under an everlasting shell fire, which became unendurable and was thoroughly nerve-destroying.

We knew what a desperate business the advance would be, because the Germans greatly outnumbered us, and they had planted vast numbers of guns. They had immense bodies of men in trenches, and in a large number of the houses and buildings which commanded the ground over which we had to advance, they had placed machine guns, with their villainous muzzles directed on us from bedroom windows and holes which had been knocked in walls.

A MOST TERRIBLE BUSINESS

From start to finish the advance was a terrible business – far more terrible than any words of mine can make you realize. The whole division was on the move, stretching along a big tract of country; but of course no man could see much of what was happening, except in his own immediate locality. Neither had he much chance of thinking about anything or anybody except himself, and then only in a numbed sort of way, because of the appalling din of the artillery on both sides, the crash of the guns and the explosions of the shells, with the ceaseless rattle of the rifles and the machine guns.

British infantry of the 7th Division on the march seen here consulting maps to determine where they are and where they are heading.

At the beginning the regiments kept fairly well together, but very soon we were all mixed up, and you could not tell what regiment a man belonged to, unless he wore a kilt; then you knew that, at any rate, he wasn't a Bedford.

Some of us had our packs and full equipment. Others were without packs, having been compelled to throw them away. But there was not a man who had let his rifle go: that is the last thing of all to be parted from, it is the soldier's very life. And every man had a big supply of ammunition, with plenty in reserve.

The General himself took part in the advance, and what he did was done by every other officer present. There was no difference between officer and man, and a thing to be specially noted was the fact that the officers got hold of rifles and blazed away as hard as any private soldier.

Never, during the whole of the war, had there been a more awful fire than that which we gave the Germans. Whenever we got the chance, we gave them what they call the 'Englishman's mad minute' – that is, the dreadful fifteen rounds a minute rapid fire. We drove it into them and mowed them down. Many a soldier, when his own rifle was too hot to hold, threw it down and snatched the rifle of a dead or wounded comrade who had no further use for it, and with this fresh, cool weapon he continued the deadly work by which success could alone be won. I do not know what the German losses were, but I do know that I saw bodies lying around in solid masses, while we passed our own dead and wounded everywhere as we advanced. Where they fell they had to stay; it was impossible to do anything for them while the fighting continued.

The whole of the advance consisted of a series of what might be called ups and downs – a little rush, then a 'bob down'. At most, no one rush carried us more than fifty yards; then we dropped out of sight as best we could, to get a breather and prepare for another dash. It was pretty open country, so that we were fully exposed to the German artillery and rifle fire, in addition to the hail from the machine guns in the neighbouring buildings. Here and there we found little woods and clumps of trees and bits of rising ground and ditches and hedges – and you may take it from me, that shelter of any sort was very welcome and freely used.

A remarkable feature of this striving to hide from the enemy's fire was that it was almost impossible to escape from the shells and bullets for any appreciable time, for the simple reason that the Germans altered their range in the most wonderful manner. So surely as we got the shelter of a little wood or ditch, they seemed to have the distance almost instantly, and the range was so accurate that many a copse and ditch became a little graveyard in the course of that advance.

At one point as we went along I noticed a small ditch against a hedge. It was a dirty, uninviting ditch, deep in water ; but it seemed to offer promising shelter, and so some officers and men made a rush for it,

Reconnaissance force of the 2nd Scots Guards, October 1914.

German infantry and artillery moving up into the Ypres sector.

meaning to take cover. They had no sooner scrambled into the ditch and were thinking themselves comparatively safe than the Germans got the range of them with machine guns, and nearly the whole lot were annihilated. In this case, as in others, the enemy had been marvellously quick with their weapons, and had swept the ditch with bullets. I don't know what happened to the fine fellows who had fallen. We had to leave them and continue the advance.

The forenoon passed, noon came, and the afternoon was with us; still the fighting went on, the guns on both sides crashing without cessation, and the machine guns and the rifles rattling on without a break. The air was filled with screaming, bursting shells and whistling bullets, and the ground was ploughed and torn everywhere. It was horrible beyond expression, yet it fired the blood in us, so that the only thing that mattered was to put the finish to the work, get up to the Germans, and rout them out of their positions.

At last, after endless spells of lying down and jumping up, we got near enough to make it possible to charge, and the order went round to get ready. We saw what big, fine fellows we had to tackle. Clearly now we could distinguish the enemy infantry, and a thing that particularly struck me just then was that their bayonets looked very cruel. The Germans wore cloth-covered brass helmets, and through the cloth we could see the gleam

A group of Prussian infantry pause for a photograph during the advance.

of the brass in the sunshine. The nearer we got, the more clearly we saw what splendid chaps they were, and what a desperate business it would be when we actually reached the long, snaky blades of steel – much longer than our own bayonets – with longer rifles, too, so that the Germans had the pull of us in every way. But all that counted as nothing, and there was not a man amongst us who was not hungering to be in amongst them.

The order to fix bayonets came quietly, and was carried out without any fuss, just as a part of the day's work. We were lying down when the order came, and as we lay we got round to our bayonets, drew them and fixed them and I could hear the rattle of the fixing all along the line, just as I had heard it many times on parade or at manoeuvres – the same sound, but

now – with what a different purpose.

A few of the fellows did not fix their bayonets as we lay, but they managed to do it as we ran, when we had jumped up and started to rush along to put the finish to the fight. There was no bugle sound, we just got the word to charge, an order which was given to the entire Seventh Division.

When this last part of the advance arrived we started halloaing and shouting and the division simply hurled itself against the Prussian Guard. By the time we were up with the enemy we were mad. I can't tell you much of what actually happened – and I don't think any man who took part in it could do so – but I do know that we rushed helter-skelter, and that when we got up to the famous Guards there were only two of my own section holding together – Lance Corporal Perry and myself, and even we were parted immediately afterwards.

The next thing I clearly knew was that we were actually on the Prussians, and that there was some very fierce work going on. There was some terrific and deadly scrimmaging, and whatever the Prussian Guard did in the way of handling the steel, the Seventh Division did better.

It was every man for himself. I had rushed up with the rest, and the first thing I clearly knew was that a tremendous Prussian was making at me with his villainous bayonet. I made a lunge at him as hard and swift as I could, and he did the same to me. I thought I had him, but I just missed, and as I did so I saw his own long, ugly blade driven out at the end of his rifle. Before I could do anything to parry the thrust, the tip of the bayonet had ripped across my right thigh, and I honestly thought that it was all up with me.

Then, when I reckoned that my account was paid, when I supposed that the huge Prussian had it all his own way, one of our chaps – I don't know who, (I don't suppose I ever shall know, but I bless him) – rushed up and drove his bayonet into the Prussian and settled him. I am sure that if this had not been done I should have been killed by the Prussian; as it was, I was able to get away without much inconvenience at the end of the bayonet fight.

This struggle lasted about half an hour, and fierce, hard work it was all the time. In the end we drove the Guards away and sent them flying – all except those who had fallen; the trench was full of the latter, and we took no prisoners.

Then soon we were forced to retire ourselves, for the quite sufficient reason that we were not strong enough to hold the position that we had taken at such a heavy cost. The enemy did not know it then, though perhaps they found out later, that we had nicely deceived them in making them believe that we had reinforcements. But we had nothing of the sort; yet we had stormed and taken the position and driven its defenders away.

GROUND LITTERED WITH DEAD

We were far too weak to hold the position, and so we retired over the ground that we had won, getting back a great deal faster than we had advanced. We had spent the best part of the day in advancing and reaching the enemy's position; and it seemed as if we must have covered a great tract of country, but as a matter of fact we had advanced less than a mile. It had taken us many hours to cover that short distance, but along the whole of the long line of the advance the ground was littered with the fallen – the officers and men who had gone down under such a storm of shells and bullets as had not been known since the war began.

Retiring, we took up a position behind a wood, and were thinking that we should get a bit of a rest, when a German aeroplane came flying over us, gave our hiding-place away, and brought upon us a fire that drove us out and sent us back to three lines of trenches which we had been occupying.

We made the best of things during the evening and the night in the trenches. The next day things were reversed, for the Germans came on against us; but we kept up a furious fight, and simply mowed them down as they threw themselves upon us. We used to say 'Here comes another bunch of them!' and then we gave them the 'mad minute'. We had suffered heavily on the 31st, and we were to pay a big bill on this 1 November, amongst our casualties being two of our senior officers.

The second day of the fighting passed and the third came. Still we held on, but it became clear that we were too hopelessly outnumbered to hope for complete success at the time, and so we were forced to leave the trenches. Withdrawing again, we took up positions in farmhouses and woods and any other places that gave shelter. All the time there was a killing fire upon us, and it happened that entire bodies of men would be wiped out in a few moments. A party of the Warwicks got into a wood near us, and they had no sooner taken shelter than the German gunners got the range of them, shelled and killed nearly all of them.

There was not a regiment of the Glorious Seventh that had not suffered terribly in the advance during the three days' fateful fighting. The Bedfords had lost, all told, about 600, and it was a mere skeleton of the battalion that formed up when the roll was called.

I became a member of the grenade company of the battalion, which was something like going back to the early day of the Army, when the grenadier companies of the regiments flung their little bombs at the enemy. So did we, and grim work it was, hurling home-made bombs, which had the power of doing a terrible amount of mischief.

Improvising grenades from used food tins.

MERRY PARTY SPOILT

I was with the grenade company, behind a brick wall close to the trenches, and was sitting with several others round a fire which we had made in a biscuit-tin. We were quite a merry party, and had the dixie going to make some tea. There was another dixie on, with two or three nice chickens that our fellows had got hold of – perhaps they had seen them wandering about homeless and adopted them. Anyway, they found a good home in the stew-pot, and we were looking forward to a most cosy meal. The Germans were close enough to fling hand-bombs at us. They gave us lots of these little attentions, so that, when I suddenly found myself blinded, and felt a sharp pain in my left hand. I thought they had made a lucky shot, or that something had exploded in the fire in the biscuit-tin.

For some time I did not know what had happened; then I was able to see, and on looking at my hand, I found it to be in a sorry mess, half the thumb and half a finger having been carried away. I stayed and had some tea from the, dixie, and my chums badly wanted me to wait for my share of the chickens; but I had no appetite for fowls just then. I made the best of things till darkness came, and under cover of it a couple of stretcher-bearers took me to the nearest dressing-station.

I suffered terribly, and lockjaw set in, but the splendid medical staff and the nursing saved me, and I was put into a horse ambulance and packed off home.

31 October, 1914

THEY SAVED THE DAY AT GHELUVELT
The Worst half-hour for Field Marshal French

by Captain H. FitzM. Stacke, MC

A great gap was made in the British line when, on the morning of 31 October 1914, the Germans captured Gheluvelt. As a forlorn hope the 2nd Battalion the Worcestershire Regiment, almost all the available reserve of the whole British defence, were ordered to counter-attack and recapture the village. How three companies of the Worcesters, charging over open ground through a hail of fire, restored the British line at a time which Sir John French afterwards described as the worst half-hour of his life, is told by Captain H. FitzM. Stacke, MC, the historian of the Regiment.

Daybreak of 31 October was calm and clear. The 2nd Worcestershire, in its reserve position west of the Polygon Wood, was roused early by the crash of gun-fire. The troops turned out, breakfasts were cooked and eaten, weapons were cleaned and inspected. Then for several hours the companies lay idle about their billets, listening to the ever-increasing bombardment and

Field Marshal Sir John French, commander of the British Expeditionary Force.

watching the German shrapnel bursting in black puffs of smoke above the tree-tops.

The 2nd Worcesters were almost the last available reserve of the British defence. Nearly every other unit had been drawn into the battle-line or had been broken beyond recovery; and to an onlooker that last reserve would not have seemed very formidable. The battalion could muster not more than 500 men. Ten days of battle had left all ranks haggard, unshaven and unwashed; their uniforms had been soaked in the mud of the Langemarck trenches and torn by the brambles of Polygon Wood; many had lost their puttees or their caps. But their weapons were clean and in good order, they had plenty of ammunition, and three months of war had given them

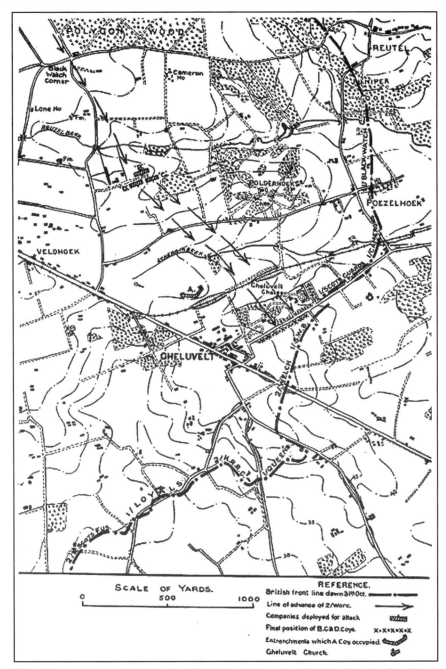

Line of counter-attack by the 2nd Battalion Worcestershire Regiment, showing the advance of the battalion from its reserve position west of Polygon Wood via Black Watch Corner to the area of the château at Gheluvelt.

confidence in their fighting power. The short period in reserve had allowed them sleep and food.

That crowd of ragged soldiers was still a fighting battalion, officers and men bound together by that proud and willing discipline which is the soul of the regiment.

Hour by hour the thunder of the guns grew more intense. Stragglers and wounded from beyond the wood brought news that a great German attack was in progress. The enemy infantry were coming on in overwhelming numbers [thirteen German battalions took part in this attack, of which six were fresh and at full strength] against the remnants of the five British battalions, together mustering barely a thousand men, which were holding the trenches about the Menin road.

Before midday weight of numbers had told. The Queen's and the Royal Scots Fusiliers had fought to the last, the Welsh and the King's Royal Rifle Corps had been overwhelmed; the right flank of the South Wales Borderers had been rolled back. Gheluvelt had been lost, and a great gap had been broken in the British line. Unless that gap could be closed, the British army was doomed to disaster. So serious was the situation caused by the loss of Gheluvelt that orders were issued for the British artillery to move back in preparation for a general retreat. At the same time it was decided that a counter-attack against the lost position should be made by the 2nd Battalion, Worcestershire Regiment.

Brigadier-General C. FitzClarence, VC, was in command of the front around the Menin road. Soon after midday he sent for the officers of the 2nd Worcestershire to take orders. Major Hankey sent his Adjutant, Captain B. C. Senhouse Clarke. Twenty minutes later Captain Senhouse Clarke returned, bringing word that the battalion would probably be wanted for a counter-attack, and that meanwhile one company was to be detached to prevent the enemy from advancing up the Menin road.

A Company was detailed for the latter duty. Led by Captain P. S. G. Wainman, the company advanced at 12.45 pm to a position on the embankment of the light railway north-west of Gheluvelt. The company held the embankment during the following two hours, firing rapidly at such of the enemy as attempted to advance beyond the houses.

Brigadier-General Charles FitzClarence, VC. He won his Victoria Cross at Mafeking, South Africa, in 1899.

At about 1 pm Major Hankey was summoned by General FitzClarence, and was given definite orders. The 2nd Worcestershire were to make a counter-attack to regain the lost British positions around Gheluvelt. General FitzClarence pointed out the church in Gheluvelt as a landmark for the advance, explained that the situation was desperate and that speed was essential. At 2 pm the battalion moved off in file, led by Major Hankey and Captain Thorne, along under cover of the trees to the south-west corner of Polygon Wood [less than two miles north of Gheluvelt].

From that corner of the wood the ground to the south-eastward is clear and open, falling to the little valley of the Rentelbeek and rising again to the bare ridge above Polderhoek. That ridge hid from view the château of Gheluvelt, and the exact situation there was unknown; but further to the right could be seen the church tower rising amid the smoke of the burning village.

The open ground was dotted with wounded and stragglers coming back from the front. In every direction German shells were bursting. British batteries could be seen limbering up and moving to the rear. Everywhere there were signs of retreat. The Worcestershire alone were moving towards the enemy. But the three companies tramped grimly forward down into the valley of the Reutelbeek.

Beyond a little wood the battalion deployed, C and D Companies in front line, with B Company in second line behind – about 370 men all told. In front of them rose the bare slope of the Polderhoek Ridge. The ridge was littered with dead and wounded, and along its crest the enemy's shells were bursting in rapid succession. Major Hankey decided that the only way of crossing that deadly stretch of ground was by one long rush. The companies extended into line and advanced.

The ground underfoot was rank grass of rough stubble. The two leading companies broke into a steady double and swept forward across the open, the officers leading on in front, and behind them their men with fixed bayonets in one long irregular line. As they reached the crest the rushing wave of bayonets was sighted by the hostile infantry beyond.

A storm of shells burst along the ridge, shrapnel bullets rained down and high-explosive shells crashed into the charging line. Men fell at every pace; over a hundred of the battalion were killed or wounded: the rest dashed on. The speed of the rush increased as on the downward slope the troops came in sight of Gheluvelt château close in front. The platoons scrambled across the light railway, through some hedges and wire fences, and then in the grounds of the château they closed with the enemy.

THEY GAVE WAY AT OUR CHARGE

The enemy was ill-prepared to meet the charge. The German infantry were crowded in disorder among the trees of the park, their attention divided between exploring the outhouses and surrounding the remnant of the British defenders; for the musketry of the defence still swept the lawn in front of the chateau. The enemy's disorder was increased by a sharp and

Gheluvelt château, with the lawns in front, where the hand-to-hand fighting took place.

accurate fire of shrapnel from British batteries behind Polygon Wood.

The Germans were young troops of newly formed units. Probably they had lost their best leaders earlier in the day, for they made no attempt to stand their ground and face the counter-attack. They gave way at once before the onslaught of the British battalion and crowded back out of the grounds of the château into the hedgerows behind. Shooting and stabbing, C Company of the Worcesters charged across the lawn and came up into line with the gallant remnant of the South Wales Borderers.

The South Wales Borderers had made a wonderful stand. All day they had held their ground at the château, and they were still stubbornly fighting, although almost surrounded by the enemy. Their resistance had delayed and diverted the German advance, and the success of the counter-attack was largely due to their brave defence.

The meeting of the two battalions was unexpected. The Worcesters had not known that any of the South Wales Borderers were still holding out. Major Hankey went over to their commander, and found him to be Colonel H. E. Burleigh Leach, an old friend.

'My God, fancy meeting you here' said Major Hankey, and Colonel Burleigh Leach replied quietly, 'Thank God, you have come.'

The routed enemy were hunted out of the hedges and across the open fields beyond the château. C and D

Major E. B. Hankey.

Companies of the Worcestershire took up positions in the sunken road which runs past the grounds. B Company was brought up and prolonged the line to the right. But the village of Gheluvelt, on the slope above the right flank, was still in the enemy's hands. Most of the German troops in the village seem to have been drawn northwards by the fighting around the château, but a certain number of Saxons of the 242nd Regiment had remained in the village, where they opened a fire which took the sunken road in enfilade. To silence that fire Major Hankey sent fighting patrols from the front line into the village. Those patrols drove back the German snipers and took some prisoners; but it became clear that the position in the sunken road would be unsafe until the village was secured. Accordingly, Major Hankey sent orders to Captain Wainman that A Company were to advance from their defensive position and occupy the village.

Captain Wainman led forward his company and, after some sharp fighting among burning buildings and bursting shells, occupied a new line with his left flank in touch with the right of the position in the sunken road and his right flank in the village, holding the church and the churchyard. From there he sent forward patrols to clear the village.

It was not possible permanently to occupy the centre of the village, for it was being bombarded by both the German and the British artillery. On all sides houses were burning, roofs falling and walls collapsing. The stubborn Saxons still held some small posts in scattered houses of the south-eastern outskirts. Nevertheless, the enemy's main force had been driven out, and the peril of a collapse of the British defence about the Menin road had been averted.

About 6 pm came fresh orders from General FitzClarence. The General had decided to withdraw his defensive line from the forward slope of the ridge at Gheluvelt to a new position farther back at Veldhoek, where the trenches would be sheltered from direct observation of the German artillery.

Arrangements were made in conjunction with the South Wales Borderers, and the retirement was begun. One by one, at intervals of ten minutes, the companies withdrew from their positions. In the darkness they assembled under cover and then tramped back along the Menin road to Veldhoek. As the last company of the 2nd Worcesters marched back out of the village, several of the houses were still burning, and the darkness was torn at intervals by the blaze of bursting shells.

The day's fighting had cost the 2nd Worcesters a third of the Battalion's remaining strength, for 187 of all ranks had been killed or wounded. Their counter attack had thrown back the enemy at a moment which the British Commander-in Chief afterwards called 'the worst half-hour of my life'. In all probability that counter attack saved Ypres from capture and the British army from possible defeat.

31 October – 1 November, 1914

LONDON SCOTTISH BEFORE MESSINES
A Territorial Battalion and its near anihilation

by Private Herbert de Hamel

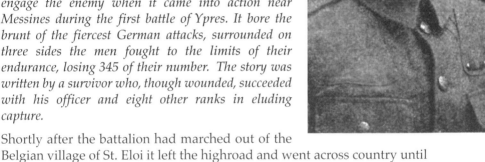

1/14th (County of London) Battalion (London Scottish) was the first infantry Territorial battalion to engage the enemy when it came into action near Messines during the first battle of Ypres. It bore the brunt of the fiercest German attacks, surrounded on three sides the men fought to the limits of their endurance, losing 345 of their number. The story was written by a survivor who, though wounded, succeeded with his officer and eight other ranks in eluding capture.

Shortly after the battalion had marched out of the Belgian village of St. Eloi it left the highroad and went across country until it reached a long, low-lying hill, with its steep side covered with trees, bracken and brambles. Here we halted and were told to lie down. The air was full of a drowsy rumbling and muttering of guns. The sound was a

Pipers of the London Scottish Battalion marching past Buckingham Palace, September 1914.

London Scottish soldiers marching to Watford Station, 15 September, on their way to the fighting in France.

Now in France, these men of the London Scottish having a bite to eat.

distant one, but full of a strange uneasiness. Personally, I found myself wishing that it were either a long way farther off, or a long way nearer.

I rolled over and went to sleep. I was awakened by my right ankle sliding down the slope, followed by the rest of my anatomy. The banging of the guns sounded far closer. I don't know if I had been dreaming of Germans, but I was by no means sorry to hear a cheery voice cry, 'Wake up, old son, we're falling in'. We marched down a grassy road between trees stripped of their bark and with their trunks strangely fluted and grooved by bullets. Then on past a prosperous-looking farm tenanted by incongruously ragged folk who reaped a harvest of discarded articles at our next halt.

From this a German aeroplane drove us to the cover of a wood. No sooner had I settled down for another sleep than we were off again, followed by the aeroplane, till we reached the village of Wytschaete. The battalion passed through, I believe, in safety, all save the last company. On our right were houses. On our left was a steep bank above which rose the church tower. Big shells began to fall round us. The first two pitched beyond us, the next three crashed among the houses, throwing up clouds of dust, smoke and debris, the next one hit the church tower.

The sight of the peasants rushing away down the main street in a panic brought home the tragic side of the bombardment.

A second shell struck the church tower, or part of the roof, and the fragments flew over us. Matters were becoming unpleasantly warm, when a staff officer was struck by an idea – and he waved us to advance. As we marched up the street a house was shattered with a deafening noise close to the section in front of us. At this point occurred, I believe, the first casualties the regiment sustained. Some were carried into the cellars of the houses and others handed over to a section of native stretcher-bearers that had waited by us.

Then on went the company across fields, where picks and shovels lying on the grass spoke of a hasty scattering under shrapnel in the open, till we reached the rest of the battalion, standing close in by a hedge-bordered wood, waiting motionless every time a Taube scout plane sailed over us.

Behind the shelter of a hill we adopted column formation. The companies extended one by one and marched over the brow. Bullets began to fly pretty thickly over us, and they and the shrapnel grew more and more frequent as company after company breasted the ridge.

As our company, the last one, came over the top, we could see our battalion ahead of us. The first two companies had closed and were lying down behind the next ridge. The others advanced in extended lines below us. The distance and the dressing were more perfect than at any field-day inspection at home. The lines marched steadily onwards through the roots.

At last we reached dead ground, closed-up, and lay down. Once again the companies rose, extended, and passed over the brow of this second hill

London Scottish moved up to the line near Hooge, the first step in their move to Messines.

into what must have been a very blizzard of bullets. In front of us sat Colonel Malcolm [Col. G. A. Malcolm, DSO, Commanding 1st Battalion London Scottish] chatting calmly to a staff officer. Every now and then he glanced half-anxiously along our line to see how we were taking it.

Near him sat two burly Life Guardsmen keeping watch and ward over a condemned man, a surly, black-bearded peasant who had worked the sails of a windmill, and so brought down the big shells on Wytschaete. This little attention had, I am told, been intended for the Lincolns, who passed through the village ahead of us.

I cannot say concerning the man's guilt, but what I can vouch for is that the shells were duly delivered.

Just as our turn came to follow on over the hill a staff officer ran up on our left and pointed back in the direction whence he had come. Wherefore the senior subaltern took his half company off to this new quarter. At first we were under cover. Then shell holes appeared in the ground and bullets began to pass us. One man sat down and commenced to bandage his legs – his expression one of surprised indignation.

Eventually we came to an open road and lay down in the ditch on the near side. It was a very shallow ditch, and we started to dig ourselves in. A sudden increase in the output of shrapnel puzzled me, till I realized that the senior subaltern had strolled along to our end of the ditch. He lay down and told us he wanted ten men to come with him to occupy a small trench in front of us. It had been held by natives [Indian troops] till their officers had been killed.

When the noise had quieted down he took the end ten men with him. We jumped up and started to double forward. 'I think we'd better walk. It looks better,' he remarked. So we walked towards a haystack that gave us some cover from sight. Once past this, things became more lively and our OC [the officer commanding this section in the field] took us on at the double.

For several hours there was an almost incessant din and concussion of shells. Through that inferno I was held by the pluck of the man next to me. In the very worst moments he was as bright and as cheery as was his usual habit of life. He must have felt afraid, as, of course, we all did, but he showed no sign of it. After one particularly lively outburst of assorted shells, he remarked, 'I suppose that after a couple more days we shall go back into a reserve trench'. 'Probably this is a reserve trench,' I said, 'and tomorrow we shall get into the real thing.' 'You always were a cheery blighter,' replied Bugler Dunlop, and we both laughed. Two days later I was told of his death.

About five o'clock the shelling ceased. The unnatural calm was broken only by the sound of occasional British shells and their distant explosion. An officer in a native regiment came up to me and asked where he could find the officer in command. I directed him to our senior subaltern. In the dim light he must have mistaken the star for a crown, as he saluted our OC most respectfully and urged him to retire to a position in rear of our trench – which latter he described as the worst shell-trap in the entire line.

Our OC. replied that he had orders to hold the trench till the last possible moment, and that he intended so doing.

The captain shrugged his shoulders.

'Very well, sir, of course if you insist on staying on here I can do nothing except hold my ground to support you.' He saluted and turned away.

We had deepened the trench and had scooped out hollow caves, but there was no cover in the event of enfilade fire. I was soon hard at work with the 229 others in hewing a traverse at right angles to the end of our trench. It was very slow work, and after a long spell, with only room for one man to work at a time, we had progressed about four or five feet to a depth of five feet, and from that point the traverse ran up to ground level in a gentle slope.

Then I ceased digging to take my hour spell at looking out. Two of us stood, side by side, peering into the patchwork of moonlight and shadow, straining our eyes for the least movement. Bullets 'phitted' over us, past us, and between us. I felt heartily thankful when my spell came to an end. Our OC, who could have rested comfortably under cover, shared the whole watch of each successive pair of look-outs. I debated whether to enlarge my little cave or to enjoy my oft-postponed sleep. I decided on the latter course. I was no sooner curled up than the order came to stand-to. A terrific rattle and crackle of rifle and maxim fire broke out. Away in front of us a line of dim figures advanced ghostlike in the moonlight. The OC told us to prepare to fire, but to wait for his command.

'Who are you?' shouted the OC.

There was no answer, and he repeated the question. As this met with no reply he sang out to us to open fire.

We blazed away into them and I wondered why they lay down in twos and threes to fire back at us. Then it struck me suddenly that they were tumbling over.

They made no attempt to rush us, but still advanced at a steady walk, falling as they came. Flashes spat out along their line, but there was no sound of shout or cry, only the crackling of rifle shots.

The bullets cut through the hedge in front of us and slapped into the bank behind us as the line came on – and all the while our new rifles jammed and stuck. It might be after one shot or after five shots that we dropped to the bottom of the trench and tugged and banged at the bolt to get it free. Then, as often as not, it would foul the next cartridge from the magazine and refuse to click home. And all the while the dim line was advancing. I am told that all the rifles in the battalion were condemned and exchanged for new ones very shortly afterwards.

After a while there were no more Germans walking towards us, though the heavy firing continued somewhere in the near neighbourhood. Our casualties were a sergeant and a lance-corporal – each, I believe, hit in the eyes. They were taken to the rear in the lull which followed.

At the time I imagined this silence to mean that the German attack had been repulsed, but, according to the journal *The Fighting Territorials*, the British line had retired under orders to take up a new position, and the message did not reach the Carabineers or the 'Scottish' cavalry, who were consequently surrounded and cut off and had to fight their way through.

I can speak only of what occurred to our own little party.

'GET READY TO CHARGE!'

To our left a light showed in the window of a house in the village. Other lights appeared in other windows, grew into a blaze and turned red. Flames poured out and burst through the roof. This happened in several houses, until the village was in flames. There was still firing going on, and we waited to see if anything else would happen. It did. There came a sound of great cheering. 'We're charging!' shouted the OC, 'Get ready to join in!' Some way behind the trench a building blazed brightly. Silhouetted against this, a crowd of dark figures ran past with a curious shambling gait, each man made in the same mould, bent forward under the weight of a heavy

A German artist's version of the night fighting at Messines, with the famous windmill prominent.

pack and crowned with a spiked helmet. It was not our men charging. Those men were advancing in the wrong direction.

'They are after the Carabineers,' said the OC, 'Double out and open fire on them. We'll try to draw them off, to give our poor beggars a chance of making a stand.'

I stopped behind long enough to grab an extra couple of bandoliers, and doubled out after the others. Moonlight is a deceptive form of illumination, and I lay down in careful alinement with a row of turnip-tops and opened fire. After a while it occurred to me that I might be masking the fire of the man next to me. I jumped up and ran back (instead of crawling), and as I was lying down again the old proverb about more haste and less speed hit me a bang in the ribs and thigh with a red-hot poker, and I sat over backwards instead.

Then somebody discovered that the Germans were coming up in a solid mass behind us – so the others doubled back to hold the trench. The people we had fired on had turned on us and were also advancing – and a third lot were bearing down to enfilade us. I got on my feet and proceeded to hunt diligently for a clip of cartridges which I had dropped. I was festooned with bandoliers and my pouches were full of ammunition, but that clip was the one thing which mattered. Had I hunted about for my sporran, which contained all my worldly wealth, there would have been some sense in the proceedings; but I had not then realized that the bullet which tore away my water-bottle had also robbed me of my sporran, leaving in place of the former an enormous charred hole in my greatcoat.

When I returned to the trench, I sat on the floor. Fortunately there was not room to lie down, or I should, perforce, have remained in that position. The others were firing over both sides of the trench. The Germans blazed away at us from three sides.

There was just one solid sound of bullets, a steady wail of changing notes. The junior subaltern, looking back from the ridge, saw a ring of fire round the trench and gave us up for lost.

The other sergeant's rifle jammed permanently. He took mine, but it had jammed also. Then, good fellow that he was, he cut off my greatcoat and my serge to get at my side. Thereby I lost many treasured possessions in exchange for a small avalanche of sand.

Before he could get at my first-aid bandage the garrison began to evacuate the position. Matters had been hopeless a second before. Then – so I am told – the smoke from a burning stack blew over the trench and hid it from sight after the most approved mythological fashion. I groped for my coat; I groped for my serge, but could not find them. They were very precious to me, but time was more precious still. Wherefore I left them sadly and, holding on my kilt, climbed the easy slope of the thrice-blessed traverse and joined the OC, who had stopped to make quite sure that all his men were out.

MY OC SAVED ME

We then made for a high hedge in front of us. The party scattered a little. The sergeant and some of the men found a sunken road and reached our lines in safety.

When we reached the fence the fire opened again. I found a gate and shouted to the others. We went through it and ran into another party of advancing Germans. Turning sharply back along the other side of the fence, we passed through a farmyard unseen by the men who were inside the house, setting fire to it. Then we reached a nine-foot fence with barbed wire strung through it. The others went over it like a troop of professional monkeys. The OC, hailed me softly from the far side and refused to go on without me. I cursed him inwardly, because the muscles in my right side were not intact, and I had not even considered the question of gymnastic

A photograph of the kilted warriors taken after the fighting.

The roll call taken at Wulverghem after the fighting at Messines. Only 150 officers and men answered it. In the following days stragglers turned up and the final casualty count was 394 men dead or missing.

A group photograph taken following the battle. With minimal training and time at the front; lacking maps and with mal-functioning rifles and without support of their machine guns, this Territorial battalion put up a strong fight.

effort. I managed to climb up the wires with two feet and one hand, reached the top and took a header down into the dark. The OC fielded me, and we sat down together in a heap.

In the next field we ran across a company of Germans advancing in line upon our left. On our right hand was a hedge, so we were forced to keep straight on. The moonlight was brilliant. We could see their uniforms and their faces and their *Pickelhaubes*, and could hear them talking together. Our men's bayonets were gleaming on the ends of their rifles and we must have been as plainly visible to them as they to us.

They made no attempt to rush us, and let us reach a road about 200 yards away; then they opened fire on us. I can only conclude they deliberately waited until they were out of reach of our bayonets before molesting us. Our OC was so indignant about it that he was with difficulty restrained from hurling himself and his nine able-bodied followers at them with the bayonet. He left the place with the utmost reluctance, but although a sudden charge might have thrown that company into confusion, the place was crawling with additional Germans.

We walked down a road between small trees and struck out again across country. In front of us lay a village. An enormous shell came rattling and snoring over us just as we approached the village. It burst in a blaze of light, and the houses became instantly a mass of flames. Three more shells followed, and two minutes later the whole place was a furnace.

We turned back. After a while we found ourselves on a road with high banks and walked along it. I had dropped back a little behind the others, and so first heard a wild rattle of hoofs on the road. I shouted a warning that there was an Uhlan coming. They promptly took up ambush positions. A cloaked figure galloped round the corner and pulled his horse back on its haunches as he suddenly found himself looking down nine rifle barrels, and at two bayonets which had jammed and refused to come unfixed.

I think we were all both relieved and disappointed when he turned out to be a corporal in the Household Brigade, riding for reinforcements. He told us that the Germans had simply poured over his regiment and broken through, and that the day was lost. He pointed out the direction of Ypres, set spurs to his charger, and galloped on again.

Following his instructions, we struck out across a dreary, open plain, intersected by water dykes, for all the world like the Norfolk marshes. As we approached the high road on the far side of the marshes we saw a signal lamp winking from the base of a windmill, but as we knew not if the place was held in force by the enemy, or if the flashes were the work of a spy, or if they owed their being to one of our own signallers, we decided to make inquiries before we entered the village beyond.

Accordingly we halted on the road a little way out. We had not long to wait before a motor car approached us. We stopped it and found it was driven by an English soldier, who told us that there was a staff officer and a dressing-station close by. The OC turned me over to the dressing station and then hurried to report to the staff officer. From there he and his nine men joined in, I believe, with the force that stormed Messines a few hours later.

A London Scottish lance-corporal in full marching order.

11 November, 1914

THE HORROR of SANCTUARY WOOD

by Corporal John Lucy

In this grim picture of the horrors of war Corporal Lucy, 2nd Battalion Royal Irish Rifles, tells of the fighting round Sanctuary Wood on 11 November, a most critical day in the history of the First Ypres battle, when the most violent attacks of the German army were resisted. He tells how he first encountered men of the London Territorial battalions thrown into the tortured battle line.

We stood-to in the wet shell holes and crumbling trenches under the thunder and blasting flashes of German high explosives. There is no need to describe his bombardment, except to say that it was the worst in my experience. A few of our fellows broke under it, and one poor chap entirely lost his head and ran back out of his trench. He did not have a chance in the open. The earth was vomiting all round us and he tumbled over after a few yards. Better to have kept to the trench. No trained, sane, soldier in his right mind would leave like that.

A corporal, a burly fellow, fell near me with a shrapnel bullet in the back of his head. He lay unconscious all the day, nodding his holed head as if suffering only from some slight irritation, and did not become still until evening. Earlier in the day one youngster said 'What about putting him out of his misery?' A more experienced man explained that there was no pain. The small stirrings and little moans came from a man who was already as good as dead.

Another soldier had his belly ripped open and sat supporting his back against the trench, while he gazed with fascinated eyes at large coils of his own guts which he held in both hands. It was almost the ghastliest sight I ever saw. However, its sequel was better. The man's entrails had not been penetrated. He got safe out of the trench, was washed, tucked in, and mended well in hospital.

Maimed men passed crouching and crawling behind me, leaving trails of blood on the ground on their way to a ditch which led back through woods behind. Some of them were moaning too loud, unlike our old men. One young militiaman in particular came by roaring, and seeking sympathy for a broken arm from everyone he met.

A lance-corporal told him 'for God's sake to put a sock in it', and that 'if you was ever badly wounded you would have no breath left to howl'. That stopped his hysterics. I should say that the non-commissioned officers of the old army had their work cut out keeping an eye on the inexperienced men in circumstances like these.

Some of the newer men could not even fire a rifle properly, and at times our hearts quailed for our safety and theirs. The few officers we had no doubt saw all that we did, but they were free to move about, and this was a great advantage from the point of view of a junior NCO pinned to his sector, to the bit of trench he was given to defend, and always under the close scrutiny of the men he was supposed to lead and encourage.

A runner pushing past gave me a nasty shock: 'God, are you alive?' he blurted out. 'We heard down at headquarters you had been killed.'

'No hope!' I said, hardly daring a longer sentence lest instant death should finish it.

The trenches were filled with the acrid smell of shell smoke. Heavy shrapnel burst right down on us, its pall of smoke roofing the trench and blotting out the sky. I was flung about by the concussion, and thrown flat against the trench bottom. My whole body sang and trembled. One ear was perforated by the concussion, and I could hardly hear.

The runner came over to me, and we held each other with our hands. 'Are you all right ?' I nodded, unable to utter a word. The message I am taking is, 'Stand-to!' because the enemy is massing just in front of us,' he said. 'Nasty spot, this.' And he hurried along, two more close bursts

Northumberland Hussars in Sanctuary Wood, 1914.

adding to his speed. Before the shelling ceased we were ordered to man the trench: 'Stand-to! Stand-to! Every one,' and our rifles lined our broken parapets. The man of my section on my immediate left kept his head down. I grasped his arm and shook him savagely: 'For Christ's sake, get up, you bloody fool. The Germans are coming.' He fell over sideways and on to his face when I released him, and saw that his pack was covered with blood. He was dead. My eyes moved off him to my shoulder, which was spattered with his brains and tiny slivers of iridescent bone.

The soldier on my right, wincing like most of us, standing head and shoulders exposed to the fury of the shells, said desperately: 'Mother of God! This is terrible.' A tall old sweat farther along shouted grimly: 'Ha-ha, me bhoys! Now we're for it.'

Six German army corps were marshalled in the open, advancing like they were on parade towards the weak British Army.

The magnificent Prussian Guards made a review of it. They executed their famous goose-step in the sight of their foe, and the field-grey waves came on. The Kaiser was close behind in some neighbouring town, ready to receive reports of the great break-through when it came.

THE PRUSSIAN GUARD

The left of the Prussian Guard attack caught us. Farther to our left the line broke, mended, broke, and mended again. A counter-attacking English regiment went through a temporarily victorious enemy like a knife through butter, and recaptured a lost village with great dash.

We stopped the Germans on our front, and they were the finest troops of Germany, led by the flower of her noblest houses.

That was all: a weak night attack was repelled. The next morning we found a German alive at our wire. He dropped his wire-cutters and made a friendly motion with his hand, intending surrender. Our desperate fellows covered him with their rifles. I called out: 'No! Save him!' A bitter voice replied: 'No bloody fear. No Sergeant Benson tricks here.' And the brave German was swiftly killed. [Sergeant Benson had been killed by the Germans when attempting to rescue a wounded enemy soldier.]

We stayed in the line for two more days, easily checking weaker attempts to drive us back, and then once more we went out to reserve. We ceased to fight as a battalion. We were too weak. We were told off to be ready to relieve the regiments in the line at a moment's notice. A Scottish Territorial regiment with a similar duty twice went up, and twice recaptured trenches and reinstated another battalion. They were unbelievably cheerful.

One young Highlander going back out of the line a second time called out: 'Give us a shout if ye want us again'. The Terriers had arrived. The part-timers, the supposed Saturday-night soldiers. Another regiment of them from London did great work. Although we Regulars got just a bit weary at reading their recorded deeds in every newspaper we managed to scrounge.

While in reserve I was detailed one morning to escort a sick party to Hooge. On the way back I got caught in a barrage and bolted into a dug-out. It was the headquarters of a Regular battalion in reserve. The commanding officer growled at me: 'Who's that?' I gave my rank and regiment and asked permission to stay a minute until the shells stopped. 'Get out of here,' he ordered, and he sent me out into the shelling. The next morning some of our men assisted in digging him and his adjutant from the dug-out, which had been blown in on them. They were both dead.

Now, in a weak moment, I thought I would go sick myself. I had developed haemorrhoids, and they bled rather badly. A sergeant with a perforated ear like mine said he would join me and go to the field-ambulance to be dressed, hoping to be detained there. We had other minor cuts, and a good many bruises too, and the skin was inclined to go dirty. The knuckles of our trigger fingers were cut open from constantly firing our rifles. A calloused knuckle on a forefinger is the hallmark of the 1914 men.

On the way we had to dodge a good many shells, and in an interval of sheltering behind a house we answered some call we could not resist, and returned, feeling ashamed, to our reserve trench. On our way we pulled a young frightened lance-corporal from shelter and made him join up with us. He later turned out to be the most distinguished soldier in the regiment; and he was four times decorated for valour.

On 19 November we were again in the line, because a battalion that had suffered worse than ours had to be given a rest; but that evening the London Territorial Regiment, fresh and strong, came to relieve us – a relief that was to take us away from that battlefield of Ypres, right back to the Belgian village of Westoutre.

This time only forty men of my battalion were able to march away. The rest had been killed or wounded. Forty of us left out of two hundred and fifty, and only about three weeks after there were only forty-six left out of an entire battalion. I searched my mind for total figures, and roughly reckoned that in three months ninety-six men out of every hundred had been killed oi wounded. I was too weary to appreciate my own luck. I was so completely dazed that I lingered in the front line, while a London Territorial congratulated my battalion on giving the Germans 'Denbigh'. He was a cultured man in the uniform of a private soldier. But – Denbigh – I did not know the word. I still do not know its meaning. [The Earl of Denbigh was Colonel Commandant of the Honorable Artillery Company and personally aimed a gun at the Battle of Tel el-Kebir in 1882, causing the fleeing Egyptians to be halted.] The Londoner looked for praise, he liked talking to me, a Regular corporal of the line. He asked if I thought his battalion would, one day, be as good as those of the old army.

I said, 'Yes. Every bit as good.' My eyes weakened, wandered, and rested on the half-hidden corpses of men and youths. Near and far they looked calm, and oven handsome, in death. Their strong young bodies thickly garlanded the edge of a wood in the rear, a wood called Sanctuary. A dead sentry at his post leaned back in a standing position against a blasted tree, keeping watch over them. Proudly and sorrowfully I looked at them, the Macs and the O's, and the hardy Ulster boys joined together in death on a foreign field. My dead chums.

A silence more pregnant than the loudest bombardment stole over the country, the evening silence of the battlefield. A robin sat in a broken bush on the parapet and burst into song.

"The Londoner said quietly, 'You'd better hurry up, Corporal. The Irish are falling in on the left.' I slung my rifle over the left shoulder.

'So long, chum. Good luck!'

' So long,' said the Londoner.

I left him with our dead. The roll was being called when I joined our small party, but there was no zest in this roll-call. All the men stood heavily and answered listlessly. Information about dead and wounded was murmured. Our curiosity now was not for the out-numbering dead, but for our few selves, and in a dazed way we inspected each other's faces, because every survivor was a phenomenon in himself. We exchanged half-smiles of appreciation and silent congratulations. Then we slouched off across the cold, barren, wintry fields, without talk, to join the main road at Hooge and, arriving there, got into step once more on the hard, paved

British troops in Ypres main square as the destruction of the town by German artillery is getting underway.

road. Hooge was wrecked. South of it the Menin Road from Ypres was stiff with French cavalry. They were drawn up in long lines on the west of the road, with their horses' heads facing inwards toward the centre of the road – massed in thousands and standing by, mounted, to check the Germans in case the British broke.

They were not wanted.

The first battle for Ypres was over, and Ypres was saved.

As we drew nearer to the old moated town we thought it had not been worth defending, for it was already in ruins and it looked as if every house had been destroyed by shell or flame.

The First Battle of Ypres. A house near to the entrance of the Cathedral deanery used as a makeshift hospital in Cathedral Square, completely destroyed by a shell.

25 December 1914

THE HISTORIC CHRISTMAS TRUCE OF 1914

By Captain Sir Edward Hulse, Bart.

Despite the bitter fighting which had been going on for over four months, a remarkable armistice was observed in many sectors on Christmas Day 1914. British and German soldiers ceased killing each other for a couple of days and fraternized in a most genuine manner. A captain of the Scots Guards described the extraordinary scenes enacted between the lines during that unofficial truce.

On the 23rd we took over the trenches in the ordinary manner, relieving the Grenadiers, and during the 24th the usual firing took place, and sniping was pretty brisk. We stood to arms as usual at 6.30 am on the 25th, and I noticed that there was not much shooting; this gradually died down, and by 8 am there was no sustained shooting, except for a few shots on our left (Border Regiment). At 8.30 am I was looking out, and saw four Germans leave their trenches and come towards us; I told two of my men to go and

British and German soldiers meet half way between the lines. Meetings like this took place all along the Front.

A group in the middle of No Man's Land gather to exchange gifts and chat.

meet them, unarmed (as the Germans were unarmed), and to see that they did not pass the half-way line.

We were 350 to 400 yards apart at this point. My fellows were not very keen, not knowing what was up, so I went out alone, and met Barry, one of our ensigns, also coming out from another part of the line. By the time we got to them they were three-quarters of the way over, and much too near our barbed wire, so I moved them back.

They were three private soldiers and a stretcher-bearer, and their spokesman started off by saying that he thought it only right to come over and wish us a happy Christmas, and trusted us implicitly to keep the truce. He came from Suffolk, where he had left his best girl and a three and half

horse-power motorbike. He told me that he could not get a letter to the girl, and wanted to send one through me. I made him write out a postcard in front of me, in English, and I sent it off that night. I told him that she probably would not be a bit keen to see him again. We then entered on a long discussion on every sort of thing. I was dressed in an old stocking-cap and a man's overcoat, and they took me for a corporal, a thing which I did not discourage, as I had an eye to going as near their lines as possible.

I asked them what orders they had from their officers as to coming over to us, and they said none; they had just come over out of goodwill. They protested that they had no feeling of enmity towards us at all, but that everything lay with their authorities, and that being soldiers they had to obey. I believe they were speaking the truth when they said this, and that they never wished to fire a shot again. They said that unless directly ordered they were not going to shoot again until we did. We talked about the ghastly wounds made by rifle bullets, and we both agreed that neither of us used dum-dum bullets, and that the wounds are solely inflicted by the high-velocity bullet with the sharp nose, at short range. We both agreed that it would be far better if we used the old South African round-nosed bullet, which makes a clean hole.

They think that our Press is to blame in working up feeling against them by publishing false 'atrocity reports'. I told them of various sweet little cases which I had seen for myself, and they told me of English prisoners whom they had seen with soft-nosed bullets, and lead bullets with notches cut in the nose. We had a heated and at the same time good-natured argument, and ended by hinting to each other that the other was lying.

'TIPPERARY' FOR THE GERMANS

I kept it up for half-an-hour, and then escorted them back as far as their barbed wire, having a jolly good look round all the time, and picking up various little bits of information which I had not had an opportunity of doing under fire. I left instructions with them that if any of them came out later they must not come over the half-way line, and appointed a ditch as

British soldiers climb out of their trenches to join their enemies in a brief period of peace.

the meeting place. We parted after an exchange of Albany cigarettes and German cigars, and I went straight to headquarters to report. On my return at 10 am I was surprised to hear a hell of a din going on, and not a single man left in my trenches; they were completely denuded (against my orders), and nothing moved.

I heard strains of 'Tipperary' floating down the breeze, followed by a tremendous burst of 'Deutschland über Alles' and as I got to my own company headquarters dug-out I saw, to my amazement, not only a crowd of 150 British and Germans at the half-way house which I had appointed opposite my lines, but six or seven such crowds, all the way down our lines, extending towards the 8th Division on our right.

I bustled out and asked if there were any German officers in my crowd, and the noise died down (as this time I was myself in my own cap and badges of rank). I found two, but had to talk to them through an interpreter, as they could neither speak English nor French. I explained to them that strict orders must be maintained as to meeting half-way, and everyone unarmed; and we both agreed not to fire until the other did, thereby creating a complete deadlock and armistice (if strictly observed).

Meanwhile Scots and Huns were fraternizing in the most genuine possible manner. Every sort of souvenir was exchanged, addresses given and received, photos of families shown, etc. One of our fellows offered a German a cigarette; the German said, 'Virginian?' Our fellow said, 'Aye, straight-cut', the German said, 'No, thanks, I only smoke Turkish.' It gave us a laugh.

A German NCO with the Iron Cross – gained, he told me for conspicuous skill in sniping – started his follows off with some marching tune. When they had done I set the note for 'The Boys of Bonnie Scotland, where the heather and the bluebells grow', and so we went on singing everthing from 'Good King Wenceslaus' down to the ordinary Tommies' song, and ended up with 'Auld Lang Syne', which we all, English, Scots, Irish, Prussian, Württembergers, etc., joined in. It was absolutely astounding, and if I had seen it on a cinematograph film I should have sworn that it was faked.

Rain and wet previously, the weather had cleared up the night before to a sharp frost, and it was a perfect day, everything white, and the silence seemed extraordinary after the usual din. From all sides birds seemed to arrive, and we hardly ever see a bird generally. Later in the day I fed about fifty sparrows outside my dug-out, which shows how complete the silence and quiet was. I must say that I was very much impressed with the whole scene, and also, as everyone else, astoundingly relieved by the quiet, and by being able to walk about freely. It is the first time, day or night, that we have heard no guns or rifle-firing since I left Havre and convalescence.

Just after we had finished 'Auld Lang Syne' an old hare started up and, seeing so many of us about in an unwanted spot, did not know which way to go. I gave a loud 'View Holloa', and one and all, British and Germans, rushed about giving chase, slipping up on the frozen ploughed land, falling about, and after a hot two minutes we killed in the open, a German and one of our follows falling together heavily upon the completely baffled hare. Shortly afterwards we saw four more hares and killed one again. Both were a good heavy weight, and had evidently been out between the two rows of trenches for the last two months, well fed on the cabbage patches, many of which are untouched in the No Man's Land. The enemy kept one and we kept the other.

It was now 11.30 am, and at this moment George Paynter arrived on the scene with a hearty, 'Well, my lads, a merry Christmas to you'. This is damned comic, isn't it?' George told them that he thought it only right that we should show that we could desist, from hostilities on a day which was so important in both countries; and he then said: 'Well, my boys, I've brought you over something to celebrate this funny show with.' And he produced from his pocket a large bottle of rum (not ration rum, but the proper stuff). One large shout went up, and the nasty little German spokesman uncorked it and, in a heavy, ceremonious manner, drank our healths in the name of his 'kamaraden'. The bottle was then passed on and polished off before you could say 'knife'. During the afternoon the same extraordinary scene was enacted between the lines, and one of the enemy told me that he was longing to get back to London. I assured him that so was I. He said that he was sick of the war, and I told him that when the truce was ended any of his friends would be welcome in our trenches, and would be well received, fed and given a free passage to the Isle of Man. Another coursing meeting took place, with no result, and at 4.30 pm we agreed to keep in our respective trenches, and told them that the truce was ended. They persisted, however, in saying that they were not going to fire, and as George had told us not to unless they did, we prepared for a quiet night, but warned all sentries to be doubly on the alert.

During the day both sides had taken the opportunity of bringing up piles of wood, straw, etc., which is generally only brought up with difficulty under fire. We improved our dug-outs, roofed in new ones and got a lot of useful work done towards increasing our comfort. Directly it was dark I got the whole of my company on to improving and re-making our barbed wire entanglements all along my front, and had my scouts out in front of the working parties to prevent any surprise. But not a shot was fired, and we finished off a real good obstacle unmolested.

On my left was the bit of ground over which we attacked on the 18th, and here the lines are only 85 to 100 yards apart.

The Border Regiment were occupying this sector on Christmas Day, and Giles Loder, our adjutant, went down there with a party that morning on hearing of the friendly demonstrations in front of my company, to see if he could come to an agreement about our dead, who were still lying out between the trenches. The trenches are so close at this point that, of course, each side had to be far stricter. He found an extremely pleasant and superior stamp of German officer, who arranged to bring all our dead to the half-way line. We took them over from there and buried 29 exactly half-way between the two lines. Giles collected all personal effects, pay-books and identity discs, but was stopped by the Germans when he told some men to bring in the rifles. All rifles lying on their side of the half-way line they kept carefully.

They apparently treated our prisoners well and did all they could for our wounded. This officer kept on pointing to our dead and saying, *'Les braves, c'est bien dommage'* [The brave men, that's a shame].

When George heard of it he went down to that section and talked to the nice officer and gave him a scarf. That same evening a German orderly came to the half-way line and brought a pair of warm, woolly gloves as a

Some German soldiers had worked in London before the war and chatted with ease. A British soldier seen here surrounded by Germans.

present in return for George. The same night the Borderers and we were engaged in putting up big trestle obstacles, with barbed wire all over them, and connecting them, and at this same point (namely, where we were only 85 yards apart) the Germans came out and sat on their parapet and

Christmas Day 1914 at Rue de Bois. Men of a Highland regiment constructing a breastwork of mud and hurdles. They are were in full sight of the German line in the trees on the left, but not a shot was fired. Sir Edward Hulse describes how he saw Germans sitting on the parapet of their trenches, indifferent spectators to the work being carried out .

watched us doing it, although we had informed them that the truce was ended. All was quiet that night; and next morning, while I was having breakfast, one of my NCOs came and reported that the enemy were again coming over to talk. I had given full instructions, and none of my men were allowed out of the trenches to talk to the enemy. I had also told the NCO of an advanced post which I have up a ditch, to go out with two men, unarmed; if any of the enemy came over, to see that they did not cross the half-way line, and to engage them in pleasant conversation. So I went out, and found the same lot as the day before; they told me again that they had no intention of firing, and wished the truce to continue. I had instructions not to fire till the enemy did; I told them and so the same comic form of temporary truce continued on the 26th, and again at 4.30 pm I informed them that the truce was at an end. We had sent them over some plum-puddings, and they thanked us heartily for them and retired again, the only difference being that instead of all my men being out in the No Man's Land, one NCO and two men only were allowed out, and the enemy therefore sent fewer.

Again both sides had been improving their comfort during the day, and again at night I continued on my barbed wire and finished it right off.

WHAT A DESERTER TOLD US

We retired for the night all quiet, and were rudely awakened at 11 pm. A headquarters' orderly burst into my dug-out and handed me a message. It stated that a deserter had come into the 8th Division lines and stated that the whole German line was going to attack at 12.15 midnight, and that we were to stand to arms immediately, and that reinforcements were being hurried up from billets in the rear. I thought, at the time, that it was a damned good joke on the part of the German deserter to deprive us of our sleep, and so it turned out to be. I stood my company to arms, made a few extra dispositions, gave out all instructions, and at 11.20 pm George arrived. Suddenly our guns all along the line opened a heavy fire, and all the enemy did was to reply with 9-in. shells (heavy howitzers), not one of which exploded, just on my left. Never a rifle shot was fired by either side (except right away down in the 8th Division), and at 2.30 am we turned in half the men to sleep and kept the other half awake on sentry.

Apparently this deserter had also reported that strong German reinforcements had been brought up, and named a place just in rear of their lines, where, he said, two regiments that had just been brought up were in billets. Our guns were informed, and plastered the place well when they opened fire (as I mentioned). The long and short of it was that absolutely *nixt* happened, and after a sleepless night I turned in at 4.30 am, and was woken again at 6.30, when we always stand-to arms before daylight. I was going to have another sleep at 8 am when I found that the enemy were again coming over to talk to us (27 December). I watched my NCO and two men go out from the advanced post to meet them, and hearing shouts of laughter from the little party when they met in front, I again went out myself. They asked me what we were up to during the night, and told me that they had stood to arms all night and thought we were going to attack them when they heard our heavy shelling; also that our guns had done a lot of damage and knocked out a lot of their men in billets.

I told them that a deserter of theirs had come over to us, and that they had only him to thank for any damage done, and that we, after a sleepless night, were not best pleased with him either. They assured me that they had heard nothing of an attack, and I fully believed them, as it is inconceivable that they would have allowed us to put up the formidable obstacles (which we had on the two previous nights) if they had contemplated an offensive movement.

Anyhow, if it had ever existed, the plan had miscarried, as no attack was developed on any part of our line, and here were these fellows still protesting that there was a truce, although I told them that it had ceased the evening before.

So I kept to the same arrangement, namely, that my NCO and two men should meet them half-way, and strict orders were given that no other man was to leave the lines. I admit that the whole thing beat me absolutely. In the evening we were relieved by the Grenadiers, quite openly (not crawling about on all fours, as usual), and we handed on our instructions to the Grenadiers in case the enemy still wished to pay visits.

16 December, 1914

Lieutenant Colonel L. Robson Royal Garrison Artillery, Battery Commander, Hartlepool Batteries, December 1914. His actions against the German battle cruisers are described here.

GERMAN BOMBARDMENT OF HARTLEPOOL

Britain's First Bombardment in 250 Years

On the morning of 16 December, 1914, German vessels Seydlitz, Moltke *and* Blücher *bombarded the Hartlepools, killing and wounding 420 civilians and soldiers in 43 minutes. This account is told by the officer in command of the forts at the time of the raid.*

Michiel de Ruyter

Not since 1667, during the reign of Charles II, had a British soldier been killed by enemy action whilst serving in England. During the Second Anglo-Dutch War, Michiel de Ruyter, one of the most skilled admirals in Dutch history, conducted a raid on the Medway. He bombarded and then captured the town of Sheerness, sailed up the River Thames to Gravesend, then up the River Medway to Chatham. It was the worst defeat in the Royal Navy's history.

Hartlepool, or rather the Hartlepools, for the new town of West Hartlepool immediately adjoins its ancient sister, possesses fine mercantile marine shipbuilding yards, and is the home port for a large fishing fleet. There are also immense marine engineering works. These were cogent reasons for arming the place, and so it had been a defended port many years previous to the Great War.

But a pretty weak armament it was: two forts, one containing two six-inch guns, the other, a hundred yards to the south, one of the same calibre. Three and a half miles farther south, across Tees Bay, lay the mouth of that river, defended by a fort containing two 4.7 guns. The steel works, dotted up its banks as far as Middlesbrough, were too far inland to attack, though the river-mouth was an important anchorage for in- and out-going vessels.

In other words, the authorities, in arming the place, never contemplated this sort of attack. But nothing in war ever happens as per book. During the night of 15-16 December, 1914, five German cruisers, *Seydlitz, Moltke, Derfflinger, Von der Tann*, and *Blücher*, all battle-cruisers except the last-named, gathered off the North East Yorkshire coast in two divisions. The northern consisted of the *Seydlitz, Moltke,* and *Blücher*. These must have edged in a bit closer to the shore, as they were inside our extended patrol – two destroyers and a gunboat – by dawn.

Somewhere off Saltburn seems to have been the spot where the attackers hung about until they steamed off in line ahead to the attack of Hartlepool.

The other two, *Derfflinger* and *Von der Tann*, steamed south, and at about 8 am, on the 16th, fired upon Scarborough and Whitby.

Shortly before 8 am, 16th, *Seydlitz, Moltke, Blücher*, in that order, steamed across Tees Bay from the South East. The December morning was cold, but there was not a breath of wind, the smoke going straight up from the funnels, for the hostile vessels were easing down their speed. The sea was like oil, and the tide dead low – a combination which considerably helped the defence.

Pocketed in the bay was a dense mist which slowly thinned, but never quite dispersed. It persistently hung about Tees mouth, which locality appears to be the permanent catchpan for all fumes coming down river from the steel works. These conditions considerably hampered the style of South Gare, the 4.7 battery.

Defending patrol boats destroyers HMS *Doon* and HMS *Hardly*, plus the gunboat HMS *Patrol*, pluckily closed with the three monsters, who naturally 'bashed' them unmercifully, quickly causing damage to personnel and material. It was a hopeless fight from the first, and the boats had to draw off.

Royal Navy ensign

Imperial German Navy ensign

Shrouded in smoke from the ships' funnels, the two flags appeared similar from a distance.

It was difficult to distinguish the ensign. Both flags at a distance, especially when fouled by funnel fumes, appear the same. I refer, of course, to the old Imperial German ensign. Personnel at South Gare, in consequence, hearing the firing and seeing what they thought to be three British cruisers attacked by German destroyers, (the Germans were only using their seaward, or starboard armaments), swarmed on to the parapet and took what they thought were front stalls for a most interesting fight. Only when they saw later these same ships firing on the Hartlepool forts did they realize their mistake. By that time South Gare was out of range.

Out of the mist, and almost head-on, at a range of only 4,000 yards, came the leading ship. Identification was difficult under such conditions. In a few seconds the position was clarified. A large

SMS *Seydlitz*, commissioned May 1913.

SMS *Moltke*, commissioned August 1911.

SMS *Blücher*, commissioned October 1909.

German battle-cruisers steaming across the North Sea.

red light suddenly showed from the foremast of the *Seydlitz,* and the Germans opened immediately with some ranging rounds. The ships between them had twenty 11.2 guns, eight 8.2, eighteen 5.9, besides a host of lesser armament available for 'port-side' fire.

To reply, we had three 6-inch, two at Heugh and one at Lighthouse. All three German ships ranged quickly; the forts even more speedily. The two guns in Heugh engaged the leading ship, while Lighthouse took on *Blücher,* the last ship in the line, and the only one in the arc of fire from this battery.

Hartlepool at the turn of the century; her shipyards and other industrial enterprises made the town a prime targe for an attack from the sea.

The third round from the Lighthouse was a 'juicer'. An immense sheet of flame shot up from the *Blücher's* after-deck. The deck supply for one 5.9 gun had been detonated by our lyddite shell, and the effect passed on to the next gun, whose ammunition did ditto. Half the after-bridge was brought down, and eleven seamen killed.

I mentioned the fact of it being low water. Both Heugh and Lighthouse are very low-sited batteries. The range was short, the mean range during the in-fighting being only 5,300 yards; consequently the trajectories of the hostile guns, designed for fighting at 20,000 yards, were, at this distance, absolutely rigid, i.e. straight lines – the smallest error in laying was a miss. Each of our 6-inch guns had to receive a direct hit to damage it, and each presented a relatively small target, even at short range. Clods of earth and chunks of masonry there were in plenty, but the guns remained intact, though the three had several hair-breadth escapes.

FORTS ESCAPED, BUT PEOPLE DIED

To render things more difficult for the Germans, a few days previously a camouflage extension had been placed along the rear fort wall of Heugh. It gave a jagged skyline from the sea – an appearance of false height. This and low water gave a most exaggerated height to the battery, and the enemy projectiles hummed over – only just over – the fort, to burst in the houses behind.

Naturally, the enemy then shortened the range; one shell burst just in front of the guns. Here the defences were advantaged, for the Germans used delay armour-piercing projectiles, which struck only to bounce and burst far above in the air. The shrapnel, however, killed and wounded many civilians, who were in the streets heading inland to escape.

A pilot cutter, becalmed half-way between the combatants, was in a somewhat unique position. The Germans left her alone. Her captain could actually see some of our six-inch projectiles whirring away after they had failed to penetrate the tough armour of the battle-cruisers. When the range

Gun drill at Fort Heugh.

was adjusted to hit the upper works, considerable damage was seen on funnels and upper structures.

An excited voice shouted:

'Go o-n-n-n ! Shove 'em through! Shove 'em through! Give the b.......rs hell!'

Then came a calming voice to the excited junior officer:

'Mr so-and-so, do stop dancing about, and save your breath for your gun corrections!'

The worst thing of all was seeing each ship momentarily lit up by a nasty yellow glare, that seemed to trickle along her side, and having to wait for the result. It was only a matter of a few seconds at that range. Each salvo as it arrived was preceded by an appalling 'onde-de-choc' – that curious double report which occurred when you are stationed in line with a high velocity gun at short or medium range. The shells were so low that the wind of each salvo knocked down any men that happened to be on the manning parade, and caps were snatched off heads and whirled away like leaves.

Behind the Lighthouse Battery, marching on his post in the approved Buckingham Palace style, was a sentry belonging to the 18th Battalion Durham Light infantry (1st Durham Pals). His sentry drill undisturbed by the enemy bombardment: forwards one, two, three, four, halt; about-turn and back again, one two three four, halt.

His officer asked him why the hell he had not gone under cover. His reply was classic, that of a Durham pit-man:

'E-ee, booger! I was that there feart if I 'ad done nowt, I'd ha' roon aw-a-ay!'

The little fellow's beat, I may add, was fully exposed. The opening salvo had bashed up the row of houses in front of which he had to pass continually throughout the action.

Our total casualties among the two forts were extraordinarily light – thanks to the enemy's delayed-action projectiles. Direct-action fuses would

Some of the projectiles which failed to explode: 11.2 and 5.9 calibre shells

have wiped everything and everybody out, as naturally by now the range had been found exactly, and the Germans had been for some time at 'fire for effect'. Four gunners, one sapper and eight infantrymen were killed, and between twenty and thirty of the garrison wounded – these mostly in reserve at billets.

Four infantrymen, manning a machine gun behind the beach, close to the entrance to Heugh Fort, were wiped out by the first salvo. Two gunners who rushed out to render possible assistance were killed by the next salvo.

Seydlitz, and *Moltke* now moved north to swing round and rake the Hartlepools. This ended the second phase of the opening fire from the Germans, which commenced at 8.05 am, the concentration ceasing at 8.20 am. In spite of the close range, no material damage had been done to the defences, except that the scarps and parapets of each fort were a mass of ruined masonry.

Had it been a clear morning, with an enemy at, say, 18,000 yards – their normal fighting range and hopelessly beyond that of our guns – it might have been a very different story. British weather and the forces of Nature were, for once, on our side. Had the tide been the other way – Spring high – so that the ships could have judged their 'overs' relative to some background, they would not have had to waste so much ammunition.

The calm state of the sea made perfect shooting conditions for us, as did the complete lack of wind. It was no superior marksmanship that we scored hit after hit at that absurd range, but the penetrating power of our shells against that type of armour was hopeless. It was most surprising the damage we did do – all to the superstructure.

The two battle-cruisers then left the *Blücher* to engage the two forts with harassing fire. This ship, either by lucky chance or design, had, towards the end of the bombardment, taken station so that she was directly in line with the Lighthouse itself, thereby causing the single gun of the Lighthouse Battery to go out of action for something like twenty minutes.

With one gun short, the battery commander could only follow the leading ship *Seydlitz* with the two artillery pieces in Heugh until she passed out of that fort's arc of fire, then he switched to the *Moltke*. When she, likewise, had disappeared he swung on to the *Blücher*. Lighthouse Battery never had a chance of switching on to the other ships after she had been blanketed, but they had, throughout the action, always been just out of its extreme left arc, so that her one and only target had to be the *Blücher* the whole time.

Directly Fort Heugh engaged the *Blücher* the ship began to move out to sea. She cleared the Lighthouse, and that battery came into action, immediately engaging her again. A dense white cloud issued from near one of her funnels, some thought it might have been steam from a damgaged pipe. Others, however, thought it to be as a result of 'the Black squad' (stokers) raising a good head of steam for the run home, and that it was only the safety-valves lifting. Before being engaged by Heugh, the *Blücher*, in order to blind that fort from firing on the other two ships, had been firing salvos of old pattern powder-filled 8-inch, projectiles at the rocky foreshore just beneath the battery. Owing to the absence of any wind a quite efficient smoke-screen was put up – the first of its kind. It cut down the rate of fire tremendously, but our gunners, availing themselves of every opening in the screen, still continued to fire on the *Seydlitz* and *Moltke*, until these drew out of the arc of fire and so enabled attention to be drawn on the harassing ship.

The work of destruction now began upon the two boroughs. A group of enormous gasholders were the first to go, colloquially described as 'picked off as clean as a whistle'. Each became a roaring column of flame.

No area seemed to have been untouched. It was as if a gigantic rake had been drawn across each spot, a gigantic 'search and swoop'. Shipyards, marine engineering works, railway stations, churches, schools and streets, even the private houses of heads of businesses on the low ridge above West Hartlepool, received shells of various calibre. A total of 119 killed and 300 wounded, both sexes; 600 houses destroyed or damaged, the result.

The Germans claimed the silencing of an old battery known as 'Cemetery' by either *Seydlitz* or *Moltke*. As this work had been dismantled in 1906, they merely wasted their salvos. Another useful lesson gained in the use of dummy positions.

As soon as the *Blücher* was well under way the other two vessels ceased fire on the Hartlepools and steamed off, converging on her. As they once more crossed the arcs of the batteries, they gave Heugh and Lighthouse a

Ruins of one of the two gasometers destroyed at Hartlepool.

few parting salvos. These were replied to, and as the last ship disappeared in the mist our final round was fired at a range of about 9,300 yards, the batteries continuing to pepper their opponents up to the last possible moment.

The whole action lasted forty-three minutes, i.e. from the first opening round at 8.5 am until cease fire at 8.48 am. The Germans had evidently worked to a carefully timed programme – 15 minutes' concentrated fire on the forts plus half an hour's destructive fire on the yards, etc., combined with harassing fire on the forts.

The *Blücher* had to refit in Kiel after this action. The Germans admitted to eleven killed aboard the *Blücher*.

In the whole squadron there were 80 killed and 200 wounded. This information became available later from Dutch sources, and ex-service German seamen who in post war years visited the port as members of mercantile crews, and who were aboard the cruisers that memorable morning.

Cleveland Road, Hartlepool.

A page from *The War Budget* magazine with photographs and details of the women and children killed and wounded in the raid on Hartlepool.

The Hartlepool attack killed 86 civilians and injured 424. Seven soldiers were killed and 14 injured. 1,150 shells were fired at the town, striking targets including the steelworks, gasworks, railways, seven churches and 300 houses.

Scarborough and Whitby were attacked by the cruisers *Derfflinger, Von der Tann* and *Kolberg*. Above an artist's impression of the bombardment of Scarborough. Left: hits on the castle keep and right, the lighthouse at Scarborough. Below: The barracks at Scarborough Castle severly damaged.

The Abbey of St Hilda at Whitby, with shell damage. The ruins
were targeted during the East Coast Raid, 16 December 1914.
The British used the German raid as a recruiting tool for
Kitchener's New Army.